高等学校交通运输专业教材

西南交通大学研究生教材（专著）立项项目

U0616511

Data-driven Train Dispatching Theories in a High-speed Rail System

数据驱动的高速铁路列车运行调整理论

Chao Wen　Ping Huang　Zhongcan Li

文　超　　黄　平　　李忠灿　　著

西南交通大学出版社

·成　都·

图书在版编目（C I P）数据

数据驱动的高速铁路列车运行调整理论 = Data-driven Train Dispatching Theories in a High-speed Rail System: 英文 / 文超，黄平，李忠灿著. —成都：西南交通大学出版社，2020.1

高等学校交通运输专业教材

ISBN 978-7-5643-7303-0

Ⅰ. ①数… Ⅱ. ①文… ②黄… ③李… Ⅲ. ①高速铁路 – 列车组织 – 高等学校 – 教材 – 英文 Ⅳ. ①U284.48

中国版本图书馆 CIP 数据核字（2019）第 293011 号

高等学校交通运输专业教材

Shuju Qudong de Gaosu Tielu Lieche Yunxing Tiaozheng Lilun

数据驱动的高速铁路列车运行调整理论

Data-driven Train Dispatching Theories in a High-speed Rail System

文超　黄平　李忠灿 / 著

责任编辑 / 张文越
封面设计 / 何东琳设计工作室

西南交通大学出版社出版发行

（四川省成都市金牛区二环路北一段 111 号西南交通大学创新大厦 21 楼　610031）

发行部电话：028-87600564　028-87600533

网址：http://www.xnjdcbs.com

印刷：四川煤田地质制图印刷厂

成品尺寸　185 mm×260 mm
印张　16　字数　518 千
版次　2020 年 1 月第 1 版　印次　2020 年 1 月第 1 次

书号　ISBN 978-7-5643-7303-0
定价　58.00 元

前 言// PREFACE

The large-scale construction and operation of the high-speed railway have achieved remarkable results in improving the scale and quality of network, alleviating the tightness of the transportation capacity, and enhancingthe quality of transportation services. Railwayhas played an important supporting role in sustained and rapid development of national economy. Chinese high-speed railway has entered an era of a large-scale network operation characterized by high speed, high density, high traffic volume, and the complexity of the transportation organization has ranked numberone all over the world.

High security, high speed, and high density arethe competitive advantages that high-speed railways become more and more popular among passengers. At the same time, passengers are paying greater attention to the operational reliability of high-speed railways. Under the premise of safety, providing reliable quality and excellent services is the primary task during the development of the railway transportation industry. However, the train encounters a large number of random disturbances during operation, which cause the delays. The anti-interference capacityof the timetable and the delay recovery ability after adisturbance directly affect the service quality of high-speed railway. The exclusivity and competitiveness associated with the use of railway transportation resources mean that such delays will havecumulative effects (horizontal and vertical) and networked propagation characteristics. The horizontal propagation of atrain delay will affect the operation of subsequent trains (possibly delay them). Vertical propagation may delay trains at subsequent stations. Serious delays may spread over a large area of the line and local railway network, affecting the normal execution of the train's operation plan and reducing the quality of transportation services.

An efficient resolution to the problem of high-speed train delays is a daily priority for dispatchers. Existing research at home and abroad mainly focuses on modeling and algorithms for adjustments to train operations at the macro level. These models are based on certain train disturbances and delay distribution assumptions; therefore, they do not fully reflect the actual delay distribution characteristics of high-speed trains. Most of the problems are excessively abstracted and simplified to a certain extent, and a lack of research on the propagation and micro-mechanism of late trains means that the relevant research results are still in the laboratory stage. A certain distance from the application of railway dispatching practices still exists. The station, interval buffer time, and inter-line redundancy time (hereinafter referred to as "redundancy time")—set in the timetable—are resources that the dispatcher can use to recover from adelay. The quality of the redundant time layout directly affects the efficiency of delay recovery, and it is related to the degree of the delay'sinfluence. The current redundant time layout mainly relies on simple statistics regarding historical layout schemes and lacks systematic research basis for recovery capabilities. According to the specific operating conditions of the line and station, determining the efficiency of redundant time and optimizing the corresponding layout scheme will help improve the robustness of the high-speed railway train timetable and enhance delay recovery capabilities.

Chinese railway informatization has developedrapidly. Actual train operation performance, which is the main manifestation of railway transportation production performance,can be documented and saved effectively (actual train timetable, delay cause record, equipment operation status, etc.).The performance recordincludes important information, such as train running status, advanced and late arrival information, and the relationship between trains and equipment utilization status. If legislation regardingtrain operations can be extracted based on operation performance and if the train operation process model is established, the dispatcher will be able to predict future trendsin train operations more effectively. Furthermore, the dispatcher can predict and estimate developing trendsrelated to high-speed train delays andmake relevant dispatch decisionsbased on the delaying possibility. Thus, a more accurate operational adjustment plan and implementation of predictive scheduling can be expected.

Based on global data regardingtrain operations and considering the mutual influence ofadjacent trains, it wouldbe beneficial to analyze the interactiverelationship between trains and the comprehensive formulation of decisions and schedules. The benefits from the development of big data technology, artificial intelligence, and data-driven methods include advantages in theoretical research and operational practices in many fields. Under the conditions of sufficient data and a permitted method, the data-driven model enables examination of the more complicated process involvingtrains and an analysis ofthe delay propagation and recovery process. The data-driven approach does not require a prior knowledge;rather,it facilitates the discovery of laws from the data and construction ofmodels to approximate real-world rail transport production. Although there maybe some deviation between the data-driven model and the real situation, it is sufficientfor guidingpractices and overcomingthe problem inherent in existing mathematical models (i.e.,difficult to apply to production practices). Data science provides a new solution to the problem of high-speed raildispatching. The trend in usingdata-driven methods to study high-speed railway train operation adjustments and automation will provide effective support for high-speed railway dispatching decisions.

Based on high-speed train operation performance andthe combination of macroscopic law exploration and micro-mechanism research, the data-driven method is used to establish the delay propagation model, revealing the horizontal and vertical propagation mechanisms of train delays and put forward a proposal forenhancing the anti-interference and delay recovery capability of the timetable by laying out redundant time. How to improve robustness of the timetable is a key scientific problem that needs to be solved by the high-speed railway traffic control. Moreover, it is necessary for the intelligent high-speed rail dispatching to become a reality for the high-speed railway.

This book aims to introduce the theories of data-driven methods in train dispatching management. It includes 6 chapters, which are: Train dispatching management with data-driven approaches: A comprehensive review and appraisal; Data-driven delay distributions of HSR trains; Data-driven delay propagation mechanism on horizontal; Data-driven delay propagation mechanism on vertical; Confliction management of HSR; and 6) Delay recovery and supplement time allocation. This book is written by WenChao, Huang Ping, and Li Zhongcan from Southwest Jiaotong University, and the students Yang Xiong,Mou Weiwei,Hou Yafei, Feng Yongtai, Li Jin,Xu Chuanlin, Hu Rui, and Zhang Mengyin have collected some materials.

This book is supported by the National Natural Science Foundation of China [grant number 71871188 and U1834209]. We acknowledge the support of the Open Research Fund for National Engineering Laboratory of Integrated Transportation Big Data Application Technology [grant number CTBDAT201909]. This book is also listed in the Graduate textbook (Monograph) Cultivation Project sponsored by Southwest Jiaotong University in 2018.

In the process of writing this book, Tian Rui, a senior engineer inthe dispatching department of China National Railway Group Co., Ltd.; Zhuang He, the general manager of China Railway Wuhan Bureau Group Co., Ltd.;and senior engineers of the China Railway Guangzhou Bureau Group Co., Ltd.—Chen Liquan and Zhou Zhiheng—provided practical experience and valuable guidance. Professor Fu Liping from the Department of Civil Engineering at the University of Waterloo and Professor Yang Xianyi from the College of Engineering at the University of Guelph provided valuable guidance. The relevant data used in this book has received strong support from the technical personnel of the dispatching office of China Railway Guangzhou Bureau Group Co., Ltd. Here, we would like to express our sincere gratitude to them.

目 录// CONTENTS

Chapter 1

Train dispatching management with data-driven approaches: A comprehensive review and appraisal

Train dispatching (TD) is at the forefront of all rail operations no matter transporting passengers or goods. Recent technological advances and the explosion of digital data have introduced data-driven methods (DDMs) in rail operations. In this study, DDMs on the TD problem are briefly explored, focusing on relevant studies on delay distribution, delay propagation, and timetable rescheduling. Data-driven TD methods, including statistical methods (SM), graphical models (GM), and machine learning (ML) methods are reviewed. Then, key issues on establishing different data-driven models for the TD problem are addressed. Subsequently, ML methods are considered to be among the most promising DDMs leading to innovative TD methods, which relies on rich data obtained from train operations. This study emphasizes the potentials on designing new alternatives in the three key fields of interest and provides directions for further research on TD.

1.1   Introduction

Robust train operations and effective management of unexpected incidents are critical for quality of service (QoS) and competitiveness of rail services in the transportation sector. Delays affect users' expectations about reliability, punctuality, and QoS. Moreover, delays cause missing transfers and extend working hours of crews and locomotives, which leads to increased operational cost for operators. Consequently, rail operating companies are given high priority in avoiding and reducing the negative influence of delays[1]. A significant number of models and algorithms have been proposed to improve train services in response to unexpected incidents during rail operation[2]. Recently, several railway traffic control (RTC) projects were launched to improve train operations and services for the ever-increasing rail travel demand. The Europe ON-TIME project, which began in November 2011, defines two out of eight targets mainly related to disturbance management[3]. The project titled Safety, Reliability, and Disruption Management of High-Speed Rail (HSR) and Metro Systems (Grant No. T32-101/15-R) was granted to enable dependable train operation, performance, and service through the advanced design of rail system operations with the help of train operation data[4]. In case of a delay incident, a train dispatcher who is responsible for facilitating the train movements over an assigned territory follows a set of dispatching decisions that are provided in the timetable or adjusts them according to critical decisions. Train dispatching (TD) is a multi-criteria decision-making (MCDM) problem [5, 6]. Although several MCDM approaches are available, each has its advantages and disadvantages. As reviewed in [7, 8], TD has become an active research area mostly due to delay reduction priority. However, a gap remains in the number of models that can handle TD in a real-time RTC system. In addition, most of the proposed solutions are based on abstracted models and simplified assumptions. Most of the recent practices in TD are still dominated by predetermined rules, contingency plans, intuition, and personal expertise. In practice, dispatchers need to integrate real-time structured and unstructured information (supporting data) when making dispatching decisions in response to unexpected incidents and displaced operations. This phenomenon is the main limitation of conventional mathematical models because they can hardly handle real-world, large-scale models in real-time, thereby leaving aside the gap between the experimental results fromly, these models and the actual operations.

Recent rapid advances in monitoring and communication systems and data technologies enabled a wide range of possibilities, such as data-driven train dispatching (DDTD) for operations management in rail transportation [9]. Train operation records from control and monitoring systems are a valuable resource to mine and assess realized operations to improve train operations based on data-driven decisions. The applications of big data in railway operations, maintenance, and safety have attracted the attention of researchers and practitioners [10]. Admittedly, data-driven decisions are remarkable, practical, and reasonable. In this regard, TD-related activities and decisions can be supported by hidden knowledge extracted from train operation records to make better decisions and actions in response to delayin future train operations.

The rest of this chapter is organized as follows: Section 1.2 briefly introduces some related concepts of TD, and presents the collection of dispatching data and summarize dimensions that are reviewed. Subsequently, Section 1.3 categorizes three types of data-driven models that have been applied in TD, covering 153 relevant papers focusing on data-driven methods (DDMs) in TD. Then, the review results, the future research direction, and the potential applications of DDMs in TD are presented in Section 1.4. Finally, Section 1.5 draws.

For reading convenience, all the abbreviations and their full forms in this paper are listed alphabetically conclusions in Table 1-1.

Table 1-1   Index Of Phrases Have Abbreviation

Full forms	Abbreviation
Artificial neural networks	ANN
Buffer Index	BI
Buffer time allocation optimization	BTA

Full forms	Abbreviation
Conflict detection	CD
Conflict detection and resolution	CDR
Convolutional Neural Networks	CNNs
Conflict Resolution	CR
Centralized Traffic Control	CTC
Deep Belief Networks	DBNs
Data-Driven Methods	DDMs
Data-Driven Train Dispatching	DDTD
Deep Extreme Learning Machines	DELM
Deep Learning	DL
Designer of Network Schedules	DONS
Deep Reinforcement Learning	DRL
Data-Driven Dynamic Train Delay Prediction System	DTDPS
Extreme Learning Machine	ELM
Fuzzy Petri net	FPN
Graphical Models	GM
High-Speed Rail	HSR
Linear Programming	LP
Least Square Method	LSM
Least Square Support Vector Machine	LSSVM
Multilevel Advanced Railways Conflict Resolution and Operation	MARCO
Multi-Criteria Decision Making	MCDM
Machine Learning	ML
Neural Networks	NN
Non-Parametric Bayesian Network	NPBN
Passenger information Control System	PIC
Quality of Service	QoS
Recurrent Neural Networks	RNN
Railway Traffic Optimization Using Alternative Graphs	ROMA
Railway Traffic Control	RTC
Real-World Train Operation Data	RWTOD
Schweizerische Bundesbahnen	SBB
Statistical Methods	SM
Support Vector Machine	SVM

Full forms	Abbreviation
Support Vector Regression	SVR
Train Dispatching	TD
Train Delay Prediction Systems	TDPS
Traffic Management System	TMS
Train Observation and Tracking System	TROTS
Timetable Rescheduling	TTR
Weighted Average Distance	WAD

1.2 Data-driven train dispatching

1.2.1 Train dispatching

A train dispatcher (United States, Japan, and China), rail traffic controller (Canada), train controller (Australia), or signalman (United Kingdom) is obliged to make real-time decisions to command trains. For the sake of safety and efficiency, train operations are governed by strict rules. Once delay occurs, the operations should be recovered as soon as possible at the first possible position with the greatest care to avoid affeeting the subsequent operations. Thus, dispatchers should make critical dispatching decisions on the basis of available data and previous experiences. First, they need to collect relevant data from operational circumstances. Secondly, they need to process the data to gather useful information. Thirdly, dispatching knowledge and personal experiences lead to decisions in train operation dispatching strategies. Traditional dispatching works are highly experience-oriented, thereby resulting in many uncertainties and inconsistencies in decision making in response to similar circumstances. Although the proposed mathematical models for TD perform well in experiments and provide remarkable results in the academic field, their application in real-time TD situations is difficult because they are not able to consider the knowledge and expertise of dispatchers. This phenomenon is mainly due to the hidden factors and interdependencies that models can hardly cover, which a dispatcher can do.

1.2.2 Train dispatching data

Recent technological advances and developments in rail transportation have enabled operators to store, access, and mine enormous real-world train operation data (RWTOD) from realized train processes. These kinds of RWTOD can come in three forms. The first form is structured data (e.g., arrival and departure time at stations), which is mainly reserved in the centralized traffic control (CTC) system [11]. The second form is semi-structured data, which can be obtained from recorded videos, images, and event notes [12, 13]. The third form is unstructured data (e.g., dispatching command and other literal event records), which can be captured by monitoring systems. Researchers and practitioners can use a host of data processing tools to process the numeral structured data. However, semantic and syntactic data models, which offer greater capabilities for data integration, extensibility, and compatibility over traditional approaches, are often applied to process semi-structured and unstructured data [14]. Train operation appearance is analyzed and estimated to a certain extent using train operation records of the Japanese railway, whether in the form of tables, texts, graphs, images, and videos [15]. Goverde and Hansen confirm that delay propagation and conflicts in the Netherlands can be analyzed by using train operation records [16]. Graffagnino visualizes train operation data in Switzerland to study delays [17]. For instance, TRENO in OPEN TRACK performs an extremely detailed graphical analysis of train movements, train speeds, acceleration, braking curves, and dwell times using RWTOD tools [18]. Moreover, train operation data in other countries, such as Germany [19], Italy [20], Denmark [21], Finland [22], UK [23], Japan [24], India[25], Turkey[26], US [27], Serbia [28], and China [29, 30], have been used in data-driven TD modeling.

1.2.3 Data-driven train dispatching issues

1.2.3.1 Delay distributions

Train operations are assumed to be stochastic processes [31]. Dispatchers need to capture the characteristics of delays on specific lines or local railway network. Delay distributions usually provide basic rules on delay causes that the trains follow and assist dispatchers in obtaining the delay probabilities and duration online and offline. Figure 1-1 shows the decision making based on delay distribution models, which may include delay cause distributions, arrival/departure delays at stations, running time delays in sections, delay aggregation distributions, and delay influence distributions. The upper part outlines what dispatchers do, and the lower part illustrates some delay distribution examples at stations and in sections. Overall, dispatchers need to estimate the potential delay probabilities and their influences based on delay-specific causes according to historical delay distributions in the approaching journey. When a delay occurs to a train, various strategies, such as adjusting running speeds, altering dwell times, and changing overtaking could be considered by dispatchers to absorb delays.

1.2.3.2 Delay propagation

Delay propagation is a function of delay aggravation caused by disturbances and delay recovery activities conducted by dispatchers. A delay may spread out in vertical and horizontal orientations, leading to delay propagation on the line or even on the network and contributing to the complexities of train operations. Delay propagation has been the main source of displacements in the railway system; thus, minimizing delay propagation takes high priority [32]. Analyses of microscopic and macroscopic approaches show that most of the studies consider the railway system at a microscopic rather than at a macroscopic level, and almost all papers have focused on minimizing delays of passengers or freight. Delay prediction is one of the most popular issues in these studies. It is a typical data-driven process because the following arrival or departure time is subject to its current status and the adjacent leading train. Thus, dispatchers can determine the arrival and departure times one after another. Figure 1-2 shows that determining train status is a recursive, iterative process. The time axis (red line) denotes the current time, and dispatchers need to use known data on the left of the time axis to predict unknown events on the right of the time axis. The origination departure time p_4 of train $i+1$ is determined by p_1, and p_5 is derived by p_2 and p_4. Similarly, p_7 is derived from p_5 and p_6. Train $i+1$ is mostly subject to the status of train i, whereas train $i+2$ is mostly subject to the status of train $i+1$, whose predicted points of p_4, p_5, and p_7 are considered historical data. Major disturbances can propagate to other trains in the network, thereby requiring short-term adjustments in the timetable to limit delay propagation [33].

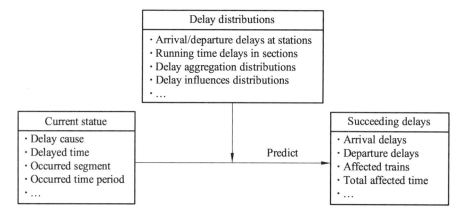

Fig 1-1　Decision-making based on delay distributions

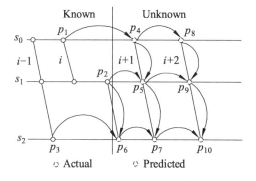

Fig.1-2　Recursive iterative processes of delay prediction

1.2.3.3 Timetable rescheduling

TTR is what dispatchers mainly deal when the effect of unexpected displacements on train operations are adjusted. TTR is usually considered the decision of altering succeeding train arrival, departure, and running times, which are previously planned timetable. Conflict detection (CD) and resolution (CDR), minimizing delays, minimizing delay costs, and buffer time allocation (BTA)optimization are the mainly proposed objectives in TTR. Figure 1-3 summarizes the strategies that are mainly used by dispatchers and proposed objectives in TTR in the existing literature.

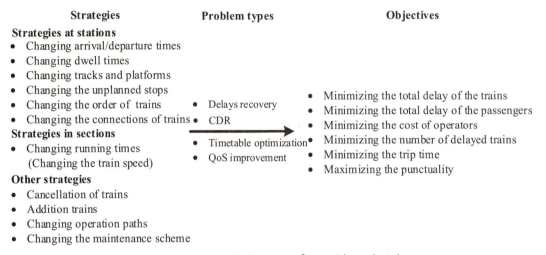

Fig.1-3   Strategies and objectives of timetable rescheduling

Several problems, such as delay recovery, conflict detection and resolution, timetable optimization, and QoS improvements, are investigated as the main issues of TTR. Fang et al. [34] surveyed nine types of models and solution approaches on TTR in railway networks, addressing problems of conflict resolution (CR), disturbance/disruption recovery, TD, and some data-driven associated methods in general. A review of recovery models and algorithms for real-time railway rescheduling of recent decades can be found in the work of Cacchiani et al. [7]. Here, the most recent papers on the DDMs employed in TTR are specifically considered.

When delays occur, the main problem that dispatchers focus on is CDR because the delay of only one train may cause an entire cascade of delays to other trains over the entire railway network and further delays and conflicts at train interactions and transferring points [35, 36]. The delays may lead to conflicts due to the competition of resources, and conflicts tend to lead to delays because of the time loss and the hindrance between trains. Conflict chains and trees should be prevented by dispatchers [37]. A conflict occurs when an overlap occurs between two or more time windows due to deviations of train events [38]. The total solutions for trunk lines in European railway networks include identifying and resolving conflicts automatically are the bases of the European Rail Traffic Management System [39]. One of the ultimate goals of TTR isCR, of which the detailed loop is presented in [40], and the detailed loop of CD is proposed by [41].

In practice, a certain amount of buffer times is mostly added to the timetable. However, this method can affect operational capacity in heavily utilized networks by contributing to longer travel times. Furthermore, the unused buffer times in sections (or stations) cannot be used by trains in the downstream sections (or stations) due to its non-storage property. Therefore, various BTA schemes can have different impacts on delay propagation and recovery and the operational capacity of the railway system,even with the same amount of buffer time [42]. To this end, two main issues need to be addressed. The first issue is how and to which extent the buffer times affect delay recovery and CR. The second issue is how to distribute the buffer time among different stations and sections to achieve the highest utilization ratio of buffer time. The timetable planners and dispatchers design or reschedule timetables with historical data using the empirical buffer times used in previous timetables with certain delay scenarios. On the one hand, planners may create a new BTA scheme for a new operation based on the statistics of historical timetables that are used for the line. They may use the statistics of timetables of another line with similar operating conditions for a newly opened line. This process can be considered a long-run period BTA to boost the robustness of the timetable. On the other hand, dispatchers adjust timetables according to the historical performance of a certain day to resolve probable delays or conflicts. This process can be considered a short-term BTA.

1.2.3.4   Outline of data-driven train dispatching issues

DDMs or data-oriented and data-based models are built by analyzing the actual data obtained from an operating system, particularly in finding connections between the subsystems and state variables (input, internal, and output variables) without requiring many details and explicit knowledge from the physical behavior of the system. DDMs have strong modeling abilities for complex systems, digging out relationships among system indices and establishing models that can fit different situations [43]. The survey shows that DDMs are multifunctional and are important in the development of intelligent transportation systems [44].

The rail industry has been a pioneer in using and implementing big data analytics. In this regard, the recently published book on big data application has shown practical aspects of DDMs in rail transportation [45]. The RWTOD has been widely used in many countries, supporting the improvement of rail traffic control qualities. For example, a data-driven train delay prediction system is developed with the help of big data analytics [20]. In Table 1-2, some of the case studies on TD issues based on the RWTOD in typical countries are summarized. Some trained models based on RWTOD have been used in many simulations in the last decade via commercial software, such as Opentrack [46] and RailSys [47], and laboratory software, such as railway traffic optimization using alternative graphs (ROMA) [32] and TNV-Conflict [37], to figure out the precise behavior of trains and improve train operation qualities.

Table 1-2   Case Studies On Train Dispatching

Literature	Country	Data	Addressed issues	Methodologies or systems
[19]	Germany	Train position data Arrival and departure time	Delay distribution, Evaluation of timetable quality	Open Timetable
[21]	Denmark	Train delay records	Assess and layout of timetable supplements	Statistical methods
[22]	Finland	Train actual timetable	Delay chains	Data-mining approach
[23]	The UK	Train delay data Meteorological data	Impacts and propagation of disruption	Statistical methods, Visualization
[24]	Japan	Train actual timetable	Delay causes Delay distributions	Visualization
[25]	India	Track occupation data Train actual timetable	Robustness evaluating of railway networks	Stochastic delay propagation models
[26]	Turkey	Train actual timetable	Train states and steady-state delay probabilities estimation	Markov chain model
[27]	USA	Freight data Train operation records	Optimization of rail capacity and congestion	Statistical methods
[28]	Serbia	Track occupation data Train actual timetable	Estimating train delays	Fuzzy Petri net
[29]	China	Train actual timetable of HSR	Delay distribution models	Statistical methods Regression models
[32]	Netherlands	Track occupation data Train delays	Short-term traffic prediction	ROMA dispatching system
[37]	Netherlands	Track occupation data Train actual timetable	Dispatching decisions Delay propagation chain	TNV-Conflict TNV-Statistics
[48]	Netherlands	Track occupation data Train actual timetable	Train delay propagation prediction	Analytical model
[49]	Netherlands	Track occupation data Train timetable	Knock-on delays estimation	Analytical stochastic model
[50]	Germany	Train actual timetable	Delay Dependencies, delay propagation	Correlation statistics
[51]	Denmark	Train position data Train actual timetable	Analysis of train deviations	Punctuality Reporting System
[52]	China	Train actual timetable of HSR	Primary delay recovery	Regression model Random forest model

Turner et al. [53] reviewed some studies on timetable planning and scheduling that applied DDMs, such as data mining, knowledge engineering, and expert systems. In this work, we look into the most popular DDMs, namely, statistical method (SM), Graphical models (GM), and machine learning (ML) methods [43]. The SM, including correlation analysis, regression models, and visualization methods, mine relationships among variables embedded in the data. The GM methods attempt to derive knowledge or rules from the data to establish the arc weights of the alternative graphs, the matrices of the Markov model, the probability chains of the Bayesian network, and the fuzzy numbers of the fuzzy network. These models include fuzzy logic, expert, and probabilistic graphical models. ML is a method used to produce reliable, repeatable decisions and to uncover hidden knowledge by learning from relationships and trends in historical datasets. The support vector machine (SVM), reinforced learning, deep learning (DL), and artificial neural networks (ANN) are also typical ML methods. Figure 1-4 shows that three different key subjects in TD, including delay distributions, delay propagation, and TTR and optimization, are reviewed using the aforementioned DDMs.

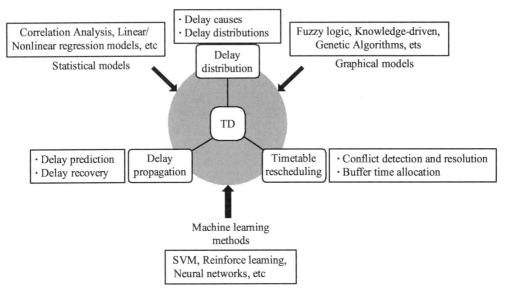

Fig.1-4　Outline of data-driven train dispatching issues

1.3　Data-driven models in train dispatching: Literature

1.3.1　Data-driven delay distributions: literature

In this section, we review studies on delay causes and distributions based on DDMs. Train delay distributions highly depend on the varying operating conditions of specific lines and networks. Although developing universal distributional forms that can be applied everywhere is difficult, data from specific lines can be used to reveal the general principles for other similar areas. Conte[54] pioneered the systematic study of dependencies among delays using data-based methods; his application-oriented thesis deals with identifying dependencies among delays through a stochastic analysis based on the measured arrival and departure delays that have been considered observations of random variables.

1.3.1.1　Delay causes

SM

Observations show that external factors are the main causes of primary delays, and operation interference is the main cause of knock-on delay, according to the data of on-schedule ratios. The number of passengers, occupancy ratio (passengers/seats), infrastructure utilization, cancellations, temporary speed reductions, railway construction, departure and arrival punctuality, and operational priority rules are the main factors that may affect train operations [55]. Palmqvist et al. [56] applied SM to quantify how severe weather, timetable, operational, and infrastructure-related variables can influence the punctuality of passenger trains.

From the aspect of external factors, poor weather condition has always been the main cause of primary delays. A novel exploration of the impacts of extreme events has been conducted [23, 57]. Punctuality statistics on the Norway railway show that more than 4000 delay hours, which was approximately 30% of the total amount of delay hours, was caused by infrastructure conditions [58].

Internal and congestion-related factors, such as crosses, passes, overtakes, prior time period train counts, total train hours, train spacing variability, and train departure headway were investigated by using SM for freight trains in the US [27]. The study found that the primary congestion factors (crosses, passes, and overtakes) consistently have the largest effect on congestion delay. Positive and statistically significant relationships between reactionary delays and capacity utilization conclude the exponential relationship between adding trains onto a congested network and capacity utilization, which is an important internal factor of delay[59].

The experience from Taiwan HSR shows that shortening the maintenance cycle can effectively alleviate the problem of train delay caused by signal failures [60]. Recently, over 1,200 train operation records were obtained from the "delay events record chart" of Wuhan–Guangzhou HSR in China, and seven categories of external causes that lead to primary delays are identified [29], and a similar relationship plot between capacity utilization and delays are also obtained from the Chinese HSR operation data. Statistics also show that almost 90% of disruptions are due to bad weather [61]. All these results help dispatchers to know the overall causes of delays in HSR.

Data-driven visualization based on train operation records can help determine delay causes. Timetable planners can intuitively determine the situation of train operation and obtain helpful information for analysis by visualizing the historical train operation data [24]. Chromatic Diagram, a helpful software to visualize the raw data, is abstracted and plotted to determine the delay causes [17, 62]. Moreover, the bubble diagram, incremental delay diagram, 3D diagram, and other information visualizations, such as box diagrams, dwell times, running times, headways, and scatter diagrams for delays, are applied to visualize historical train operation records [24]. Causes and effects of delay can be analyzed, and delay reduction measures can be evaluated by comparing results with the help of these skills.

GM

The fault trees are generally used for estimating the risk and development of railway facility failures. Port and Ramer [63] stated that fault trees may be helpful in estimating earthquake-induced failure probability and downtime of critical facilities, including in railway systems. Liu et al. [64] employed a fault tree combined with quantitative analysis to investigate the fault of HSR accidents. The fault tree analysis is also used to determine where the risks are, the dangers they pose, and what factors have the most significant effects on the rail system by analyzing all possible basic events. All wind-, rain-, and snow-related adverse weathers along with human-related factors can potentially cause great risks. A hierarchical analytic process is used to calculate the weights among indices for each adverse weather factor. A fuzzy synthetic evaluation process is then conducted to identify the risk level of an evaluation target [65].

ML

ML is not popularly used in studies of delay causes. So far, large amounts of historical detector data together with failure events, maintenance action, inspection schedule, train type, and weather information are used to predict railway facility maintenance [66]. Several analytical approaches, including correlation analysis, causal analysis (e.g., principal component), time series analysis, and ML techniques (e.g., SVM), are applied to learn rules automatically and build failure prediction models. Oneto et al. [67] proposed a train delay prediction system (TDPS) using ML to predict delays, considering exogenous weather data. The model can be further improved by including data from exogenous sources, particularly on the weather information provided by national weather services. Results of real-world data from the Italian railway network show that the recommendations of this study can remarkably improve the current state-of-the-art train delay prediction system. The delay cause discovery model is constructed in four phases, including data preprocessing and analysis, decision tree based on ML methodology, delay analysis with key delay factors, and spatiotemporal lateness topology analysis [68].

1.3.1.2 Delay distributions

SM

Several standard distribution models are often used to fit data-driven probability distributions and regression models. Delay elements, indices, and distributions can be easily observed using data-driven visualization methods. The chromatic diagram is used to visualize where a delay emerges and how it develops [69]. Then, dispatchers can easily identify the frequency and severity of delays and the effectiveness of the respective delay reduction measures. The proposed open timetable used in Schweizerische Bundesbahnen (SBB) helps railway timetable planners to evaluate actual schedule adherence data and assist dispatchers in identifying delays [19]. Delay distributions show the number of trains in various groups and different delaypatterns using real data with clustering methods [70].

An estimation of the duration of disturbances using SM [71] or other sophisticated techniques usually happens in railway networks [72]. The third quarter distributions of actual running times and delays are investigated using historical data [21]. A percentile approach, which assists the punctuality reporting system of RDK to work effectively, helps dispatchers to aggregate delay percentiles on train numbers (or groups of trains), geography (measuring points), time period, percentile, or as a combination [73]. Several reports have been developed to help RDK locate systematic causes of delays. These approaches can be used to achieve improved punctuality. Furthermore, on the most important lines of RDK, aggregations of data for analysis of dynamics of delays and queuing effect on single lines between stations are investigated using the data from the digital CTC [74].

So far, delay disturbances of trains in most studies are approximated by exponential distribution. A shifted exponential distribution for the free running time of each train is proved, and the effect of headways on knock-on delays of trains is simulated in [75]. Goverde [76] fitted the distributions of train arrival time, departure times, and dwell times in the Netherlands railway, and Yuan [77] investigated the departure and arrival times at Hague HS station with RWTOD. Both of their studies concluded that train operation interference time follows a negative exponential distribution. The exponential distributions, which are assumed for inter-arrival time and minimal headway times, are used in a queueing network model to predict the average waiting time of trains [78]. Later, Briggs and Beck [79] used the q-exponential function to demonstrate the distribution of train delays on the British railway network.

The Weibull, Gamma, and lognormal distributions have been adopted in several studies [80, 81]. Buker and Seybold [82] evaluated the suitability of a group of existing distribution models, such as modified exponential phase-type, theta-exponential, and polynomial distributions, to approximate arrival delays. The operation data from the Wuhan–Guangzhou HSR suggest that the probability density distribution of different disruption sources and distributions of affected trains due to delays are plotted in general [61]. The log-normal distribution can fit the primary delay duration distribution, and the inverse model can fit the affected number of train distributions [29, 83]. In addition, the log-logistic probability density function is the best distributional form to approximate the empirical distribution of running times [84]. For the fitting models, several model test methods are applied, Kolmogorov–Smirnov test, for instance [61, 84, 85].

Similarly, punctuality data from automatic registrations in the signaling systems have been used for regression studies, and correlation coefficients are found to be significant at 0.01 level between arrival punctuality and the number of passengers, occupancy ratio, and departure punctuality [55]. The nonlinear regression model generated by train operation records is used to calculate the expected times under certain delays [75]. Specifically, the developed models can be incorporated into a dispatching decision support system to improve real-time train traffic control. This method would provide dispatchers with accurate estimates of the occurrence of possible disruptions and the potential effects of a given disruption event.

GM

Train operations were described by a set of processes, including train running, dwell, and waiting times caused by conflicting train routes, in which dependencies between events and processes are graphically represented by timed event graphs [86]. The running and dwell time and headway arcs are all generated by sorting all events using the same train number of their date and time of occurrence, containing all arc modeling delay dependencies among events.

Furthermore, arc weights that reflect the minimal time between two adjacent events have been derived by calculating a small percentile of all observed arc weights in the track occupation data.

Zilko et al. [87] developed a probabilistic model to estimate the railway disruption duration using non-parametric Bayesian network (NPBN), which strongly depends on the empirical distributions of each dependent variables that were generated by historical data in the entire Dutch railway network. However, the Bayesian network strongly relies on the accuracy of the information, which updates over time.

ML

So far, papers dedicated to studying delay distributions using ML methods are limited. An ML method is proposed for the automatic calibration of disturbance parameters for railway operation simulation to generate stochastic disturbances. Supported by ML, efforts toward calibrating parameters have been greatly reduced with ensured consistency between simulation models and actual railway operations [88]. The proposed calibration algorithm has been implemented and integrated into the new simulation software, DoSim. A remarkable improvement in system performance is observed. The software has been tested on an example for a real railway network in Germany with 71 stations. The recently published paper in TRB meeting presents statistical and ML models to build the relation between delay duration and cause and statistically predict delay time [89]. The models of MLR, decision tree, and SVM are applied, in which SVM performs best in estimation accuracy. In addition, the SVM models are applied to investigate the relationship between the primary delays and their affected trains based on the train operation records obtained from Guangzhou Railway Bureau in China, and the ε-SVR and υ-SVR models show remarkable performance to predict the possibilities of the number of affected trains [90].

1.3.1.3 State-of-the-art on delay distributions

This is not an easy task for dispatchers given their heavy workload. The delay information should be provided with an easy-to-understand way so that the information can be used without increasing hassle. Delay distributions and relationships between delays and their causes help manage delays during train operations. They can help dispatchers to understand the delay mechanism to improve the management of train delays in practice. Table 1-3 presents a summary of the literature on data-driven delay distributions.

Table 1-3　Summary of the State-of-the-art studies on data-driven delay distributions

Literature	Data	Methodologies or systems
[54]	Harz Region in the center of Germany:598 stations, 92 vehicles and 31 lines	Data-based methods,GM
[55]	Trains of IC1900, IC2100 and IC2400 of Norwegian: 594, 340 and 327 records respectively during 2001 and 2003	Statistical analysis

continued

Literature	Data	Methodologies or systems
[56]	32.4 million train movements for all trains in Sweden during the year of 2015	Statistical methods
[23]	Delay trains which have 10,000 weather-related minutes from the UK rail networks on June 28, 2012	Case study
[27]	Delays records for freight trains in eight train districts in the western USA from January 2001 to August 2006	Statistical methods
[57]	Over 6,000 train departures from metropolitan commuter rail based upon the Dublin Area Rapid Transit rail system	Statistical analysis
[58]	96, 319 and 92 records respectively of stations Høn, Oslo, and Sandvika in Norway railway from June 01, 2005 to May 31, 2006	Statistical analysis
[59]	Data from 24 routes across the Railtrack network in the UK between April 2001 and June 2002	Statistical analysis
[60]	Data from the Taiwan HSR	Linear regression
[29]	Over 1,200 train operation records from February 24, 2015, to November 30, 2015, from Wuhan-Guangzhou HSR in China	Statistical analysis
[61]	More than 86,000 trains from January 2013 to May 2014 from Wuhan–Guangzhou HSR	Statistical analysis
[24]	Train numbers, arrival times, departure times at stations, track and other related information	Visualization methods
[17]	3-year rolling window for around 1,000 stations and 10,000 trains per day in SBB	Mathematical methods; Visualization methods
[62]	Data from TOZAI Line in Japan	Visualization methods; Simulation algorithm
[63]	Fragility parameters in 50 years	Fault-tree analysis methods
[64]	Data of train D301 and train D3115 on 20:30, July 23, 2011	Fault-tree analysis methods; Quantitative analysis
[65]	Data from the Beijing URT Line 8 Olympic Center Station	Fault tree analysis, AHP evaluation model
[66]	7 or 14 days historical readings in USA Class I railroad in 2011	Correlation analysis, Causal analysis, ML methods
[67]	More than 1,000 trains and several checkpoints in more than 6 months in Italy	Kernel methods, Extreme learning machine
[68]	More than 360,000 records from TRA from April 04,2011 to May 31, 2012	Decision tree, Topology analysis
[69]	27 hourly trains between Urayasu Station and Kayabacho Station on weekdays in the most congested morning rush hours in June 2008	Visualization methods
[19]	Passenger trains at the LN station during the entire day for the week of June 16-20, 2003 in Swiss Federal Railways	Visualization methods, Statistical methods
[70]	The *Kystbanen* (coastline),north Copenhagen, Denmark from April to December 2014	K-MEANS clustering
[71]	Data corresponding to the regional railway network in Asturias	Statistical methods
[72]	More than 1,000 trains and several checkpoints in more than 6 months in Italy	Deep extreme learning machine
[21]	Data from the line Copenhagen-Roskilde in Rail Net Denmark from 2014	Statistical analysis

Literature	Data	Methodologies or systems
[73]	Approximately 1,400 trains operating daily on Rail Net Denmark's network from January 2009 to March 2010	Percentile approach
[74]	Data from Sweden to Copenhagen Central Station in February 2012	Statistical analysis
[75]	18 simulation generated data from Rotterdam C to Den Haag	Stochastic simulation, regression analysis
[76]	1846 trains in Eindhoven during one week in September 1997	Statistical analysis
[77]	Nearly 10,000 trains during September 1999 at Hague HS station	Statistical analysis
[78]	Two parts of the Dutch railway network between 1997 and 1998	Queueing network model
[79]	Over 200,000 departures records from 23 major stations for the period September 2005 to October 2006 on the British railway	Super statistical model, Q-exponential function
[80]	Around 10,000 trains during September 1999 in the Hague HS station	Statistical analysis
[81]	Nearly 10,000 trains during September 1999 at Hague HS station	Statistical analysis
[82]	Data from Basel in Swiss railway network	EM-algorithm, Iteratively optimize
[41]	Data from the corridor Rotterdam-The Hague of Dutch railway during February 2009	Data mining, Statistical analysis
[83]	29,662 HSR train records of Wuhan-Guangzhou HSR from February 24, 2015, to November 30, 2015.	Distribution models
[84]	Train operation records of Wuhan-Guangzhou HSR from February 2015 to November 2015	Distribution models
[85]	"Kystbane", the coastal railway running north from Copenhagen, from the period September through November, 2014	Distribution models
[86]	Data from Dutch train describer during March 2000 between Zwijndrecht and Rotterdam Central	Statistical analysis, Linear regression analysis, Robust regression
[87]	Data in the entire Dutch railway network from January 1, 2011, to June 30, 2013	Probabilistic model
[88]	72 trains in Germany Railway network with 71 stations.	ML methods
[89]	602 train delay events from January 1, 2010, to June 30, 2016, of Taiwan High-speed Rail	Decision tree, SVM
[90]	High-speed trains' records from April 21, 2014, to November 21, 2016, of HSR in Guangzhou Railway	SVM

The actual operation can be affected by various of factors, over 50 broad attributable reasons have been listed in the UIC 450-2 that will lead to train delays, such as weather, facility failure, and drivers' and travelers' behavior [91]. The reviewed studies have shown the roadmap of modeling delay distributions based on RWTOD (Figure 1-5). Two layers of indices obtained from RWTOD should be used in the modeling. First, dual-index models should combine delay causes and one of the indices in the "second layer indices." Second, multi-index models can be formed using several or all indices that can be obtained. In this light, spatiotemporal delay distribution models, delay aggravation, and recovery distribution models, as well as comprehensive models that involve all the elements above, can be established. ML methods should be employed because more data have become available, and the big data have provided a broad vision in data mining.

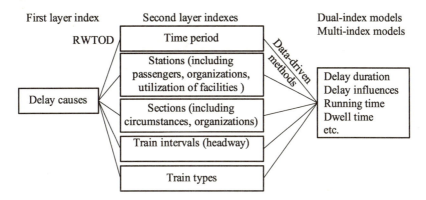

Fig.1-5 Roadmap of the data-driven approach for delay distribution modeling

The existing studies have four deficiencies concerning delay distributions, which are:

(1) Researchers have focused on delay-distribution modeling based on specific lines, lacking general models that can fit multiple lines.

(2) Cause-based models of delays are scarce; many specific causes for which the data can not be obtained have not been studied. More detailed relationships between delay distributions and their causes based on rich RWTOD should be determined. As stated by the International Union of Railways, the availability of delay causes is urgently required to optimize international train networks [21]. Primary and secondary delays should be explicitly recorded, thereby making the development of algorithms possible to link primary and secondary delays and to determine how delays develop and how trains may auto-correlate their delays.

(3) The studies tend to focus on a single line or even a segment. It is necessary to study the delay distributions for the entire railway network involving many types of trains, especially the systems comprised of cross-line trains.

(4) The models can fit the delay data well, but they can not tell us the mechanisms causing the delays. Also, most of the statistic models need to be established based on some prior assumptions.

1.3.2　Data-driven delay propagation: Literature

Delay prediction and recovery are the main issues in addressing the problem of delay propagation. Delay propagation factors, such as interaction among primary delays, knock-on delays, exogenous events, delay aggravation, and recovery can be approximated using probability functions that can consider factors from sections, stations, time, and train interactions.

1.3.2.1 Delay prediction

Train operations are highly dependent on running and dwell time variations [92]. The estimation of running times requires predicting the effect of disturbances and subsequent buffer time adjustments that may be experienced during their operations.

SM

Results supported the strong correlation between arrival delays and dwell times, focusing on a statistical analysis of running times between stations to make predictions of the delay propagation in a railway system [86]. Phase-type distributions that can derive secondary delay distributions from primary delay distributions have been proposed [93]. Yuan and Hansen [49] presented an analytical stochastic model for estimating the propagation of train delays, and the key issue is how to estimate the convolution of individual independent distributions. Validation results reveal that the proposed analytical stochastic model effectively estimates the propagation of train delays and consequently, the punctuality of train arrivals, departures, and knock-on delays of trains. Correlation statistics are used to mine delay dependencies in large-scale real-world delay data obtained from the SBB network during two months of the timetable [50]. However, without any assumption on the statistical distribution of data, algorithms that efficiently find systematic dependencies in large-scale railway delay data are proposed.

Regression models obtained from delay distributions can serve as prediction models [55, 75]. Therefore, advanced minimum running time estimations may be used as a piecewise linear function that consists of the maximum number of regression lines for small delays and a small percentile for large delays. Passenger boarding and alighting events contribute to the dwell time prediction of trains [94, 95]. Murali et al. present a delay regression-based estimation technique that models delay as a function of the mix of trains and the network topology [96]. Guo et al. [97] consider the train operation as a sequence of discrete events and apply a linear regression model when modeling the delay prediction. The delay interpretation and dependencies are learned from historical data obtained from five stations on the Beijing–Shanghai HSR. A combination of linear regression and combinatorial model is generated from the online train delay monitoring data and is tested on the basis of a regional corridor from Lucerne, and resulted in low prediction error, although capacity constraints within stations are not considered [98].

Most recently, Kecman and Goverde [99] presented models that were developed by collecting all running and dwell time data from the training set and creating a separate predictive model to estimate each type of process time. This model confirms that regardless of departure delays, the majority of running times seem to be weakly affected by peak hours and do not have a remarkable daily variation. Li et al. [100] developed parametric and non-parametric regression models to estimate dwell times at shortstops for real-time scheduling, which is driven by train detection data from the Netherlands. Peak-hour dwell times are estimated using a linear regression model of train length and dwell times at previous and preceding trains. The off-peak-hour dwell times are estimated using a non-parametric regression model, particularly the *k*-nearest neighbor model.

A visualization and analytic system that can perform delay forecasting for the passenger information control system has been used since July 2003 [101]. This system generates delay status information that can show delay propagation.

GM

Difficulty in delay prediction is mainly due to unpredictable factors that affect train event times, and the key issue is to model uncertainties during train status transition. To this end, computation theories such as graph theory, Markov chain, fuzzy network, and Bayesian network are employed.

A data-mining approach is used to analyze rail transport delay chains with data from passenger train traffic on the Finnish rail network; however, data from the train running process are limited to one month [22]. Also, event graphs are used to forecast running, arrival times, dwell times, and headways [48, 86]. Kecman and Goverde [102] employ a timed event graph with dynamic arc weights to set up a microscopic model for the accurate prediction of train event times. Through this model, train interactions are modeled with high accuracy by involving operational constraints and following the actual headway time between adjacent trains.

A laboratory version of the real-time dispatching system called ROMA was developed and tested on an offline dataset to automatically recover disturbances and proactively detect each time interval [32, 103, 104]. The alternative graph is a suitable model for the job shop problem and can easily model several real-world constraints. The main value of the alternative graph is the detailed representation of the network topology at the level of railway signal aspects and operational rules, which can provide fruitful data and rules for other modules.

Barta et al. [105] developed a Markov chain model to evaluate the evolution of freight train delays at their successive terminals and classify terminals in terms of the roles of the trains. Şahin [31] established a Markov chain model to illustrate delay propagation and recovery using the observed historical data collected from a single-track line of the Turkish State railways. When the data-driven status transition matrix is available, predicting train states at certain event time steps and estimating steady-state delay probabilities will be possible. However, data used for modeling in this paper were 6-h and 18-station train-graphs of seven days, and only six delay cause classes that distinguish delay states are used. Based on the assumption that the probability of a state change depends on the moment of transition, train delay predictions are modeled by using a non-stationary Markov chain [106].

A fuzzy Petri net (FPN) model in which expert knowledge is used to define fuzzy sets and rules, transforming expertise into a model to calculate train delays, is proposed to estimate train delays [28, 107]. The proposed dispatching rules, which is empirically verified under different circumstances, can serve as training documents of the central training center and can be a basis of the decision-making system for dispatchers by interviewing dispatch experts with more than

10 years of experience in the central train control center of Taiwan railways [108]. In the triangular fuzzy number workflow nets of high-speed train running state models, the fuzzy time for train activities are generated on the basis of data for June 21–24, 2012 at five stations between Beijing South and Dezhou East of the Beijing–Shanghai HSR [109]. The probability of different deviation times are obtained by initially using least squares linear regression.

The transition matrix is generated from actual records of train movements when applying the Markov chain to model the delay propagation [31]. The Bayesian networks can timely update train running status based on new operation data. Zilko et al. [87] first attempted to apply the NPBN, which represents the joint distribution among variables that describe the nature of the disruption to predict the disruption length to the Dutch Operational Rail Control Centre. Later, they extended a new model with copula Bayesian networks, which consider the factors that influence the length of disruptions and models the dependence between them [110]. We proposed a hybrid Bayesian network model to predict HSR delays using the train operation records of Wuhan–Guangzhou HSR. The proposed model on overage can achieve over 80% accuracy in predictions within a 60-min horizon [111]. Of course, the joint method with Bayesian Reasoning and Markov model can be used to predict the delay state in different station [112, 113].

ML

Kecman and Goverde [99] proposed a statistical learning method that combines the SM and ML methods. The modeling is divided into three steps, namely, least-trimmed squares robust linear regression, regression trees, and random forests. The complementary advantages of these three types of models enabled the statistical learning methods to outperform other models. A supervised decision tree method that follows the ML and data mining techniques is designed to estimate the key factors in knock-on delays [68]. The proposed model can be used in predicting lengths of railway disruptions with high accuracy using delay history data. A hybrid approach that combined decision tree and random forest regression is also used to predict the running time, dwell time, train delay and penalty costs, which merges the data-driven model and experience-based models approaches [114].

ANN, as a basic ML method, learn from historical data to make predictions about future [115]. Peters et al. [116] applied ANN to process existing delays abstracted from known operation data to generate delay predictions for depending trains shortly; this method performs well when predicting future (secondary) delays based on existing (primary) delays, and it outperforms the traditional rule-based method. Yaghini et al. [117] also presented an ANN model with high accuracy to predict the delay of passenger trains in Iran; the comparison of the proposed ANN, decision trees, and multinomial logistic regression models confirm that the ANN model has high accuracy, low training time, and remarkable solution qualities.

Also, support vector regression (SVR) in passenger and freight train arrival delays prediction is implemented in [118, 119]. The comparison between the proposed SVR model and the ANN model shows that the SVR outperforms ANN because it achieves higher average R^2 than ANN on the test data. The models, based on the least-squares method, SVM, and least square SVM were trained and tested by using the field data collected in Wuhan–Guangzhou HSR and were proposed to predict train positions. These methods enabled the prediction of the HSR train position and the running time [120].

Most recently, the shallow and deep extreme learning machine (DELM) was proposed, along with the rapid development of big data technologies. Oneto et al. [20, 67] presented a data-driven TDPS for a large-scale railway network to provide useful information to RTC processes by using state-of-the-art tools and techniques; this system can extract information from a large amount of historical train movement data using the most recent big data technologies, learning algorithms, and statistical tools. The described approach and prediction system have been validated on the basis of real historical data in six months. The results show that the DELM outperforms the current technique, which is mainly based on the event graph proposed by Kecman and Goverde [102]. Using the findings of Oneto et al. [20] as a basis, Oneto et al. [72] developed a data-driven dynamic train delay prediction system (DTDPS), which can integrate heterogeneous data sources to deal with varying dynamic systems using DELM. Exploiting state-of-the-art tools and techniques, this system is entirely data-driven and does not require any prior information about the railway network.

1.3.2.2 Delay recovery

SM

The majority of recent studies have focused on the area of delay recovery models and algorithms. Three classes of real-time schedule recovery, namely, vehicle rescheduling for road-based services, train-based rescheduling, and airline schedule recovery problems, are reviewed in [121]. Another overview of recovery models and algorithms for real-time railway disturbance and disruption management that mainly summarized methods on real-time TTR of the rolling stock and crew duties is presented in [7].

Naohiko [122] briefly discussed the recovery measure of disruption in train operations in the Tokyo metropolitan area and apply three kinds of data, namely, train accident, train operation record, and delay certificate data. Interviews with 19 transportation staff of 9 companies with regard to rescheduling methods at the time of the accident with casualty provided recovery effects of the various strategies conducted by dispatchers. Although this study only proposed an interview result and statistics on delay recovery, it presented a data-driven method of the measurement of delay recovery.

Liebchen et al. [123] introduced recoverable robustness into train delay recovery to jointly optimize the plan and strategy for limited recovery. Based on the assumption of uncertainty at the running and dwell times of trains, different recovery possibilities can be obtained from the historical data. Recoverable robustness integrates timetabling and the so-called disturbance management under different scenarios with various recovery possibilities.

GM

The alternative graph can be generated after all the necessary information has been elaborated by the loaded information, and the disruption recovery module of the ROMA checks if block sections in the network are unavailable and automatically recovers disturbances [32, 103, 104]. Cadarso et al. [124, 125] proposed a two-step approach that combined passenger demand pattern anticipated by a discrete choice model and an integrated optimization model for the timetable and a rolling stock to deal with recovery disruptions in large-scale rapid transit networks. The data-driven multinomial logit model was computed and validated by the Spanish rail operator RENFE based on passenger counts, inquiries, and historical data fittings.

Khadilkar [126] proposed a data-enabled stochastic model for evaluating the robustness of timetables by considering delay prediction and recovery. Regarding the time supplements, the running time between two stations is frequently used to absorb previous delays, and the delay recovery effectiveness is statistically estimated based on the empirical data. The average recovery rate of 0.13 min/km was used for the delay recovery ability obtained from more than 38,000 train arrival/departure records from the Indian Railway network. However, only the empirical data for 15 days were available for the study. Such a constant average recovery rate can hardly reflect the actual recovery potentials of different sections and stations.

ML

Recently, Wen et al. [127] presented two DDMs, namely, multiple linear regression models and random forest regression model, to address the problem of predicting delay recovery of HSR trains due to primary delays. Models were trained and tested using the 10-month train operation records from the Wuhan Guangzhou HSR line in China. The researchers examined the relationships between train delay recovery (dependent variable) and four independent variables, namely, primary delay duration, total scheduled dwell time for all downstream stations, total supplements in all downstream sections, and a binary variable. The validation tests indicate that both models can achieve considerable performance, whereas the random forest model outperforms the multiple linear regression models in delay recovery prediction accuracy. Moreover, the proposed random forest regression is superior to the extreme learning machine (ELM) and stochastic gradient descent methods [128] and [129] under the same explanatory variables and dataset.

1.3.2.3 State-of-the-art on delay propagation

Existing studies on delay propagation show that data-driven delay prediction and recovery are universally concerned with theory and practice. Table 1-4 shows a summary of state-of-the-art studies on data-driven delay propagation.

Table 1-4 Summary of the state-of-the-art studies on data-driven delay propagation

Literature	Data	Methodologies or systems
[33]	Trains locally rerouted to bypass the disruption, canceled services in the Den Bosch, Nijmegen, Arnhem, and Utrecht stations	ROMA dispatching system
[92]	30 trainsin 14 stations	Fuzzy expert systems
[93]	Actual timetable in a part of the Netherlands intercity railway network with four lines	EMPHT program
[94]	Passenger boarding and alighting data from seven busy stations in the Netherlands	Statistical methods
[95]	Broader data from door sensors, passenger counters, and train event recorders	Statistical methods
[96]	Trains' state data from Downtown Los Angeles-Inland Empire Trade Corridor in the USA	Simulation-based technique
[97]	Historical data from 5 stations on the Beijing-Shanghai HSR	Linear regression model
[98]	Train delay monitoring data of Swiss Railways	Linear regression
[99]	Running times of nine train lines over 143 blocks and the dwell times of 9 train lines in 19 stations in 82 days from the areas Rotterdam and the Hague	Statistical learning method
[100]	A train detection dataset ofDutch railway line from September 1, to November 30, 2012	Parametric regression, Non-parametric regression model
[101]	Train tracking information of Tokaido Sanyo Shinkansen	Delay forecasting system
[102]	Historical track occupation data of a busy corridor in the Netherlands	Statistical model
[32]	Train timetables in 2007 of the route Utrecht Den Bosch	Real-time dispatching system
[103]	Secondary delays based on the Schiphol dispatching area	Branch and bound algorithm
[104]	Records of the Dutch signaling system NS54	Heuristic algorithm
[105]	Historical data of the Hupac transportation network from February to June 2011	Markov chain model
[31]	Data of the TCDD during 14-20 July of 2002	Markov chain model
[106]	Traffic realization data between Beijing and Shanghai from December 2013 to March 2014	Non-stationary Markov chain model
[28]	Track occupation data and practical train timetable from the year 2012 of the Belgrade railway node	Fuzzy Petri net model
[49]	Track occupation data and train timetable of the Dutch railway station The Hague Holland Spoor	Analytical stochastic model
[50]	Several important operating points of the SBB network during two months of 2008	Correlation statistics
[22]	Data from passenger train traffic on the Finnish rail network during September 2009	Data mining
[107]	Passenger loads, fluctuation of a passenger load and bus encounter probability in four terminals.	Fuzzy Petri net model
[108]	Train dispatching data of a line section of Taiwan's network	Fuzzy Petri net
[109]	Data at five stations between Beijing South and Dezhou East of Beijing Shanghai HSR during June 21-24, 2012	Triangular fuzzy number workflow nets model
[110]	Track circuit disruptions in the Dutch railway network	Copula Bayesian Networks model
[111]	378510 arrival and departure events from February. 2015 to November 2015 on Wuhan-Guangzhou HSR	Hybrid Bayesian Network Model
[112, 113]	a very small section of the Great Western Rail line in UK	Markov model

Literature	Data	Methodologies or systems
[114]	12 months (the whole 2016 solar year) of train movements of one big Italian Region (Liguria)	Decision tree and random forest regression
[115]	the data of Thailand for six months from June 1, 2013 to November 30, 2013	KNN algorithm
[116]	Operation data in the network	Neural networks
[117]	Data of passenger train delays from 2005 to 2009: 18 174 hours per year and 30□minutes for each train	Artificial neural network model
[118]	Train arrival delay data of different routes of Serbian Railways	Support vector regression
[119]	The CSX Transportationdata from December 1, 2014 through January 31,2017	Support vector regression
[120]	Data from February 2015 to November 2015 on Wuhan Guangzhou HSR	LSM、SVM、LSSVM
[20]	Historical train movements data of the Italian railway network	Data-driven dynamic train delay prediction system
[122]	Actual train operation data from 9 railway companies in 2012	Data-driven method of delay recovery measuring
[123]	Recover time of original method and recovery robust approach in Palermo Centrale station.	Recoverable robustness methods
[124]	Passengers' and operators' costs based on realistic cases in Madrid for 2008	Two-step approach
[125]	Passengers' and operators' costs based on realistic cases in Madrid for 2008	Two-step approach
[126]	Empirical data for 15 days of operations of the Mumbai New Delhi railway	Stochastic delay propagation model
[127]	Train operation records from the Wuhan Guangzhou HSR line in 10 months	Multiple linear regression models and random forest regression model

Figure 1-6 depicts the research roadmap of data-driven delay propagation. Dispatchers need a continuous estimation of succeeding train status, including the arrival and departure time at stations, running time in sections, and delays at stations and sections. The primary and knock-on delay models should be set up, and how delays are recovered should be revealed based on delay distributions, delay and aggravation, and recovery effectiveness obtained from experiences and historical data. Attention should be paid to the ML/DL in delay propagation estimation and evaluation without any assumption on statistical data distributions to reveal the mechanism of delay development.

The reviewed studies have four shortages regardingdelay propagation:

(1) Researchers tend to study the issues of delay propagation and recovery with GM methods, such as Petri Net with Fuzzy Logic, which rely too much on the prior dispatching knowledge.

(2) Studies involvingdelay propagation due to different causes and delay durations are lacking. It is necessary to study the influence of delays, including the affected trains and time intervals.

(3) The models of primary delays and knock-on delays should be set up respectively, and how delays are recovered should be revealed lying on delay distributions, delay and

aggravation, and recovery effectiveness that obtained from the experiences and historical data.

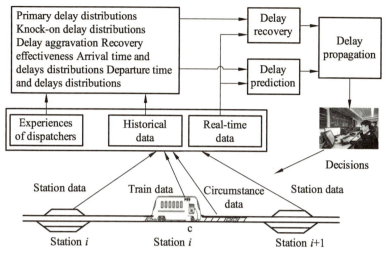

Fig.1-6   Roadmap of data-driven delay propagation

(4) Researchers mainly study the delay propagation for a specific railway line instead of a complex network. The interaction between the delay propagation in the horizon direction and the vertical direction need to be studied in-depth, and how a delay propagates on a railway network should be more significant.

The ML/DL needs to be paid more attention to delay propagation estimation and evaluation, without any assumption on statistical distributions of data, revealing the mechanism of delay development.

1.3.3   Data-driven timetable rescheduling: Literature

1.3.3.1   Conflict detection and resolution

As reviewed in [130], over four decades have passed since the conflict management problem in train operations around the world was first studied, and several systems and the CDR module have been developed. Existing studies on CDR mainly apply CI methods, especially knowledge-based methods and graph theories as well as ML, which are effective methods for dealing with CDR using train operation data.

SM

Chen and Harker firstly model the probability of a train's historical dispatching data, delaying a particular train due to actual conflicts, and the conflict delay between two trains is based on this probability and the probability of the two trains interfering with each other [131]. The latter probability is dependent on the outcome of prior conflicts in the schedule and unforeseen events. Train operation conflict number is usually used to study the characters of delays and conflict severity between trains; for example, the delay risk and reliability of train arrival times [132, 133]. The number of conflicts has been considered as one of the most important indexes to measure the severity of delays.

GM

Hansen et al. [48] presented a delay propagation model in which train path conflicts and dispatching decisions are considered and estimated the parameters through the offline statistical analysis of historical train operation data. Medeossi et al. [134] defined conflicts regarding probability by calibrating the motion equation with the train tracking data obtained from GPS or train event recorders, using performance parameters and calibrated motion equations with initial delay and stop time distributions from building stochastic blocking times. A set of tools for CDR were proposed by the Multilevel Advanced Railways Conflict Resolution and Operation (MARCO) project, which pioneered the development of tools, algorithms, and technologies for CDR [135]. Designer of Network Schedules was developed to design a conflict-free timetable in Dutch [136]. The COMBINE and COMBINE2 projects aimed to develop a traffic management system (TMS) based on MARCO [39, 137]. The dispatching support system, ROMA, which aims to compute flexible conflict-free timetables, detect and resolve conflicts, and terminate delay propagation, was proposed in [138, 139]. Another set of tools called TNV was developed, which mainly consisted of TNV-Prepare, TNV-Conflict, and TNV-Statistics [140]. Subsequently, the train observation and tracking system (TROTS) was developed to use operation data from Dutch train describers, thus serving as a dispatching support system [141].

Knowledge-based DDM systems that rely on artificial intelligence were utilized to deal with CD and CR during the 1990s. The expert system for real-time train dispatching, in which computer-aided technologies are employed to process the human expertise and train operation data, is used in detecting and resolving train conflicts [142]. In this system, the CD is triggered by the automatic train tracking system, and CR is conducted based on a highly detailed data modeling of train operation constraints. Subsequently, the knowledge extracted from human experts is used to search for a reasonable conflict resolution [143]. Similarly, the work experiences of dispatchers for more than 10 years are used as the basic rules for CDR in the knowledge-based system [108].

Furthermore, the fuzzy network theory is widely used to solve CDR problems. Fay [144] proposed a dispatching support system with expert knowledge in fuzzy rules of "IF-THEN" type and used an FPN notation to model the rule-based expert knowledge in a decision system. The modeled expert knowledge was used as the rule for the "selection of feasible actions" for conflict classification and resolution, which would affect the development of conflicts directly. Then, Zhuang et al. [145] applied a timed Petri net to model the HSR train timetable to study conflict prediction using the fuzzification of time intervals in a train timetable based on historical statistics. Based on the temporal fuzzy reasoning method, a new conflict prediction method is proposed, and the results under two scenarios of HSR in China prove that conflict prediction after the fuzzy processing of the time intervals of a train timetable is reliable and practical. Conflicts between successive stations and within stations are identified and solved with the fuzzy logic system, where expertise is used to establish fuzzy rules and adjust train dwell times [146]. The fuzzy rules from this knowledge after fuzzification could express their actual meaning effectively.

As reviewed in the part of delay prediction, pre-loaded data and accurately updated data are used by ROMA in predicting delay and then identifying conflict; the conflict identification can usually be the direct result of delay prediction. In an alternative graph, a fixed arc is a fixed precedence relation, an alternative arc represents an alternative precedence relation, and the weights of both kinds of arcs that are calculated by historical data are considered the arc lengths [147, 148]. After loading all data and determining all arc weights, offline conflicts can be detected using a topological visit of the alternative graph, and alternative arcs are used to avoid conflicts between trains [32].

TNV systems maintain a real-time record of train description steps and received events from the safety and signaling systems, with the precision of a second [16]. The TNV-Prepare tool generates TNV-tables that provide various opportunities to analyze railway operations, including capacity analysis, punctuality analysis, and assessment of stochastic railway processes. Subsequently, the TNV-Conflict tool was developed to identify all signaled route conflicts automatically, including critical sections and conflicting trains [140]. Later, the TNV-Statistics tool was developed and added to TNV-Conflict to determine chains of route conflicts with associated secondary delays and rank signals according to the number of conflicts, time loss, or delay jump [37]. The TNV system was recently replaced by TROTS, a process mining tool based on event data records from the Dutch train describer system, which aims to minimize train disruptions and improve operation safety in railway systems [40].

ML

Most recently, artificial intelligent DDMs were proposed to deal with CDR problems. The D-Agent method was developed to study CDR problems and support dispatchers in making decisions on station operation [149]. The D-Agent was designed to learn from its history in applying different decisions experimentally and evaluating skills by the preference weights of alternative solutions in a particular task. It is composed of five basic modules: local database, knowledge base, skill base, reasoning mechanism, and communication interfaces. Then, Zhu and De Pedro [150] proposed an approach to traffic state prediction and conflict detection that is based on proper state transition maps and corresponding relation matrices (anomaly analysis) to study the CD issue; the researchers used the corresponding state domain tables to maintain empirical data-driven traffic state sequences, which mainly concern infrastructure status and train movement information expressed as segment and route state vectors. The representative (statistical) state transition maps integrate timetable requirements to predict concrete traffic trends in a short period and detect abnormal states and irregular times. Then, conflict detection is conducted through the state transition under the restrictions of train operation principles and operational limitations.

1.3.3.2 Buffer time allocation

SM

After analyzing historical data and distributing the buffer times in a complex and busy junction with minimum delay propagation, Yuan and Hansen [49, 151] concluded that as buffer times between trains decrease, knock-on delays increase exponentially; this condition confirms that the BTA is necessary to reduce the behavioral response and waste of resources. To investigate the quality of timetable supplement allocation and assess whether the timetable supplement in existing timetables fits the actual need and is properly used, Fabrizio et al. [21] presented a statistical approach to analyzing the historical data of train timekeeping in Denmark; their study shows that actual supplement times can be detected in a train path using historical data.

To measure the effectiveness of buffer times, weighted average distance (WAD) and buffer index (BI) were proposed. Vormans [152] defined WAD as the weighted average distance of supplements from the starting point of the train line, which can be calculated using the historical trips of trains. Based on the analysis of historical data in [152], strategies of buffer time distributions were proposed; namely, the uniform distribution of margins, shifting margins toward the beginning or end, placing margins at or near strategic locations, and locating buffer times where disturbance occurs most frequently. WAD aims to describe how supplements are distributed along the journey and attempt to optimize this process, using both analytical and numerical methods. Similarly, WADs are applied in the approach that combines linear programming (LP) with stochastic programming and robust optimization techniques to improve the robustness of a timetable [153]. The strategy of placing margins at critical points was developed by Andersson et al. [154]. Kroon et al. [155] introduced a stochastic optimization model that can be used for modifying a given cyclic timetable in which WAD is used as a measure. The authors concluded that with the optimal allocation of different amounts of total slack, the distribution favors early buffer supplement (low WAD) when a small total buffer supplement is available. Recently, Palmqvist et al. [156] employed the analytical method to study the problem of BTA strategies that depend on the effectiveness of margins on the punctuality of passenger trains. Results imply that every additional percentage point of margins improves punctuality by approximately 0.1%, and approximately the same for every percent increase in the WAD of margins. The BI is calculated from a delay and a buffer time for each train and station and represents a characteristic of the delay due to knock-on delays [62]. By calculating the BI for all trains and stations, the existence of a train whose BI is larger than those of the surrounding trains at a station can be determined, and a delay is likely to propagate rapidly to the succeeding trains from that train at the station.

To increase the robustness of a timetable against delay propagation, the scheduled running time in sections and the dwell time at stations are often larger than the minimum required running and dwell times [157]. However, allocating excessive time supplements can extend the travel times for trains and increase the infrastructure capacity loss [1]. Therefore, the BTA should be addressed during timetable scheduling and rescheduling with consideration for delay occurrence and recovery factors. According to the UIC CODE 451-1 OR published by the International Union of Railways, regular running time supplements are added to every train path in the timetable in three ways: based on the distance driven (min/km), travel time (%), and fixed supplements per station or junction (min) [158]. Supplements vary in different countries due to local circumstances. For instance, running time supplements are approximately 7% for all trains in the Netherlands and for passenger trains in Switzerland compared with 11% for freight trains in Switzerland.

GM

Dispatching decisions partly focus on allocating sufficient amount of time supplements to train operations on the network [159] to compensate for stochastic arrival and departure delays of trains [160]. Goverde and Hansen emphasized that time allowance (buffer times) is a significant indicator of timetable stability, that is, the effectiveness of avoiding or reducing delay propagation to another train [157]. They presented the recommended BTA principles in German railways and Netherland railways that are set as the basis of their operation experiences. Meanwhile, in the UK, the runtime and dwell time allowances (supplements) are not explicitly defined but are optimized according to the past performance obtained from historical operation data on the particular railway section [161]. The BTA problem is modeled as a knapsack problem, and Jovanović et al. [42] inferred that the recent increase in the availability of historical traffic data could be exploited to prioritize candidate places in the schedule for buffer time assignment and the DDMs can be applied for BTA.

Vansteenwegen and Oudheusden [162] first investigated the desired buffer times in a timetable and then established an LP problem that penalizes the positive and negative deviations from the desired values. The ideal buffer times are calculated to safeguard the connections and transfers between trains. These buffer times are based on the delay distributions of arriving trains and on the weighting of different types of waiting times obtained from the Belgian train operation data.

ML

Huang et al. established a data-driven BTA model based on the Wuhan–Guangzhou high-speed railway. A ML model named ridge regression model is proposed to explain delay recovery time regarding buffer times at stations, buffer times in sections, and the severity of the primary delays [163]. Based on the utilization of buffer time, the model redistributes buffer time, which provides a new research method for BTA. The proposed ML model has aroused a new method to incorporate real-world timetables performance indices such as the buffer time utilization ratio and delay probability derived from historical records using ML methods.

1.3.3.3 State-of-the-art on timetable rescheduling

TTR is the carrier of decisions by which dispatchers regulate the train operation constantly in their domain. The important issues on TTR, CDR, and BTA have received considerable attention and seem to be promising research fields. Several tree-based or knowledge-based rules are obtained from data to determine the optimal input-output patterns and make better real-time decisions during operation disturbances in HSRs, timetable design, and optimization [164]. Table 1-5 presents a summary of the state-of-the-art studies on data-driven timetable rescheduling.

Therefore, integrating methods combining both optimization and DDMs for TTR are necessary for real-time train control. The research roadmap of data-driven TTR can be depicted in Figure 1-7.

Knowledge-based models, alternative graphs, and fuzzy logic are the most popular DDMs that have been applied in CDR. The key challenges of these approaches are mining conflict identification principles, obtaining conflict resolution rules, and dependence on historical data. The review of the studies listed above reveals that the BTA mainly relies on measuring the effectiveness of buffer times based on historical data, such as WAD, and searching for an approach to optimize the allocation of buffer times, combining the effectiveness of buffer times on delays or disruptions.

Table 1-5 Summary of the state-of-the-art studies on data-driven timetable rescheduling.

Literature	Data	Methodologies or systems
[131]	Arrival and departure records from a portion of single track from a major U.S. Class I railroad	Probability models
[132, 133]	Data from a 89km-length single track rail corridor with 14 stations/sidings	Analytically based models
[134]	Train tracking data from approximately 100 trains on the Trieste–Udine rail line in Northeast Italy	Motion equations, Stochastic blocking times
[135]	Arrival and departure times of 300 trains passing through terminus at peak hours of Milan Metro	Conflict detection and resolution
[136]	Train timetable and railway infrastructure status data of the Dutch Railway	Decision support systems
[137]	Simulation data from the actual Dutch railway network connecting Antwerpen – Breda – Rotterdam – Vlissingen	Traffic management system
[138]	Real-time data and train characteristics of rail network between Leiden and Amsterdam.	Intelligent conflict detection and resolution system
[139]	140,000 respondents of the questionnaire survey of commuting traffic in Tokyo Metropolitan area in 2005	Time-space network
[140]	Chronological infrastructure and train description messages of the railway line from Rotterdam to Dordrecht	TNV-Conflict
[141]	Chronological infrastructure and train description messages of the railway line from Rotterdam to Dordrecht	Colored Petri net
[142]	Passenger trains with different speeds (90 km/h up to 200 km/h) in North west German	Analytical conflict detection, Decision tree
[143]	Train operation data of 102 stations and 350 trains of the Taiwan Railway network	Job-shop scheduling

Literature	Data	Methodologies or systems
[144]	Data of the railway traffic fuzzy traffic control operation and rule-based operation results	Fuzzy Petri Net
[145]	6 stations and 15 HSR train trains of the Beijing South–Jinan West	Timed Petri net, Temporal fuzzy reasoning
[146]	Actual timetable of South East Asian single-track bi-directional railway	Fuzzy inference
[147]	Arrival and departure data recorded of 100 timetable perturbation instances by ProRail at Utrecht Central in April 2008	Alternative graph, Space-time diagram
[148]	Actual timetable at Schiphol bottleneck in 2007	Traffic management system
[16]	The actual speed, arrival and departure times of the Dutch train	TNV-tables data analysis
[37]	Real-time data on a busy railway corridor in the Netherlands	TNV-Statistics, Conflict trees
[149]	Detailed infrastructure data, planned and actual train sequence, route table, arrival and departure time of railway network	D-Agent simulation, MILP formulations, Decision support system
[150]	Data of the train actual train movement information, track occupation, original infrastructure states of a station SA with 16 segments	State transition maps
[151]	Primary delays, knock-on delays, and buffer times between scheduled trains at railway bottlenecks	Analytical approach
[152]	Arrival times of each train in the 800-line-from Haarlem to Maastricht and the 900-line-from Haarlem to Heerlen	Analytical approach
[153]	Four single-line medium-size instances in the Italian railway	Stochastic programming Robust optimization
[154]	Empirical observations data of the Swedish timetable and the Swedish Southern mainline during 2011	Robustness measure analysis
[155]	500 realizations of trains on the corridor Haarlem–Maastricht/Heerlen under stochastic disturbances	Stochastic optimization model
[156]	Almost 46,000 distinct timetable versions and over 1.1 million departures in 2015 in Swedish railway network.	Margins assigning Strategies
[157]	Records of primary delays and the settling time absorbed in timetabling	Classification method
[160]	Estimated waiting time, the occupation of different track sections and buffer time within the station of Den Hague HS	Queuing theory
[161]	67,000 train runs on approximate 4,500 km during 4:00 pm-9:00 pm in the timetable of 2001-2002 of the network of Hannover and Mannheim	Analytical approach, RailSys
[162]	Passenger flow and train running data in a small part of the Belgian railway network	Linear programming
[163]	Over 64,547 HSR train operation records from during 49, to 10 November 2016, from Wuhan Guangzhou HSR in China	Ridge regression model
[164]	Basic train operation data in THSR Company	Tree-based operation Linear programming

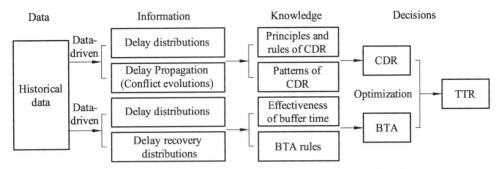

Fig.1-7 A research framework of data-driven timetable rescheduling

The reviewed studies have four shortcomings concerning the data-driven timetable rescheduling:

(1) The rules of the evolution of train conflicts need to be studied in-depth, and the theories of intelligent CDR need to be developed.

(2) The issues need to be addressed concerning how a disturbance leads to conflict, how buffer time absorb delays, and how to resolve the challenges. The modeling of conflict chains has been proved to be a hard but significant problem.

(3) There is a lack of models that can incorporate real-world timetable performances indices such as different buffer time utilization rates and delay probabilities obtained from historical records. Since delay propagation and recovery problems are highly dependent on operational factors and conditions that are realized during train operations, in practice, the BTA should be carried out by considering characteristics of implemented timetables. The BTA scheme needs to obtain better recovery effectiveness against delays.

(4) Assessments of dispatching qualities of different strategies are lacking.

Considering these issues, ML and DL methods have advantages in learning principles and rules for CDR. These can provide more patterns of CDR schemes based on the ML and DL methods that can learn much from more cases. In this way, more detailed and specific solutions are expected and possible for usage in CDR. The BTA scheme must obtain better recovery effectiveness against delays. Given rich train operation records, models can be established from past performances to describe the effectiveness of buffer times rather than using indicators, such as WAD and BI. Models, such as regression models of BTA against delay recovery, can be used as input to BTA. Models that apply ML should also be considered to learn BTA rules from historical data and optimize BAT schemes automatically.

1.4 Review results and further discussions

1.4.1 Development of data-driven train dispatching theories and implementation

High punctuality of trains is an important factor considered by railway companies.

However, trains are influenced by bad weather, mechanical failure, and organizational strategies during operation, which could lead to disruptions. Accurately predicting train-delay propagation and the scope of influence can assist train dispatchers in estimating the train operation states accurately. The detailed assessment can provide a theoretical basis for rescheduling strategies, facilitate more scientific and reliable rescheduling decisions, and improve the theories of automatic train operations and the intelligent dispatching of railways.

According to section 3, we summarize the reviewed papers in Figure 1-8, which indicates that few ML methods and studies focus on TD. This summary illustrates the existence of a gap, which necessitates further research on the modeling of CDR and BTA with ML approaches. The distribution of reviewed articles by year is shown in Figure 1-9. The figure indicates that the application of DDMs in TD presents a generally increasing trend in the last two decades. ML methods have become more attractive in the last five years as big data has played a crucial role in DDMs, while many studies have focused on SM and GM from 2004 to 2013.

In summary, the DDTD theory was first proposed in the 1980s, and the knowledge-based expert systems for train-traffic control, named ESTRAC-I, II, and III were developed and implemented consequently in the 1980s and 1990s [92, 165, 166, 167]. "IF-THEN" knowledge was used to represent the decision-making rules of dispatchers. Almost at the same time, the distributed approach to railway traffic control was described with the help of artificial intelligence, and a knowledge-based interactive train scheduling system-aiming at large-scale complex planning expert systems was developed [168, 169]. The development of ROMA in the 2000s has great contributions to the DDTD as reviewed above [138, 140]. The fuzzy logic and many other GM methods have been applied before 2014 [28, 108]. And the ML methods have been widely and rapidly applied in DDTD in the latest 5 years, based on RWTOD [20, 23, 127].

In other words, TD is an issue that belongs to the problem of job-shop scheduling and system control [170]. Through data-driven methods, dispatching rules are discovered from the data for job-shop problems. The literature review shows that ML approaches have been widely applied over the last 20 years in the scheduling of manufacturing systems [171, 172]. This condition means that the ML approach based on preference learning can perform in uncovering train dispatching rules [173]. One of the most promising ML approaches is neural networks (NN) and variants, such as convolutional neural networks (CNNs) in image processing [174], deep belief networks (DBNs) in audio recognition [175], and recurrent neural networks (RNN) in sequence analysis [176]. RNN-based models have been successfully applied in travel time estimation in highways [177, 178] and air transport [179], but the applications in railway train delay/travel time prediction are limited. DL discovers the complex structure in large datasets by using the backpropagation algorithm to indicate how a machine should change its internal parameters used to compute the representation in each layer from the representation in the previous layer [180]. DL approaches have shown strong abilities in analyzing, evaluating, and predicting the performance of a complex system [181, 182]. To minimize the job scheduling time, a deep reinforcement learning method was proposed for studying multi-resource multi-machine job scheduling, revealing that deep reinforcement learning method has the potential to outperform traditional resource allocation algorithms in various complex environments [183].

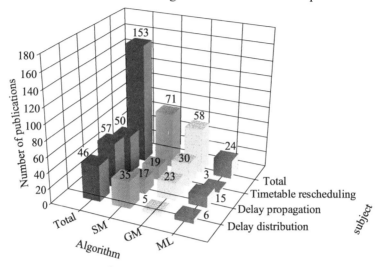

Fig.1-8   Number of publications reviewed on data-driven methods in TD

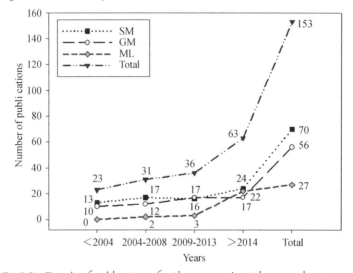

Fig.1-9   Trends of publications for the reviewed articles in each category

1.4.2   Further discussions: opportunities and challenges

1.4.2.1   ML/DL driven TD

Based on RWTOD, with the advantages of ML/DL in data processing and modeling, there will be several potential applications in TD:

(1) Integrated models of temporal, spatial, and cause-specific distribution models of delays must be established using detailed RWTOD during longer periods. More complex investigations regarding the delay distributions are required to determine the characteristics of delays. The modeling of the frequency and duration of the initial interruption and the

subsequent knock-on delays are essential to assist the dispatchers making decisions. The compound distribution model, which consists of the occurrence time, sections, and stations of delays, are more valuable than the currently used models. The delay duration distribution model and the temporal and spatial distribution model of cross-line trains would be helpful to capture the basic delay features of the rail network. Using these models, dispatchers can obtain the real-time and future status of trains under certain operation circumstances. Clustering methods, such as k-means, can be used to classify delay categories, and the delay patterns can be derived from data and data-driven models. Delay distributions can also be used as input in data-driven simulation studies and distributional functions in predictive modeling for delay propagation.

(2) DDMs can support dispatchers in having better predictions of delay propagation patterns and possible delays under specific situations to adjust train operations. The implementation effects of TDPS and DTDPS based on big-data technologies have shown good performance in terms of delay prediction [20, 72]. ML and DL methods can be used to model propagation patterns, in-train interactions, and the spatial and temporal relationship between adjacent trains. Exploring the delay rules and the propagation mechanisms and enhancing the delay-recovery capacity of the timetable are the critical issues required to be addressed to improve the efficiency and quality of train dispatching. Theories of train delay propagation and recovery using data-driven methods based on operational records are needed. Based on the RWTOD, studying delay propagation rules and evolution mechanisms, combined with delay and buffer time on a network, will continue to be crucial, especially for cross-line trains. After analyzing the mechanisms of delay propagation in the horizontal direction on the rail network, the influencing factors should be determined, including the number of affected trains and the event's duration time. Various categorizations should be taken into account, and a quantitative of prediction model of train delay influence indicators should be established separately. The delay propagation in horizontal direction model can be used for estimating the severity of delays and how they affect the operation of trains on the rail network. The model can also provide support in creating dispatching strategies.

(3) DDMs can uncover more precise rules for CDR and BTA from RWTOD, including conflict identification principles, conflict resolution rules, and the effectiveness of buffer times. ML and DL models can be used to classify, model, forecast, and then optimize CDR and BTA on the basis of RWTOD. Moreover, rules for CDR and BTA are more likely to be obtained on the basis of RWTOD. For example, some conflict reasoning rules and conflict resolving rules can be mined by DL. Currently, the scheduling of a train timetable scarcely considers the impacts of the implementations, which has adverse effects on the transport quality and capacity of the railway. Executing train timetable feedback optimization is a significant step in improving the quality of the timetable theoretically and practically. It is possible to reveal the evolutionary trend's structure concerning potential conflicts based on the train's operational data. When detecting a delay, a method to calculate the potential conflict situation is required.

This situation can be considered as the optimized object in the data-driven CDR model, establishing the feedback optimization theory for timetable rescheduling using DDMs.

(4) Delay recovery effectiveness measures can be obtained from RWTOD by CNN to update WAD. The BTA model based on deep reinforcement learning can be established to maximize the delay recovery capacity and increase the buffer time effectiveness. The delay recovery effectiveness measures can be obtained from RWTOD by CNN to update WAD. The BTA model based on DRL can be established to maximize the delay recovery capacity and increase the buffer time effectiveness. For different types of delays, based on RWTOD, modeling of temporal and spatial distributions of delay recovery due to buffer time need to be carried out first, and the characteristics of recover time under different BTA scheme should be investigated. DDMs will be used to calculate the buffer time distribution matrix and the delay recovery coefficient matrix. These matrices can be used to determine the timetable buffer time utilization efficiency and to identify significanttrains, sections, and stations. Then, the delay-recovery chains should be established to derive the effectiveness of buffer times. Because of the close relationship between buffer time utilization and dispatching strategies, the assessment of the dispatching strategies can be realized [163].

1.4.2.2　Intelligent TD

Intelligent TD is an automated decision-making process in the dispatching system, controlling the train operations. The dispatchers' experience, along with the RWTOD, provides knowledge and dispatching rules regarding the assessing, developing, and protecting of transportation states, making sure that trains always run well. The sketch map of intelligent TD is as shown in Figure 1-10.

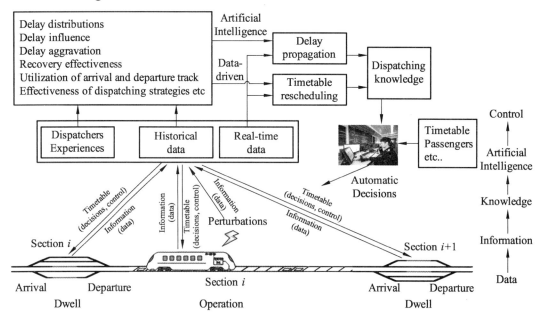

Fig.1-10　Sketch map of intelligent TD

SBB has recently started the rollout of adaptive control system (from German Adaptive Lenkung, adaptive train control) on their network since 2014 [184, 185]. However, the predictive dispatching is needed to be carried out, by considering the disturbances, estimating the running times and the potential conflicts, and predicting the delay occurrence. The distributional model and propagation of delayscan be used as a predictive tool by the dispatchers to assess the delay duration and their influences, given certain operation circumstances. With new train operation data, the models can be updated via a dynamic or predicting system for delays. This work is to establish a predictive dispatching decision support tool to help dispatchers in managing train operations.

The development of the intelligent TD will need to address the concerns of dispatching-knowledge extracting, automatic decision-making, and the assessments of dispatchers and their actions taken during train operation control. These measures would eventually contribute to the state-of-the-art, intelligent dispatching systems, enriching the theories and practice of timetable design and real-time train operation adjustment.

The intelligent TD is a critical point of intelligent train operation. Based on large-scale and complex train operation data, various advanced data science and artificial intelligence methods will be synthetically used to study the closed-loop control problem of intelligent traffic control, involving train-state assessment and deduction, train rescheduling, collaborative dispatching, emergency management, and train operating state protection. A study of the train operating state assessment and developing theories based on the multi-driven of time and events is also needed. Also, train delay propagation and recovery mechanisms are required to be revealed; data-driven train delay recovery and intelligent train rescheduling methods in various scenarios are needed to be established; and knowledge automation of intelligent train reschedulings, such as delay propagation knowledge, CDR rules, BTA schemes, and effectiveness of certain dispatching strategies, are needed to be constructed. These research area can provide the theoretical and technical support to the intelligent train dispatching and subsequently, the railway transportation science.

1.5 Conclusions

Rail system performance depends on carefully designed timetables and effective real-time train operations control. In this regard, train dispatching plays an indispensable role in train operation management. Train dispatchers deal with collecting and processing train operation information, estimating the status of trains, resolving conflicts, and rescheduling the timetable. Train operation records from train monitoring and describer systems have been valuable sources for analyzing railway performance and assessing the QoS of railways to provide feedback on train operations and improve the planning and control of dense railway networks.

To support dispatchers in decision making, various models have been proposed from which this study surveyed data-driven models and methodologies. Through the review of the relevant literature, drawbacks in train dispatching were found in the mathematical- and simulation-model-driven methods. However, the data-driven models based on train operation records can generate different solutions to support the decision-making of dispatchers. Usually, statistical analysis is employed to reveal some fundamental rules of TD or dependencies between related factors within the CI and ML models. CI is used to generate knowledge for TD or deriving the status of trains. ML models have shown potentials in the field of railway engineering, especially for delay prediction. In bridging the gap between theories and practices in TD, although DDMs have been applied, several research challenges remain in establishing innovative dispatching decisions to help dispatchers in managing train operations. Although DDMs can be useful in solving practical problems or modeling a specific system or procedure, a contemporary trend is to establish hybrid models that combine DDMs and traditional mathematical models. As reviewed in [186], the model-driven DL approach that combines model-and data-driven DL approaches can retain advantages (i.e., determinacy and theoretical soundness) of the model-driven approach and avoid the requirement for accurate modeling. Model-driven approaches have been proven to have a significant level of accuracy, relying on the objective, physical mechanism, and domain knowledge for a specific task. However, their level of generalization is limited in practice. Meanwhile, ML/DL approaches use a standard network architecture as a black box, highly relying on big data to train the black box. Model- and data-driven approaches do not oppose each other. Moreover, the model-driven DL approach can retain the powerful learning ability of the DL approach and overcome the difficulties in network topology selection. We believe that the model-driven DL approach can be widely applied in TD and the other works associated with train operation and management. Given that ML/DL approaches have shown promising abilities in data processing and modeling, they can be applied in TD modeling and classifying delays, modeling the delay propagation, solving the problems of CDR, and optimizing the BTA.

Big data analytics is at its nascent stage; a future research direction is to develop a decision support system for a network-wide RTC to continuously supervise trains that run on the network and update the operating timetable. Advanced and intelligent RTC systems are intended to monitor, predict, and control trains in real time to ensure the safety, regularity, reliability, and punctuality of train operations.

Chapter 2

Data-driven delay distributions of HSR trains

2.1 Statistical Investigation on Train Primary Delay based on Real Records: Evidence from Wuhan-Guangzhou HSR

The focus of this chapter was to conduct statistical analysis on primary delays in Wuhan-Guangzhou High-speed railway (HSR). The main statistics of primary delays were investigated, including delay causes, delay frequencies, delays' temporal and spatial occurrences, affected number of trains, and delay recovery patterns. Models that can illustrate the primary delays duration and the number of affected trains were developed. Namely, the log-normal and the Weibull distributions are tested, and the results affirm that the former one can better approximate the duration of primary delays. Subsequently, a non-linear regression model to fit the distribution of the affected number of trains was presented. The temporal and spatial analysis of primary delays and capacity utilization show that there is a high degree of dependency between the periods with high delay frequency and capacity bottlenecks. Specifically, wherever there is a high capacity utilization rate, there is a high probability of delay occurrence. This chapter provides insightful findings that help understanding the primary delays in HSR operation and conducting further research.

2.1.1 Introduction

Ever increasing demand for rail transport necessitates companies either to expand their capacities or operate at maximum capacity by aiming at service punctuality. However, even in the advanced railway networks with state-of-the-art communication facilities and well-organized operation systems, this goal is hindered mainly by disturbances and disruptions during train operations. For example in Japan, having HSR systems reputed of being very punctual, the average delay per train is 0.9 min [187]. In China, the average departure punctuality of conventional railway is 88%, and it is estimated as high as 98.8% for HSR in 2015. However, due to the disturbances in the operation process, the average operation punctuality of HSR is less than 90% in practice [188]. Basically, a railway system comprises several sub-systems, such as railway infrastructure, rolling stock, timetable, and human behavior in order to operate trains. Many uncertainties may arise from these sub-systems that can inevitably disturb trains operation with delay, and result inefficiency in utilizing the maximum capacity. For instance, the lower punctuality in Chinese HSRs operation partly is attributed to the fact that they have very long lines within complex networks in which an enormous number of trains operate. More specifically, the longest travel journey for a single train covers about 2300 km from north to south, which means that the trains run into various operating conditions with many disturbances, all of which can lead to the disposition of trains from the published timetable, and delays as a result.

Delays are categorized as primary and secondary (knock-on) delays. A primary delay happens if the delay incident related to the train concerned, i.e., the delay does not result from another delayed train. Primary delays may propagate and thus cause delays in subsequent and dependent processes, which is called secondary delay [93]. The mechanism of secondary delays is very complex, and depending on the network structure, and applied timetable, the delay propagation patterns vary, for which the secondary delay cannot readily be measured. Knowing this, the primary delays are focused on in this analysis. Various mathematical models and simulation techniques have been used for analyzing the consequence of disturbances in trains operation, and making proactive or retroactive decisions to recover from the delay. However, these kinds of methods are restricted in describing the underlying process of trains' delay [189, 190].

Train movement records and data on the arrival and departure times of trains have been realized as very rich sources to study train operations. One essential application of delay records is to mine the underlying mechanism of railway delays. Though data mining and big data technologies are becoming increasingly popular for data-driven analysis, few studies have been conducted on real train operation data from HSR. In this study, statistical analysis of primary delays using train operation records of Wuhan-Guangzhou HSR were carried out. The main contributions of this study can be categorized as follows: 1) determining the primary delay distributions of HSR trains in detail as basis for further studies and operational practices, 2) establishing models of primary delay duration and affected number of trains' distribution, which can be used in HSR simulation studies, and 3) investigating the general relationship between the temporal distribution of primary delay and the capacity utilization.

The remainder of this study is organized as follows: Section 2.1.2 briefly reviews the delay management literature and the related data-driven methods. Section 2.1.3 describes the train operation data collected from Wuhan-Guangzhou HSR. Section 2.1.4 presents the results obtained from the statistical analysis of the primary delays. Section 2.1.5 deals with developing models for the distributions of primary delay duration and number of affected trains. Section 2.1.6 discusses the relationship between the temporal distribution of primary delays and the capacity utilization. Finally, Section 2.1.7 provides conclusions and highlights future research directions.

2.1.2 Literature review

In the recent decade, data-driven methods are widely used in transportation research field based on observation records. The possibility to analyze big data has enabled practitioners to extract insightful findings and knowledge, due to drastic advances in computer science and information technology. Goverde and Hansen are two of the pioneers in analyzing train operation data using a tool named TNV-Prepare. TNV-Prepare derives detailed information of event times associated to train services from data records of the Dutch train describer systems. The data contains signaling and interlocking information of an entire traffic control area. Each train event times includes train description steps, section entries and clearances, signals, and point switches [16]. Regarding train punctuality data, there are two types of data: 1) simulation data obtained from train operation simulator, and 2) real data abstained from command system of monitoring equipment. During modeling and analyzing, simulation data is more accessible than real data, since it is easier to obtain and much simpler under some restrictive assumptions. In this regard, automatic calibration of disturbance parameters, which are used to generate stochastic disturbances in simulation tools, is developed with the support of the reinforcement learning technique [88]. A train operation simulation model is formulated to reproduce the behavior of train operation that takes into account the interaction between trains, as an attempt to reproduce the situation of train operation under the knock-on delays [190].

In summary, based on a review of the literature, the data-driven research on train punctuality can be classified, regarding the type data used, into simulation data and real data, partial data and systematic data. A classification of the works on train operation data was presented in Table 2-1.

Table 2-1　Recent literature on train delay data-based research

Literature	Simulation data	Real data	Partial data	Systematic data
[190, 191, 192, 193]	√		√	
[194, 195, 196]	√			√
[23, 79, 109, 197]		√	√	
[22, 164]		√		√

Several researchers dedicated efforts to the data-driven visualization based on train operation records. Chromatic Diagram is shown to be a helpful software to visualize the train operation records [198]. Some plots are presented based on the raw data [17]. Y. Ochiai et al. visualized train traffic record data using the Chromatic diagram, and presented experiences of applying in the Odakyu Electric Railway company [15].

In real data analyzing domain, several analytical approaches are explored based on enormous volumes of historical observation data, including correlation analysis, causal analysis, time series analysis and machine learning techniques to automatically learn rules and build failure prediction models [199]. An intelligent onboard system for the high-speed train is preliminarily implemented rest on the historical data can provide better detection ability than other models when processing real-time events stored in high-speed train Juridical Recording Unit [200]. Most of the methods perform well for the proposed particular problems.

Some studies have also made contributions on distributions of delay and finding the respective fitness models. The Weibull distribution, the Gamma distribution and the lognormal distributions have been adopted in several studies [80]. Van der Meer et al. mined several factors, such as peak hours, rolling stock, and weather data and developed predictive model for delay estimation [201]. A q-exponential function is used by Briggs and Beck to demonstrate the distribution of train delays on the British railway network [79]. The spatial and temporal distributions of freight train delays are presented based on the train departures and arrivals during 2008 and 2009 in Sweden. The 20 % largest delays contribute to about 74% of total delay minutes and more than 50% of the total arrival delay per year occurs in just 7% of stations. They found that delays at the origin can increase arrival delays to subsequent stations. However some part of the initial delay is recovered at arrival, probably due to large slack in the timetables [202]. Based on the HSR operation data, the probability density distribution of the different disruption sourceand the distributions of affected trains due to delays were plotted in general [61].

The research on modeling based on real train operation data show that the data-driven approaches and delay distributions are helpful in managing delays during train operations. A data-mining approach for analyzing rail transport delay chains is applied, using data from passenger train traffic on the Finnish rail network; however, the data from a train operation process was limited to one-month data [22]. Hansen et al. presented a delay propagation model in which train path conflicts and dispatching decisions were taken into account, and parameters were estimated by offline statistical analysis of historical train operation data [203].

Our review of the relevant literature, all together, shows that the long-run real data was hardly used and there is a lack of systematic and detailed data-mining analysis of delay dependencies. The studies listed above mainly rely on conventional lines, there are a few statistical analysis and studies on the long-run real Chinese HSRs data. Therefore, we have lack of statistical analysis on primary delays about Chinese HSRs operation. Analyzing the primary delay can be very useful for further studies and practitioners, especially for CHSRs. It can help understanding the delay mechanism and then managing train delays in practice.

2.1.3 Data description

The data used in this study are from four HSR lines in the Chinese railway network, as shown in Figure 2-1. The details about the four lines are:
  ➢ Wuhan-Guangzhou High-speed Railway (B-G HSR): Total length of 998.5 km, from Chibi station to South Guangzhou station; this includes the lines in the 14 stations on

the route and connecting lines;

- ➤ Guangzhou-Shenzhen High-speed Railway (G-S HSR): The line of 175.1 km runs from South Guangzhou station to North Shenzhen station and has five stations;
- ➤ Guangzhou-Shenzhen Intercity Railway (G-S ICR): There are six stations on the 153.4 km line from Guangzhou Station to Shenzhen Station;
- ➤ Xiamen-Shenzhen High-speed Railway (X-S HSR): The 362.5 km line connecting North Shenzhen station to Zhao'an station has thirteen stations.

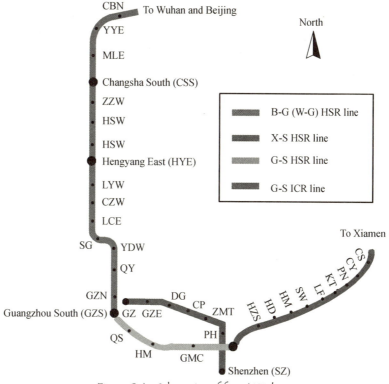

Figure 2-1 Schematic of four HSR lines

Train operation records of the Wuhan-Guangzhou HSR line that connects Wuhan (WH) to Guangzhou (GZ) with a 1096-kilometre double-track line that has 18 stations were collected. However, only data from 15 stations and 14 sections from GuangzhouSouth (GZS) to ChibiNorth (CBN) were obtained from the Guangzhou Railway Bureau as the remaining parts are administrated by the Wuhan Railway Bureau. Chinese HSRs train operations are fully under the supervision of the Centralized Traffic Control (CTC) system, which records all the running events and related data and displays the data with its exact time, to the second. As a train moves around the network, it is continuously monitored by a remote controlsystem via the occupancy reports that are logically linked to the train number. When a train passes a signal point, this event is recorded by remote control and simultaneously transmitted to the CTC system.

The records gathered from CTC include the arrival and departure times, which describe the overall running process of the trains. There are numerous records in graph and table formats. Table 2-2 shows a sample train operation records.

Table 2-2 A sample of train running records in a database

Train No.	Date	Station	Arrival time	Departure time	Scheduled arrival time	Scheduled departure time
G634	2015-2-24	GuangzhouNorth (GZN)	17:28:00	17:28:00	17:26:00	17:26:00
G6152	2015-2-24	Qingyuan (QY)	17:18:00	17:20:00	17:16:00	17:18:00
G9694	2015-2-24	YingdeWest (YDW)	19:00:00	19:03:00	19:00:00	19:02:00
G548	2015-2-24	Shaoguan (SG)	17:25:00	17:29:00	17:26:00	17:29:00

Train movements data in one direction that is from GZS to WH were considered. The data gathered from February 24, 2015, to November 30, 2015, includes 29662 HSR train records in total. In data cleaning step, delay records with more than 90 minutes delay were excluded as these instances were distributed too randomly, with a very low proportion. Ultimately from 5063 delayed train observation, 1249 records of source (primary) delay with the corresponding delay factors were obtained and used in our analysis. In addition, the following attributes were directly gathered:

- Train number, including train types distinguished by G and D,
- Name of stations,
- Unit of the time in minutes,
- Arrival times, departure times, planned arrival times, and planned departure times in the "year/month/day and hour: minute: second" format,
- Detailed information on delayed trains, including occurrence time, occurrence location, reasons, and delay duration,
- The regular train speed is 300 km/h, however this can increase to 310 km/h when a train is delayed or for other legitimate reasons,
- The minimum interval between arrivals and departures is 5 minutes at each station and 3 minutes in each section, and here is around 110 trains from GZ to WH every day (One direction).

2.1.4 Primary delay statistical analysis

2.1.4.1 Delay causes

According to the records from Guangzhou Railway Bureau, The causes of primary delays were classified into following seven categories, and the number of samples for each cause factor are shown in Figure 2-2.

(1) Failure of train control system (FA): Refers to the failure of Chinese train control system that mainly appears as failures of automatic train control system.

(2) Failure of the track (FT): Includes the failure of tracks, switches, bridges, and tunnels.

(3) Failure of rolling stock (FRS): Refers to mechanical failure of rolling stock.

(4) Failure of pantograph, signal, and catenary (FPSC): Are the failures of the pantograph, catenary of electronic multiple units, and signal system.

(5) Failure of foreign material (FFM): Refers to factors that animals or foreign matters entering the track.

(6) Fault of weather (FW): Refers to the severe weather, such as torrential rains and snow, frost, hurricane, flood.

(7) Other factors (FO): All the factors that are not listed above.

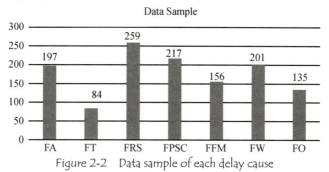

Figure 2-2　Data sample of each delay cause

2.1.4.2　Distribution of primary delay Duration

The scattergram and histogram of the distribution of primary delay durations to examine durations of the primary delay instances were directed. In Figure 2-3(a), the horizontal axis is the sequence number of delayed trains in the database, while the vertical axis is the delay duration of each train. In Figure 2-3(b), the horizontal axis is the primary delay duration in a 5 minutes intervals, while the vertical axis is the frequency of each duration interval. As can be seen, the majority of the instances have a duration less than 30 minutes, most of which fall in 5 to 20 minutes range.

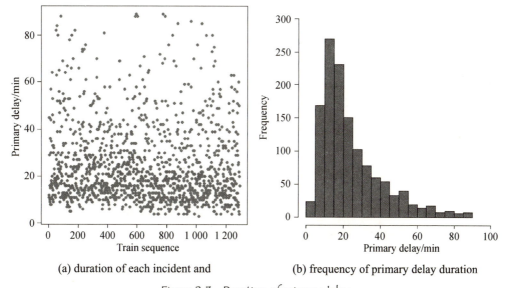

(a) duration of each incident and　　　　(b) frequency of primary delay duration

Figure 2-3　Duration of primary delay

2.1.4.3　Temporal distribution of primary delay

Figure 2-4 shows the temporal distribution of primary delay occurrence. Using this visualization, three distinct time intervals for primary delays can be distinguished:

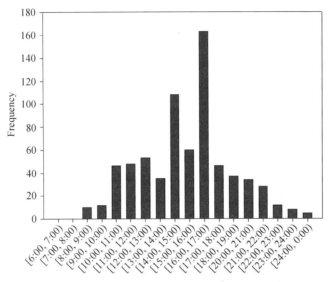

Figure 2-4　Temporal distribution of primary delay

(1) Early morning time (typically 06:00–10:00): This is the start time of train operation. In this period, the facilities have all been well prepared during the night. So the probability of delay occurrence due to relevant factors, and as a result the number of the delayed trains is minimal.

(2) Peak time (typically 10:00–17:00): In this period, the number of delays increases suddenly and remains relatively high. The delay factors may more easily lead to primary delay because of a higher travel demand and density of the operating trains in this period.

(3) Evening and night time (typically 17:00–24:00): In this period, the number of delays begins to decrease and remains relatively very low.

2.1.4.4　Spatial distribution of primary delay

Stations and sections are working under different conditions, and this results in different occurrence probabilities of primary delay. The spatial distribution of primary delays is depicted in Figure 2-5, in which the primary delay occurrence in each section is regarded as occurrence at the preceding adjacent station.

It is apparently that the stations GZN and CSS have significantly a higher frequency of primary delay occurrence. GZN is the first station that the trains depart from or pass by, and CSS is a terminal station that connects the HSRs Shanghai-Kunming to Wuhan-Guangzhou. The GZS - GZN segment and the CCS station are very busy, which could therefore be a reason for the high frequency of primary delay.

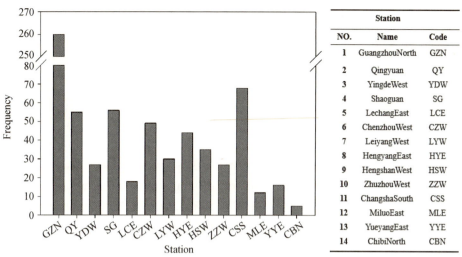

Figure 2-5　Spatial distribution of primary delay

2.1.4.5　Affected trains distribution owing to primary delay

Each instance of disturbance may have a different effect on the operation of all the trains, and because of different primary delay causes, the affected trains will differ. Figure 2-6 depicts the scattergram and histogram of affected trains' distribution.

In Figure 2-6(a), the horizontal axis is the sequence number of delayed trains in the database, while the vertical axis is the number of trains affected by each primary delay. In Figure 2-6(b), the horizontal axis shows the number of affected trains with a class interval of two trains, while the vertical axis is the frequency at which trains are affected.

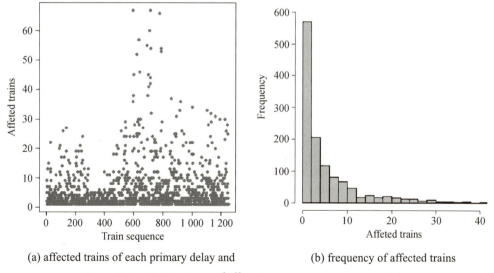

(a) affected trains of each primary delay and　　　(b) frequency of affected trains

Figure 2-6　Distributions of affected trains owing to primary delay

2.1.4.6　Delay recovery statistics of primary delay

To maintain timetable flexible and thus to recover the trains from delay, some buffer time is usually set at stations and in sections. Buffer time is the difference between the scheduled running time (dwell time) in the timetable and the minimum running time (dwell time) in practice. The buffer time helps dispatchers to manage delays by absorbing them in a particular level and recovering delayed trains.

The running times in sections and usage of average buffer times in sections and at stations are shown in Figures 2-7 and 2-8, respectively. Figure 2-7 shows the statistical results of running time of the delayed trains in each section, including the minimum running time, average running time, and maximum running time. The vertical axis is time in units of one minute. From this plot, the span of the running times in each section can be obtained, which can then be recorded in the format of (minimum time, average time, maximum time). These values can be used to estimate the running time of the trains in each section, both in practice and for studies in terms of time derivation. Dispatchers can estimate the most likely running time for a delayed train in a particular section and make a decision to reschedule the timetable and to control the traffic. These results can be used to validate the fuzzy time used in previous train delay studies, such as triangular fuzzy number and event time [109, 201]. For instance, the span of running time in YDW-SG is (15, 17.2, 20). Thus, it can be confirmed that delayed trains can travel through this section in approximately 17.2 min with a high probability. If a train departs from YDW at 10:00, the train can arrive at SG at 10:17 in general, with the earliest arrival time being 10:15, and the latest arrival time being 10:20.

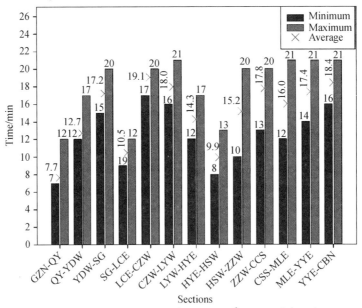

Figure 2-7　Running time in each section of primary delayed trains

Figure 2-8 compares the average scheduled running time (dwell time) and the average practical running time (dwell time) in each section (at each station). The bars on the left side show the average scheduled running time (dwell time) for all delayed trains in each section, and that on the right side show the average practical running time (dwell time). An interesting finding is that the differences between practical dwell times and scheduled ones are greater than that of the running times, which is different from previous knowledge and experiences about conventional lines. This means that the buffer times used at stations are much greater than those used in sections, due to delay incidents. It is approved that the recovery ratios of the stations are much higher than those in the sections, except for the ZZW station and the ZZW-CSS section. The average recovery time at a station is defined as the average buffer time used by the late arrived trains. The average recovery time in a section is defined as the average buffer time used by the late departed trains from a station while running over the adjacent section. Figure 2-8 shows that the average recovery times of the stations are slightly higher than those in the sections, except for section ZZW-CSS. Especially, the delayed trains have a significant recovery potential, more than 3 minutes, when they pass through the ZZW-CSS section. This shows that the ZZW-CSS section plays an important role in recovering delayed trains. This information will be used in future studies on modeling the delay recovery of HSR trains.

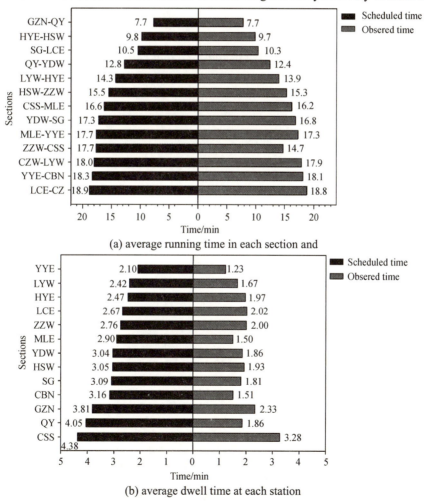

Figure 2-8 Comparing average scheduled running times (dwell times) and average practical ones

2.1.5 Statistical distribution models

2.1.5.1 Primary delay duration distribution

Considering the shape of Figure 2-3(b), the logarithmic normal distribution and the Weibull distribution are expected to show similar behavior to the histogram of the primary delays duration. In probability theory, a log-normal distribution is a continuous probability distribution of a random variable whose logarithm is normally distributed. A positive random variable x is log-normally distributed if the logarithm of x is normally distributed. Given a log-normally distributed random variable x with the mean parameter μ and the shape parameter σ, it has a probability density function as follows:

$$f(x;\mu,\sigma) = \frac{1}{x\sigma\sqrt{2\pi}} e^{-\frac{(\ln x - \mu)^2}{2\sigma^2}} \tag{2-1}$$

where μ and σ are the location and the scale parameters of the distribution, respectively[204].

The probability density function of a Weibull random variable x is:

$$f(x;\lambda,k) = \begin{cases} \dfrac{k}{\lambda}\left(\dfrac{x}{\lambda}\right)^{k-1} e^{-(x/\lambda)^k} & x \geqslant 0 \\ 0 & x < 0 \end{cases} \tag{2-2}$$

Where $k>0$ is the shape parameter, and $\lambda>0$ is the scale parameter of the distribution[205].

Consequently, the primary delay duration is fit with these candidate distributions to determine which model can approximate better. The maximum-likelihood method is used to estimate the parameters of the candidate distributions, using R-project. The results are summarized in Table 2-3.

Table 2-3　Parameterestimation of primary delay distributions

μ	σ	k	λ
3.00	0.64	1.61	27.63

Figure 2-9 represents the histogram, the density, the log-normal distribution, and the Weibull distribution curves.

The Kolmogorov-Smirnov test was used to compare the goodness-of-fit for the log-normal and Weibull distributions. The Kolmogorov-Smirnov statistic quantifies the distance between the empirical distribution function of the sample and the cumulative distribution function of the reference distribution, or between the empirical distribution functions of two samples. The hypothesis of the test is as follows:

H_0: The data follow the specified distribution

H_a: The data do not follow the specified distribution

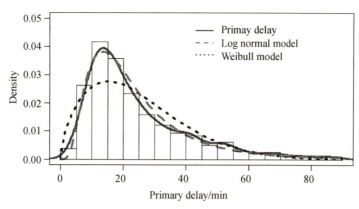

Figure 2-9   Fitting curves of primary delay duration distribution

The Kolmogorov–Smirnov statistic for a given cumulative distribution function $F(x)$ reads as follows:

$$D = \max |F'(x) - F(x)| \qquad (2\text{-}3)$$

where $F'(x)$, is the empirical cumulative distribution of the respective function. The smaller the value of D is, the better the goodness-of-fit will be; in other words, the corresponding empirical distribution fit the primary delay better.

A significance level of 0.05 was used in the test, for which the critical value of $D_{0.05}$ is derived as follows:

$$D_{0.05} = \frac{1.36}{\sqrt{n}} \qquad (2\text{-}4)$$

where n is the size of samples. The critical value of Kolmogorov-Smirnov and the D values of the two kinds of distribution modes are reported in Table 2-4.

Table 2-4   Test results for log-normal distribution and Weibull distribution

Critical Value $D_{0.05}$	D of Log-normal	D of Weibull
0.04	0.06	0.08

The hypothesis on the distributional form is rejected if the test statistic D is greater than the critical value $D_{0.05}$. From the report, it is obviously that the D valueof the log-normal distribution is small than $D_{0.05}$. Hence, H_0 cannot be rejected, whereas the H_0 of the Weibull distribution is rejected asits D is greater than $D_{0.05}$. Therefore, the log-normal distribution, with the parameters $\mu = 3.00$ and $\sigma = 0.64$, can fit the primary delay distribution better,

As explained before,the records of HSR primary delay were divided into three time periods depending on its occurrence time: before 10:00, 10:00-17:00, and after 17:00. In the same way, the log-normal distribution and Weibull distribution were considered for modelfitting according to the shape of the curve of the delay duration in different time periods, see Figure 2-10. The test results in Table 2-5 show that the log-normal distribution can fit the curve better. The estimated parameters for the log-normal distribution models in different periods are reported in Table 2-6.

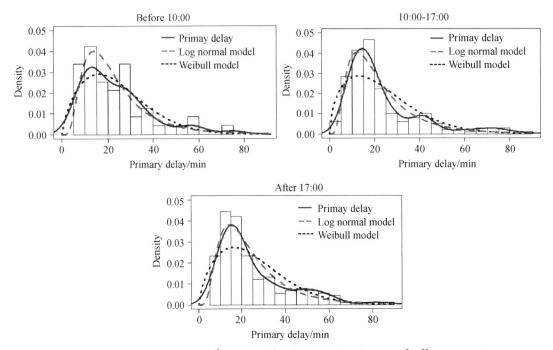

Figure 2-10   Fitting curves of primary delay duration distribution of different period

Table 2-5   Parameters of Log-normal and Weibull in different time periods

Time	μ	σ	k	λ
Before 10:00	2.98	0.60	1.71	26.86
10:00-17:00	2.93	0.65	1.52	26.03
After 17:00	3.03	0.61	1.66	28.16

Table 2-6   Test results of log-normal and Weibull distributions in different time periods

Time	Critical Value $D_{0.05}$	D of Log-normal	D of Weibull
Before 10:00	0.20	0.09	0.10
10:00-17:00	0.10	0.06	0.12
After 17:00	0.10	0.07	0.12

To conduct the spatial analysis, the records of HSR primary delay were divided into four different track segments given their occurrence location: namely, GZS-SG, SG-HYE, HYE-CSS, and CSS-CBN, where each segment includes several sections and stations. HYE and CSS are the stations that connect different HSR lines of the network, as to why they are chosen as a critical segment. While SG is almost in the middle of the segment of GZS and HYE, and it is chosen as a dividing station that balances the segments. the log-normal distribution and Weibull distribution were fitted. Figure 2-11, Table 2-7 and Table 2-8 show that the log-normal distribution fits better, with the estimate parameters in different periods that are reported Table 2-7.

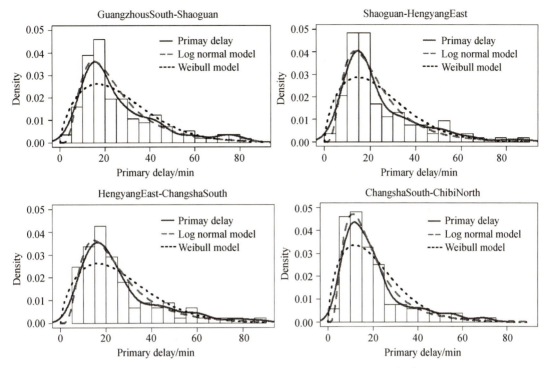

Figure 2-11　Fitting curves of primary delay duration distribution of different segments

Table 2-7　Parameters of Log-normal and Weibull of different Segments

Segments	μ	σ	k	λ
GZS-SG	3.07	0.61	1.65	29.49
SG-HYE	2.97	0.61	1.61	26.64
HYE-CSS	3.06	0.62	1.62	29.27
CSS-CBN	2.80	0.63	1.58	22.52

Table 2-8　Testing results of log-normal distribution and Weibull distribution of different Segments

Segments	Critical Value $D_{0.05}$	D of Log-normal	D of Weibull
GZS-SG	0.13	0.09	0.12
SG-HYE	0.13	0.09	0.14
HYE-CSS	0.14	0.06	0.12
CSS-CBN	0.13	0.05	0.10

2.1.5.2　Affected number of trains distribution

In this section, a model to fit the affected delayed trains' distribution was presented, see Figure 2-6(b). Regarding the shape of Figure 2-6(b), the affected delayed trains' distribution data has been fitted with a non-linear regression model. Given a random variable x and two parameters β_1, and β_2, the probability density function that models the affected number of trains distribution reads as follows:

$$y = \beta_1 \frac{1}{x} + \beta_2 \qquad (2\text{-}5)$$

Where x is the number of affected trains, and y is theprobability of a certain number of affected trains. The parameter values and test results were summarized in Table 2-9. The reported R-square value shows that the model can fit the affected number of trains' distribution well. The fitted curve of the model was given in Figure 2-12.

Table 2-9　Parameter values and test results of the inverse model

β_1	β_2	R-square	p-value
0.3106	−0.0073	0.9960	0.00

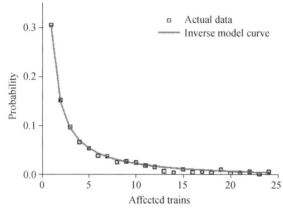

Figure 2-12　Fitting curve of affected trains' distribution

According to Figure 2-12, the affected number of trains has a non-increasing probability when the number of affected trains increase, and it can be inferred that the number of affected trains are not expected to exceed a certain threshold, as the statistical results for a long-run period reflect this situation. The cumulative probability in Figure 2-13 illustrates the range of the affected number of trains well for different values of K.

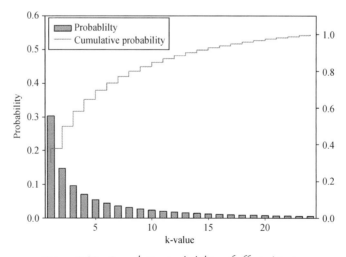

Figure 2-13　Cumulative probability of affected trains

Thus, the probability distribution model of the affected number of trains due to primary delay is as follows:

$$\begin{cases} P(x \leqslant K) = 0.3106/x - 0.0073 & x = 1, 2, \cdots 24 \quad K = 24 \\ \sum P(x > K) = 2.4\mathrm{E} - 03 \end{cases} \tag{2-6}$$

The cases where $k > 24$ have a total remainder probability less than 0.0024, in other words, the probability that more than 24 trains are involved is only 0.0024.

2.1.6 Relationship between temporal distribution of primary delay and capacity utilization

To examine the temporal distribution of delays, the capacity utilization status at different segments and times periods of BJ-GZ HSR were investigated, as depicted in Figure 2-13 and reported in Table 2-10. The capacity utilization rate C_{us}^i in per hour of section s during period i is defined by formulation (2-7).

$$C_{us}^i = \frac{c_s^i}{N_s^i} \tag{2-7}$$

where c_s^i is the actual number of trains that run in section s during period i (obtained from the timetable), and N_s^i is the maximum capacity that depends on the minimum interval $I_{\min}$ between adjacent trains in one hour. In formula (2-7), the value of N_s^i is calculated by the following formulation:

$$N_s^i = \frac{60}{I_{\min}} \tag{2-8}$$

For BJ-GZ HSR, the N_s^i is 12 as $I_{\min}$ is 5 min.

Since the delay data was obtained from Guangzhou Railway Bureau, delay data on the BJW-WH segment was not obtained. However, the capacity utilization rate and the departure time of the trains of the whole line can be obtained by the published timetable. Therefore, we depicted the relationship between delay and capacity utilization in W-GS in Figure 2-14. The shaded regions show the capacity bottlenecks where the capacity utilization is over 80% in different segments of BJ-GZ HSR at different time periods. The Wuhan-Guangzhou HSR is part of the BJ-GZ HSR, in which many trains operate. Represented by different colors, which are defined in Table 6, trains originate from different stations during 07:00 to 12:00 and 14:00 to 16:00 time periods. For instance, some trains depart from BeijingWest (BJW) during the 07:00–11:00 period and occupy the Shijiazhuang (SJZ)-ZhengzhouEast (ZZE) segment during the 08:30–12:30. Because of the accumulation of the trains originating from different stations, bottlenecks occur with very high capacity utilization in certain segments; these periods are shaded. For the segments WH-CSS and CSS-GZS, which belong to W-G HSR, there are four bottlenecks in the periods 10:00–11:00 and 12:00–17:00.

The relationship between primary delay frequency and capacity utilization is also examined and plotted in Figure 2-15. The top part of the figure shows the capacity utilization of WH-CSS and CSS-GZS according to the given period, and the bottom part shows the temporal distribution of primary delay. Figure 2-15 shows that there is a high degree of unity between the periods with high primary delay occurrence frequency and capacity bottlenecks. When there is high capacity utilization, there is a high primary delay occurrence probability, as it is expected in practice. The results of the relationship between the capacity bottlenecks and primary delay frequency help us to improve the timetable by considering a balance between capacity utilization and timetable elasticity.

Table 2-10 Correspondence between bar shape and originating train station

Shape of the bars	Trains' originated stations
	BJW
	SJZ
	ZZE
	WH
	CSS

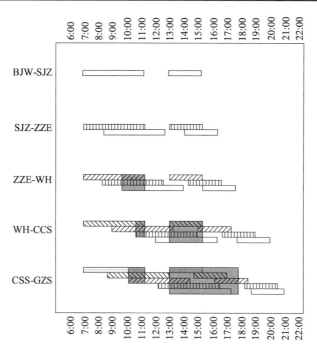

Figure 2-14 Capacity bottlenecks in different segments and periods

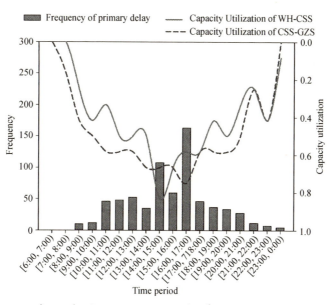

Figure 2-15　Relationship between primary delay frequency and capacity utilization

2.1.7　Conclusions

Statistical analysis on the primary delay issue of HSR trains operating were conducted in Wuhan-Guangzhou HSR line in the Guangzhou Railway Bureau. Using train operation records, key delay indicators was first examined, and showed that distribution of the frequency of primary delay could be fitted to a log-normal distribution, and the affected number of trains' distribution to a non-linear regression model. Then, the relationship between capacity utilization and primary delay occurrence were investigated. Some of the obtained results may work for the specified line, as this study was carried out based on the data of Wuhan-Guangzhou HSR. However, the methods and some of the results can be readily extended and applied to other lines. Based on observation and obtained results, the following future research activities were investigated: 1) examining the underlying mechanism of delays and including reason, influence, development and propagation pattern of each delay type, and 2) studying the relationship between trains running times in track sections and their arrival delays at stations.

This study has the following limitations: Firstly, more precise results and models would have been obtained if more records of data covering longer periods and different lines were available. Secondly, the interaction of running and dwell times with delay recovery needs to be studied carefully. Thirdly, more detailed research on the relationship between capacity utilization and primary delays' temporal and spatial distributions should be carried out. In our future studies, the spatial and temporal analysis of delay occurrences, dependencies between several delay factors, and the relationship between primary delay duration and propagated delay will be examined in details. All of these will be a part of our train delay management decision support tool.

2.2 Statistical Delay Distribution Analysis on High-Speed Railway Trains

The focus of this study is to explore the statistical distribution models of high-speed railway (HSR) train delays. Based on actual HSR operational data, the delay causes and their classification, delay frequency, number of affected trains, and space-time delay distributions are discussed. Eleven types of delay events are classified and a detailed analysis of delay distribution of each classification is presented. Models for explaining the delay probability distribution for each cause for delay are proposed. Different distribution functions, including the lognormal, exponential, gamma, uniform, logistic, and normal distribution, were selected to estimate and model the delay patterns. The most appropriate distribution, which can approximate the delay duration corresponding to each cause, is derived. Subsequently, the Kolmogorov-Smirnov (K-S) test was used to test the goodness of fit of different train delay distribution models and the associated parameter values. The test results show that the distribution of the test data is consistent with that of the selected model. The fitting distribution models show the execution effect of the timetable and help in finding out the potential conflicts in real-time train operations.

2.2.1 Introduction

Since 2008, China's high-speed railway (HSR) has grown significantly owing to its advantages over other modes of transport; these include large transport capacity, low energy consumption, and high degree of punctuality. Several railway passenger terminals and HSR lines have developed into networks; all these factors could improve the rail transport operations in terms of quantity and quality.

In the process of creating an HSR timetable, the conflicts between different trains over network resources will be eliminated. Ideally, trains are supposed to operate according to a timetable without any conflict. However, delays are often unavoidable owing to human-related errors, interference from operating environments or facilities, and equipment-related events. Compared with road and air transportation, railways have a stricter order of line resources, that is, any delay would affect several trains and cause a series of delays.

On high-speed lines in China, once the delay is more than one minute, the train would be marked as a delay train. According to the data from the Chinese Guangzhou Railway Corporation, during March to November in 2015, the total arrival and departure delay time are 54,327 minutes in Changsha station and 77,802 minutes in Guangzhou station. On the one hand, train delays would reduce the quality of transportation services and increase the cost of railway operations. On the other hand, they would increase the travel time of trains and cause inconvenience to passengers. Accurately analyzing the impact of the delay of HSR trains is conducive to improving the management level of HSR transportation, and is an important guarantee that HSR will provide quality transportation services to society.

The railway delay mechanism could be revealed by the delayed train records [84]. Using the actual train operation data, this study promotes the statistical distribution analysis of the HSR train delays, including the various distribution functions of train delays caused by different delay events. In particular, related parameters of these delay distributions were also estimated to describe the current delay statue of the high-speed trains. The following are the main contributions: 1) preliminary analysis of the causes of delays and the overall situation of HSR train delays as a foundation for further studies; 2) establishing distributions models and parameter estimations of delays to serve as the basis for timetabling and simulation studies of train operations.

The remainder of this study is organized as follows. Section 2.2.2 briefly reviews the current studies on the train operation disturbance and analyzes the actualtrain performance data. Section 2.2.3 introduces the structure of the delay record data. Section 2.2.4 presents the results of the causes and statistical characteristics of HSR train delays. Section 2.2.5 proposes the statistical models for the distribution of train delay time; Further, distribution model selection and parameter estimation results are also put forward. Finally, some conclusions and future study directions are discussed in section 2.2.6.

2.2.2 Literature Review

HSR train operation disturbance has received extensive interest, as reflected in the literature on railway transportation management and most of the scholars have focused on the prediction of disturbance, simulation research of disturbance, and the theoretical models of delay propagation. With the development of computer science and data technology, quantitative research on train performance based on operationaldata has become popular.However, owing to the difficulty of obtaining train operation records, most of these studies have been based on simulated or partial data [29].

In the simulation and theoretical researchdomain, simulation software, such as LUKS [255], RailSys, and OpenTrack [46] are generally used to simulate the operation of trains.However, the specific disturbance valuesare mostly set on the basis of qualitative methods.Keiji et al. formulated a train operation simulation model for the Tokyo Metropolitan Areaby taking into account the interaction between the trains and passenger-boarding model at each station [190]. Weik et al. provided a strict mathematical proof of the Strele formula for the estimation of knock-on delay[324]. Weng et al. established a regression tree model to predict train delays [325]. This research has focused on urban rail transit;however, the operating environment of HSR is much more complex.

In terms of quantitatively studying the effects of disturbance based on data-driven methods, the existing studies focused on the distribution of the delay time. Scholars had used the lognormal, exponential, or Weibull distributions to fit the train delay duration distribution [80]. First, Schwanhäußer et al. proved that the distribution and propagation of primary delay probability follows a negative exponential distribution [326]. Based on the historical operation data of the Dutch railway, Yuan found that the distribution of train arrival and departure delay fitted a log-normal distribution curve [81]. Based on the train operation data, Xu et al. used the zerotruncated negative binomial (ZTNB)distribution to simulate and predict the probability of the daily delay in trainoperation. However, this research did not explain themodel effect [62]. Meng put forwardan approach to reconstruct train delay propagationbased on the records of the Dutch railway operation data. However, the data was only for one month [211].

In summary, the existing studies show that there is a growing research trend of delays based on actual train data. However, there is a lack ofstatistical analysis and distribution modeling of Chinese HSR train delays.Studies of HSR train delays in Chinawould contributeto an improvement in the management of train operation.

2.2.3　Data Description

Train delay data, including data on four HSR routes shown in Figure 2-1, were derived from the train operation database of the China Railway Company. After removing invalid data (accounting for 4.4% of the total), which lack the records of the delay reasons, there are still 11,452 delayed trains. That is to say, all the trains in this work are delayed trains.

The sample period of the delayed trains is from 25 to December 17th, 2015. A sample of the data format is presented in Table 2-11. Here, we just consider the positive delays; this means that trains departing and arriving earlier than their schedule time are not taken into account.

Table 2-11　Format of the original data sample

Train number	Origin or destination	Scheduled time*	Actual time*	Delay reasons	Responsible Department	Date
D2312	North Shenzhen Station	16:55	17:14	A balloon on the catenary	None	20140501
G1135	South Guangzhou Station	18:20	18:37	Speed limitation due to heavy rain	None	20140521

* This time might be the departure or arrival time.

2.2.4　Analysis of Train Delays

2.2.4.1　Causes of delays

According to the records of the China Railway Company, there are over 40 kinds of events, such as heavy rains, catenary faults, and braking equipment failures, which cause train delays.

In this article, the causes of train delays were classified into the following eleven types: human error (HE); foreign body invasion (FBI), bad weather (BW); natural disaster (ND); passenger influence (PI); vehicle fault (VF), traction and power-supply system fault (TPSF); dispatching and control system fault (DCSF); communication and signal system fault (CSSF); line fault (LF), and other problems (OP). The detailed explanations of the causes are as follows:

(1) Human error (HE): unexpected maintenance (related departments require a temporary operation interruption, which is not scheduled, to maintain or examine the tracks, vehicles, or other facilities); physical discomfort of the driver; departure before the maintenance operation completed; and a stop at aneutral section.

(2) Foreign body invasion (FBI): hitting animals; pedestrians stepping on tracks; track or catenary faults.

(3) Bad weather (BW): heavy rain, wind,or snow.

(4) Natural disaster (ND): flood, landslide, fire, or earthquake.

(5) Passenger influence (PI): temporary stop owing to passage of key trains; passenger aid; passenger transferring,and large passenger volume.

(6) Vehicle fault (VF): fault in any component of a vehicle.

(7) Traction and Power-supply system fault (TPSF): faults of catenary, pantograph, hauling system, braking system, and so on.

(8) Dispatching and control system fault (DCSF): faults in automatic train control (ATC) system, centralized traffic control (CTC) system, Chinese train control system (CTCS), monitoring system, risk prevention system, and so on.

(9) Communication and signal system fault (CSSF): faults of signals, transponders, communication equipment, and so on.

(10) Line fault (LF): faults in tracks, switches, and tunnel drainage facilities, train shaking (owing to damage to track parts), track settlement, and so on.

(11) Other problems (OP): faults in the air-conditioning equipment and so on.

2.2.4.2 Correlation analysis of the factors

The classifications of these cause for delay were based on experience. In order to explain and evaluate the classification results, the correlation coefficients between each pair of the factors were calculated. By calculating the delay time of delayed trains owing to different causes on individual days, a date-delay time matrix was obtained. The columns of the matrix are populated by the delay time because of different causes, whereas the rows contain the dates.

The results obtained by using Eq. (2-8) to calculate the correlation matrix between different factors are presented in Table 2-12. The largest absolute value in the correlation matrix is 0.241; this means that most factor pairs are nearly uncorrelated. These results confirm that the statistical characteristics of these individual delay factors could be considered independently.

$$\rho_{i,j} = \frac{E\{[X_i - E(X_i)] \times [X_j - E(X_j)]\}}{\sigma_{X_i} \sigma_{X_j}} \tag{2-8}$$

where X_i and X_j are the delay times due to different causes on a particular day, and the subscripts i and j, which are different column numbers in the matrix, denote different causes; σ_{X_i} nd σ_{X_j} are standard deviations of the delay time owing to different causes; and $E(X)$ denotes the expectation.

Table 2-12　Correlation matrix between various factor pairs

	HE	FBI	BW	ND	PI	VF	TPSF	DCSF	CSSF	LF	OP
HE	1.000	−0.004	−0.017	−0.014	−0.016	−0.025	0.026	0.160	−0.009	−0.006	−0.008
FBI	−0.004	1.000	−0.024	−0.015	−0.007	0.015	−0.021	−0.006	0.011	−0.026	0.005
BW	−0.017	−0.024	1.000	−0.019	0.005	0.103	−0.025	−0.028	−0.014	0.198	−0.011
ND	−0.014	−0.015	−0.019	1.000	−0.006	−0.016	0.010	0.236	−0.006	0.003	−0.004
PI	−0.016	−0.007	0.005	−0.006	1.000	−0.020	0.024	−0.016	−0.008	−0.016	−0.006
VF	−0.025	0.015	0.103	−0.016	−0.020	1.000	−0.014	−0.024	−0.004	0.008	−0.006
TPSF	0.026	−0.021	−0.025	0.010	0.024	−0.014	1.000	0.023	−0.010	0.241	0.043
DCSF	0.160	−0.006	−0.028	0.236	−0.016	−0.024	0.023	1.000	−0.012	−0.004	−0.009
CSSF	−0.009	0.011	−0.014	−0.006	−0.008	−0.004	−0.010	−0.012	1.000	−0.009	−0.003
LF	−0.006	−0.026	0.198	0.003	−0.016	0.008	0.241	−0.004	−0.009	1.000	−0.006
OP	−0.008	0.005	−0.011	−0.004	−0.006	−0.006	0.043	−0.009	−0.003	−0.006	1.000

2.2.4.3　Overall statistical analysis of delay data

Based on different cause for delay, the overall statistical analysis of the delayed train data (see Table 2-13) shows that a total 1615 delay events took place during the sample period and 11452 trains were affected; this led to an average delay of 42 min per train.

Table 2-13　Overall statistical analysis of delayed train data

Causes	Frequency (%)	Numbers of delayed trains*(%)	Total delay time* (%)	Delay per train *	Max delay	Std. Deviation	Skewness	Kurtosis
HE	2.60	4.13	3.15	32	205	29.45	2.92	10.34
FBI	14.86	14.77	11.68	33	229	26.99	2.77	10.83
BW	16.78	27.69	35.12	53	333	50.45	1.90	3.85
ND	1.73	7.14	11.87	69	1199	81.23	7.50	86.93
PI	3.53	3.45	2.05	25	91	13.48	2.15	6.58
VF	13.99	9.48	7.21	32	204	26.10	2.28	6.23
TPSF	19.01	13.87	10.72	32	183	26.78	2.38	8.21

Causes	Frequency (%)	Numbers of delayed trains*(%)	Total delay time* (%)	Delay per train *	Max delay	Std. Deviation	Skewness	Kurtosis
DCSF	22.11	12.78	12.53	41	257	41.24	1.94	3.38
CSSF	1.30	1.96	1.49	32	74	17.13	0.48	-0.76
LF	3.72	4.38	3.97	38	162	26.24	1.39	1.75
OP	0.37	0.33	0.21	26	56	9.87	0.45	1.05
Sum/mean	100	11452*	476984	42	1199	43.38	5.48	90.60

* It includes primary and knock-on delays; all time units are in minutes.

Table 2-12 provides the following results. First, TPSF (19.0%) and DCSF (22.1%) have the largest probabilities of occurrence of delay; they are followed by FBI (14.9%), BW (16.8%), and VF (14.0%). These five factors accounted for 72.8% of all occurrences. Second, some of the low-frequency causes,such as ND and CSSF,lead to serious delays and affect a large number of trains. Third, some causes, such as ND (standard deviation of 81.23)exhibit greater randomness, and, thus, it is difficult to predict how long the disruptions will last. However, most of these factors generally lead to regular delays; for example, TPSF has a standard deviation of 26.78. Finally, 81.0% of the delays last for less than 60 min while 90% of the delays are less than 91 min long. A kurtosis of 90.60 for the train delays and a huge gap between maximum delay (1199 min) and 75 percentile delay (49 min) prove that the distribution is biased to the left, as shown in Figure 2-16.

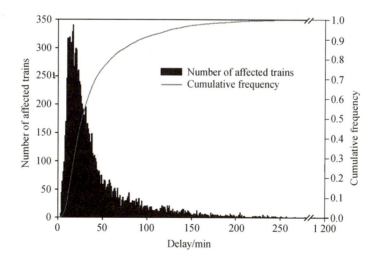

Figure 2-16　Number of delayed trains along with delay time

2.2.4.4　Chronological analysis of delays

The total delay time and the number of delayed trains are calculated for each day of a two-year period, as shown in Figure 2-17; owing to holidays and festivals, the peaks are nearly coincident. In February, May, and October, there are some grand holidays and festivals, such as Spring Festival and National Day in China. On these days, there is greater demand for transportation. More high-speed trains are dispatched, even during the night, and the regular midnight maintenance is skipped to transport more passengers. The lack of maintenance and greater train density lead to more infrastructure-related faults, and more trains are affected when disruptions occur. Second, delays take place more often in spring and summer, because the operating environment is worse in these seasons. More heavy rains and winds in these seasons cause more damage of exposed equipment, and limit train speed.

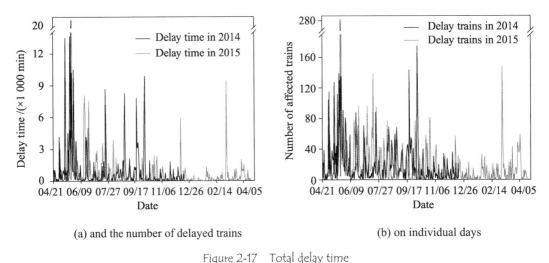

(a) and the number of delayed trains   (b) on individual days

Figure 2-17　Total delay time

2.2.5　Distribution Intensity and Parameter Estimations

To evaluate a timetable or add disturbance events in the simulation process of train operations, it is necessary to consider the intensity of disruptions or disturbances. The intensity, on the one hand, means the number of delayed trains in a time period. On the other hand, it also stands for how long the delay event lasts.

2.2.5.1　Duration distribution of delayed trains in a given time period

Primary delay probability has been proved to follow a negative exponential distribution [203,327,328].

$$f(t) = \begin{cases} \lambda e^{-\lambda t}, & t > 0, \\ 0, & t < 0, \end{cases} \tag{2-9}$$

Where λ is the rate parameter.

In addition, a zero-truncated negative binomial distribution (ZTNB), as expressed in Eq. (2-10), was applied to model and forecast the probability of the number of delayed trains per day:

$$\Pr(y_i \mid y_i > 0) = \frac{\Gamma(y_i + 1/\alpha)}{\Gamma(y_i + 1)\Gamma(1/\alpha)}(\alpha\gamma_i)^{y_i}(1 + \alpha\gamma_i)^{-(y_i + 1/\alpha)}[1 - F_{NB}(0)]^{-1} \qquad (2\text{-}10)$$

where α is the over-dispersion parameter; γ_i is the estimated number of delayed trains for the ith observation and $F_{NB}(y_i)$ is the probability of negative binomial distribution when the frequency is y_i. Moreover, γ_i is calculated as

$$\gamma_i = \exp(\beta_0 + \beta_1 x_{1i} + \cdots + \beta_n x_{ni}) \qquad (2\text{-}11)$$

where x_{ni} is the frequency of the ith cause.

2.2.5.2 Distribution of delay duration

A specific distribution should be selected to model the possible delay duration for a train. The data collected from April 21st, 2014 to 17th December 17th, 2015 were divided into two groups: the first twelve months (7,872 or 68.7% of the observations, or the so-called modeling data)were used for establishing the model and parameter estimation, and the following eight months (3,580 or 31.3% of the observations; so-called testing data) for the hypothetical test and calculating the relative values of goodness of fit. All the calculation processes followed were implemented on the R-project program.

1. Selection of Candidate distributions

Beforeproposing the suitable distributions, it is important to find the good candidates among a series of distributions. One of the typical causes, bad weather (BW), wastakenas an example to explainthe method for candidate distribution selection.

First, the empirical density histogram, nuclear curve, and cumulative distribution of BW were used to intuitivelydetermine candidate distributions. As shown in Fig. 2-18, the majority of the delay durations were less than 100 minutes, presenting a left-skewed distribution.

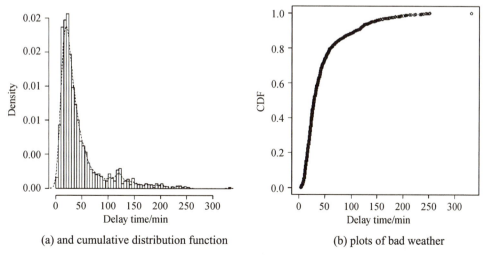

(a) and cumulative distribution function   (b) plots of bad weather

Figure 2-18 Histogram

In addition, Cullen and Frey graph (Fig. 2-19) were introduced to quantitatively compare the skewness and kurtosis of the target dataset and the candidate distributions. Owing to the uncertain distribution and skewness and kurtosisvalues of the dataset, a non-parametric bootstrap was performed in the Cullen-Frey graph by using the argument boot. Some of the distributions (normal, logistic, etc.) have only one possible value for the skewness and kurtosis, while others (lognormal, gamma, and beta) have areas of possible values, presented as lines or areas. Based on the result of BW in Fig.5, with a positive skewnessand a kurtosis not far from 5, three types of distributions were taken into account: lognormal, exponential, and gamma. With the same analysis and calculation for all the causes, Table 2-14 shows the results of candidate distributions for the remaining causes of delay.

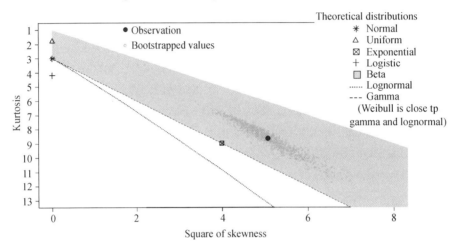

Figure 2-18   Cullen and Frey graph with a bootstrapped value of 1000 for BW data

Table 2-14   Candidate distributions for different causes

Causes	Candidate distributions
BW	Lognormal, exponential, gamma
CSSF	Uniform
DCSF	Lognormal, exponential, gamma
HE	Uniform, normal
LF	Normal, logistic
ND	Logistic, lognormal, gamma*
OP	lack of data
PI	Lognormal, exponential, gamma
TPSF	Lognormal, exponential, gamma
FBI	Lognormal, gamma
VF	Lognormal, gamma
All	Lognormal, exponential, gamma

* According to the original data, natural disaster may cause, in total, 500 minutes of delay on one train; here, onlythe delay times less than 500 minutes, which constitute the left part of the distribution, are taken into account.

2. Parameter estimation by maximum likelihood estimation (MLE)

3. Model testing

The Kolmogorov-Smirnov test (K-S) is used to evaluate these distributions. As shown in formula (2-12), the statistic is the maximum difference between the empirical piecewise function of the dataset and the empirical distribution function of a theoretical distribution.In this study, the significance level of the test is 0.05, and the critical value of D is calculated by formula (2-13) when the sample size is large enough (generally greater than 50). According to the K-S test, if D is not greater than $D_{0.05}$, the null hypothesis (H_0) is accepted. The null and alternative hypotheses in the test are:

H0-Delay time data fitting the identified distribution;

H1-Delay time data not fitting the identified distribution.

$$D = \text{Max} \, | \, F_1(x) - F_2(x) \, |, \tag{2-12}$$

$$D_{0.05} = \frac{1.36}{\sqrt{m}}, \tag{2-13}$$

where $F_1(x)$ and $F_2(x)$ are the empirical distribution functions of the modeling dataset and thecandidate distribution, respectively, and m is the sample size.

The modeling datawere applied to conduct the K-S test;because all the models passed the K-S test, the null hypothesis (H0) is accepted. Subsequently, the testing of fitting models was calculated.Using the same method, the testing data were introduced to match the specified probability distributions of every cause by the K-S test. The results are listed in Table 2-15.

Table 2-15　Results of the K-S test for testing data

Cause	Sample size	D	$D_{0.05}$	Pass
BW	976	0.038	0.044	Yes
DCSF	477	0.056	0.062	Yes
PI	124	0.018	0.122	Yes
TPSF	529	0.054	0.059	Yes
FBI	497	0.057	0.061	Yes
VF	302	0.031	0.078	Yes
ND	272	0.075	0.082	Yes
CSSF	70	0.173	0.163	No
HE	148	0.099	0.112	Yes
LF	163	0.079	0.107	Yes
All	3558	0.020	0.023	Yes

The test results show that the distribution models fitted in this study all passed the K-S test, except for CSSF. The model could accurately describe the general law of HSR disturbance affecting the train delay time distribution, and has good prediction ability and practical application. As for CSSF, the reason might be: 1) the data scale is not adequate for the precisecalculationand 2) the probability of its occurrence is too random, and, thus, the uniform distribution cannot be accurately fitted.

2.2.6 Discussion and Conclusions

In this study, the statistical train delay status and distribution models of HSR were investigated by using the actual operational data. Based on the categorization of delay events, different distribution models were fitted and the related parameters were estimated. The Main findings and contributions are as follows:

(1) Based on the actual performance of the trains onhigh-speed lines, the train operation delay status were extracted and analyzed.

(2) Distributions of delay time were modeled for elevencause for delay, and all the most suitable fittings were screened by the MLE method and *K-S* test.

(3) The models were checked with the operation data. The test results show that most of the distribution models fitted in this study had good practical applicability, and could accurately fit the impact of HSR disturbance on train delay time, which had great practical application value.

Nest, studies,such asthe clustering models of the delays, detailed studies about the primary delay distributions, and predicting delays in train operations using the hybrid Bayesian network model are proposed as future work.

2.3 Temporal and Spatial Distributions of Primary Delays in a High-Speed Rail System

Improving the quality of service of a rail transportation system, and enhancing the operation safety require aquantitative understanding of the dynamic and stochastic characteristics of its train operations, especially those caused by unexpected disruptions. In this chapter, based on historical train operation records, the characteristics of the primary delays (PDs) occurred on the Wuhan-Guangzhou (W-G) high-speed railway (HSR) are investigated, with a specific focus on the underlying behavioral and physical factors. Alternative distribution models, including Log-normal, Weibull, and Gamma distributions, are calibrated and subsequently tested using hold-out data, to investigate the temporal and spatial distributions of PDs. The Kolmogorov-Smirnov (K-S) test results show that all thecandidate models can fit the PD distribution curves, however, the Log-normal distributional form outperforms the other models. Subsequently, the model validation, carried out on the test dataset and the entire data, supported by the results obtained from the K-S two-sample test, indicate that the Log-normal model could satisfy the requirements with sufficient accuracy.

2.3.1 Introduction

Rail transport operates in a highly stochastic and dynamic setting resulting in unexpected disturbances and delays, which can influence the quality of intended services. Mining train operation records to investigate the temporal and spatial characteristics of delays, the accompanying distributions and mechanisms that produce delay propagation, can help operators make better delay management decisions. Since the circumstances are different from the time (segment) to time (segment), it is of profound significance to investigate the temporal and spatial distribution of the delay. When a train is held back on a track or at a station due to some external disturbances, the resulting delay is called primary delay (PD) or source delay. A late train, due to a PD, can affect the operations of other trains at the downstream stations and sections. The temporal and spatial distributional models of PDs can be used as a predictive tool by the dispatchers to assess the delay occurrence distributions, given certain operation time and location. Also, the temporal and spatial distributional models of PDs can support the distributions generated in simulation systems, as well as the study of delay propagation modeling.

Over the years, through advanced computerized control and monitoring technologies, train operations in W-G HSR have been well-monitored and well-recorded. This includes temporal-spatial system-wide data about train movement operations, and records of disturbance and disruption factors [206]. Based on the rich data sources, the system and the tools developed from the data can be used as a benchmark for future practitioners as they develop decision support solutions for improving train services [29, 207, 208]. The valuable train operation data can be mined to help understand and support practical and theoretical aspects of passenger rail operation such as timetable design, capacity analysis and operation simulation methodologies [209].

With advances monitoring devices and intelligent control systems, the operation data become available in Chinese HSR. It is possible and meaningful to model the delay distributions instead of the presumptive or hypothesis models. In our previous study [29], it has been shown that the distributional form of primary delays, and the affected number of trains can be well-approximated by classical methods such as the Log-normal distribution and linear regression models. This study, concerned with the primary delays, builds on the general duration distributions and statistical analysis of temporal and spatial occurrence presented in [29]. Our work studies the modeling of temporal and spatial distributions of PDs in further, based on the historical observations from February 2014 to November 2016 that obtained from W-G HSR train operations. In this work, the data during 2014 and 2015 was used for the modeling process, while data from 2016 was withheld for validation. PDs distribution models of three time periods and four segments were established as input for future research work on the specified line.

The remainder of this study is organized as follows. Section 2.3.2 briefly reviews the existing studies on causes and effects of PDs literature. Section 2.3.3 briefly describes the data obtained from W-G HSR. Temporal and spatial distributions modeling of W-G HSR PDs are carried out in section 2.3.4. Section 2.3.5 concludes and highlights future research directions.

2.3.2 Literature Review

Historical train operation records are valuable data for data-driven modeling to investigate real-world problems. A study has been done on the UK road and rail networks on the impacts of an extreme and intense storm that occurred on June 2012. They were able to find the impacts of extreme weather conditions, and help the dispatchers to assess the delay influences [23]. Similarly, a data-mining approach applied, on passenger train traffic using one-month railway data from Finland, to analyze rail transport delay chains [22]. Machine learning techniques have also been applied to increase the performance of models. For example, a recent study using data collected from Serbian railways that modeled arrival delay showed that support vector regression outperformed estimations from artificial neural networks [118]. The train delay propagates process based on the real data of the train is easy to operate and can be used to construct the actual train delay propagate process [210].

Data-driven models often provide more realistic results and more reliable models for simulation and managerial practices when compared to traditional methods that try to make assumptions on the behavior and distribution of events on the network and its subsystems. [211]. Examples of these approaches include calibration of the distributional form of different train process by using reinforcement learning [88]. The measured delays from reality and the current simulated delays resulted from the assumed distributions are compared to adjust the calibrated disturbance parameters, iteratively. To construct the actual train delay propagation process, based on real data, train delay propagation process and the relationship between the arrival delay and departure delay has been briefly addressed in [210].

There has been a growing body of research focusing on modeling of distributional forms of train processes.The detailed statistical analysis of the distribution of the train arrivals, dwell times and departures show a systematic mean arrival delay of almost every line (InterCity, InterRegio, AggloRegio) ranging up to 138 seconds per train [76]. The Weibull distribution, Gamma distribution, and Log-normal distribution have been adopted in several studies about the delay distributions and the respective fitness models have been presented in [80, 201]. A q-exponential function is used to demonstrate the distribution of train delays on the British railway network in [212]. Krüger et al. analyzed in detail how freight train delays can distribute with respect to size, location and time of their occurrence and arrival delays, using data covering all freight train departures and arrivals during 2008 and 2009 in Sweden [202]. Based on empirical data from a Dutch railway station, Yuan et al. found that the location-shifted Log-normal distribution is the best approximate model, among the candidate distributions, for both the arrival times of trains at the approach signal of the station and at the platform track, respectively [189]. To estimate delays at peak hours, the temporal distributions are investigated by Van der Meer et al.[86], and a predictive model involving the mining of track occupation data is presented in [196]. Given the HSR operation data, the probability distribution of the different disruption factors, has been investigated, however, models of (primary) delay consequences have not yet been established in detail in the literature [61].

2.3.3 Data Analysis and Processing

The train operation records are collected from the W-G HSR line. According to the relationship between frequency and capacity utilization of W-G HSR obtained in [29], the segments Wuhan-Changsha and Changsha-Guangzhou have four bottlenecks in the periods 10:00–11:00 and 12:00–17:00. This study showed that the PD distributions are different in the period of 10:00-17:00, before 10:00(including morning peak hours), and after 17:00 (including evening peak hours), owing to the differences of the timetable structure and the capacity utilization. In addition, the temporal distribution of the PDs of W-G HSR as shown in Fig. 2-19 confirms the results obtained in [29], which show that there is overall high PD frequency during 10:00-17:00, and there are increasing and decreasing trends before 10:00 and after 17:00 respectively. Therefore, the operation time of W-G HSR is divided into three periods as mentioned above.

The delay distributions should differ from section to section, and it is valuable to investigate the model the distributions to section by section. As there are not sufficient modeling samples for most of the single section, we finally merged several sections into a segment, and then we can successfully model the distributions. The CSS station connects the W-G HSR and Shanghai-Kunming HSR and a large number of arriving and departing trains stop here, and there will be fewer train in the downstream sections of CSS. Similarly, the HYE station connects the W-G HSR and the Hunan-Guangxi HSR, and there will be cross-line HYE train between the two lines, which will lead to the capacity utilization differences starting from HYE station. As the station SG is nearly in the middle of the segment of HYE-CZS, and it splits the line between Guangdong province and Hunan province, it can be selected as the division point of HYE-CZS. In this study, we ultimately take these three stations as the division points of the segments, dividing the W-G HSR into four segments: GZS-SG, SG-HYE, HYE-CSS, and CSS-CBN. The lower part of Table 2-16 shows the spatial distribution characters in the mentioned segments, and the descriptive statistics of the PDs are shown too.

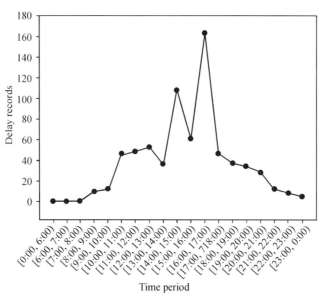

Fig.2-19 Temporal Distribution of W–G HSR.

Table 2-16 Descriptive Statistics of PDs Distributions

Temporal/ Spatial	Sample size		Minimum (min)		Maximum (min)		Average (min)		Mode (min)		Median (min)		Standard deviation	
	MD	TD	MD	TD	MD	TD	MD	TD	MD	TD	MD	TD	MD	TD
Before 10:00	47	51	7	2	75	86	23.77	27.67	29	10	20	19	15.24	22.5
10:00-17:00	197	133	4	1	88	88	23.27	24.9	16	12	17	18	16.9	19.31
After 17:00	180	87	5	3	88	82	24.66	22.76	11	10	19	16	16.3	18.15
GZS-SG	113	92	4	1	82	88	26.14	23.96	17	10	20	16.5	17.36	18.7
SG-HYE	107	63	4	4	88	83	23.64	25.52	16	10	18	18	16.19	21.04
HYE-CSS	89	59	5	2	88	81	25.98	23.98	16	10	20	19	17.53	18.23
CSS-CBN	104	54	4	1	71	86	20.03	25.44	10	10	15.5	18.5	14.02	20.9

As mentioned, we just investigated the data of a train with a difference that is no less than 1min, the on-time trains were excluded. "*MD*" denotes training data, "*TD*"denotes testing data. There are 11 records in "*MD*" are not complete, 424 records can be used in the time dimension and only 413 records can be used spatially. Meanwhile, there are 3 records in "*TD*" are not complete, there are 271 records can be used to model by temporal and only 268 records can be used by spatially. The *Mode* and *Median* show that the train operation reliability in 2016 is better than that in 2014 and 2015, since both the *Mode* and *Median* in 2016 aresmaller. They also reveal that there will be no less than 10min delay in most cases. We note from Table I that, there are higher probabilities of delays between 5min to 25min, which confirms that the PDs usually bring serious delay to the train operation.

2.3.4 Temporal and Spatial Distribution Models of PDs

Generally, a PD is a type of train delay that does not result from another delayed train or another delay to the same train during preceding operations. In this section, we present the temporal distribution models of PDs, which were investigated and represented by the models of the three periods. Next, we show the spatial distribution models of PDs, which were represented by the models of the four segments.

2.3.4.1 Candidate Models

The skewness, kurtosis, and interquartile range of the PD distribution of the W-G HSR line are shown in Table 2-17. The skewness of PD distributions in each period and segment are all greater than zero, demonstrating that the probability density functions tend to be right-skewed. Moreover, the kurtosis of the PDs is all less than three, which demonstrates that the probability density distribution functions are less steep than the normal distribution. The interquartile range in different periods and segments contains few differences, which shows that the dispersions are almost close. R-project has been applied to estimate Gauss kernel density functions and histograms, see Fig. 2-20.

According to the skewness, kurtosis, kernel density functions, and the histogram discussed above, the PD distributions show a distinct right-skewed behavior. The common right-skewed distribution models, namely the Log-normal distribution, Weibull distribution, and Gamma distribution were therefore considered as the candidate models in this study. In probability theory, a positive random variable x is Log-normally distributed if the logarithm of x is normally distributed. Given a log-normally distributed random variable x with the mean parameter μ, and the shape parameter σ, it has a probability density function as follows:

$$f(x;\mu,\sigma) = \frac{1}{x\sigma\sqrt{2\pi}}\,\mathrm{e}^{-\frac{(\ln x - \mu)^2}{2\sigma^2}}. \tag{2-14}$$

where μ and σ are also called the location and the scale parameters, respectively. The probability density function of a Weibull random variable x with, respectively, positive shape and scale parameters k, and λ is defined as:

$$f(x;\lambda,k) = \begin{cases} \dfrac{k}{\lambda}\left(\dfrac{x}{\lambda}\right)^{k-1}\mathrm{e}^{-(x/\lambda)^k} & x \geq 0 \\ 0 & x < 0 \end{cases}. \tag{2-15}$$

The probability density function of Gamma distribution with a shape parameter α, and an inverse scale parameter β is:

$$f(x;\alpha,\beta) = \begin{cases} \dfrac{\beta^\alpha}{\Gamma(\alpha)}x^{\alpha-1}\mathrm{e}^{-\beta x}, & x \geq 0 \\ 0 & x < 0 \end{cases}, \tag{2-16}$$

where $\Gamma(x)$ is a complete Gamma function, which for all complex numbers except the non-positive integers is defined as:

$$\Gamma(x)=\int_0^{+\infty} t^{x-1}e^{-t}dt .$$ (2-17)

Table 2-17 Skewness, Kurtosis and Interquartile Range of PDs

Temporal/Spatial	Skewness	Kurtosis	Interquartile range
Before 10:00	1.324	1.523	17.5
10:00-17:00	1.688	2.569	16
After 17:00	1.369	1.487	19
GZS-SG	1.399	1.433	19
SG-HYE	1.617	2.579	18.5
HYE-CSS	1.462	1.784	16
CSS-CBN	1.585	2.226	14

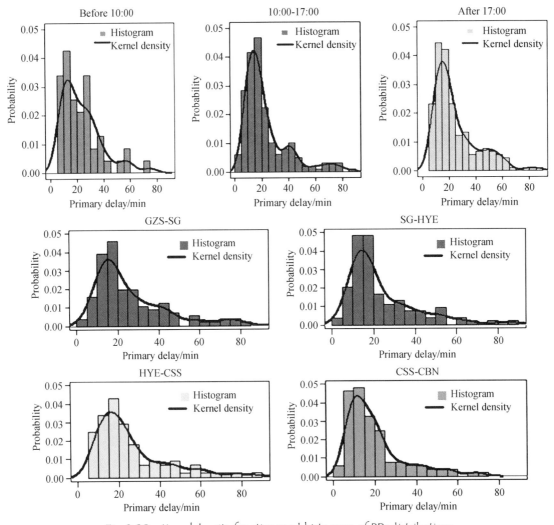

Fig. 2-20 Kernel density functions and histogram of PDs distributions.

2.3.4.2　Modeling of the Temporal and Spatial Distributions

We estimated the parameters of the Log-normal distribution, Weibull distribution, and Gamma distribution using the maximum-likelihood method in R-project, and provided the results in Table 2-18. While, the density histogram, density curves, and the fitting curves of the candidate models are shown in Fig. 2-21.

Table 2-18　Fitting Parameter Value of Temporal and spatial Primary Delay Distribution

Temporal/Spatial	Log-normal distribution		Weibull distribution		Gamma distribution	
	μ	σ	k	λ	α	β
Before 10:00	2.9873	0.5983	1.7091	26.8566	2.9188	0.1228
10:00-17:00	2.928	0.6504	1.5249	26.0316	2.4540	0.1056
After 17:00	3.0271	0.6108	1.6582	28.1596	2.7871	0.1117
GZS-SG	3.0725	0.6135	1.6496	29.4863	2.7725	0.1061
SG-HYE	2.9699	0.6116	1.6149	26.6412	2.7416	0.1159
HYE-CSS	3.0623	0.6188	1.6292	29.2747	2.7200	0.1047
CSS-CBN	2.7934	0.6295	1.5807	22.5223	2.6074	0.1302

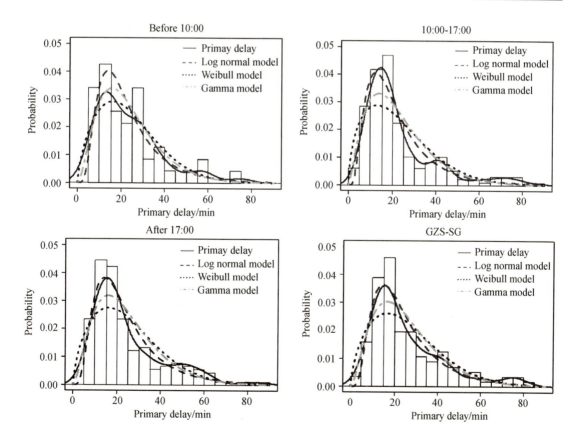

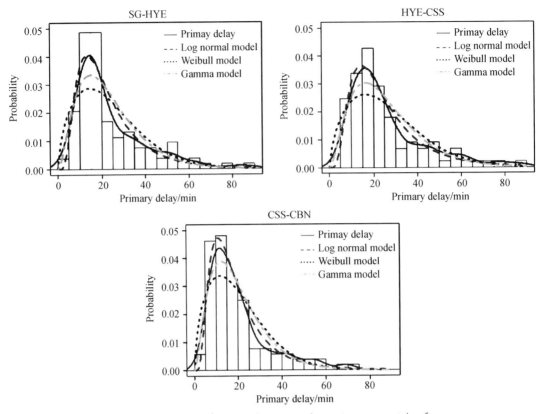

Fig. 2-21　Fit curves of temporal and spatial distribution models of PDs.

We tested the fitness performances of the candidate distribution models using the Kolmogorov-Smirnov (K-S) test as provided in the Equation (2-18). The K-S teststatistic, for a given cumulative distribution function $F(x)$, quantifies the distance between the empirical distribution function derived from the sample and the cumulative distribution function of the assumed distribution. The hypothesis of the test is as follows [213]:

H_0: The data follow the specified distribution

H_a: The data do not follow the specified distribution

$$D = \max|F'(x) - F(x)|$$
(2-18)

where $F'(x)$ is the cumulative distributions ofthe candidate distributions. The smaller the value of D is, the better the goodness of fit will be, i.e., the empirical distribution fits the primary delay better. The critical value of Dat 0.05 significance level is derived according to the Equation (2-19), where n is the sample size. The critical value of K-S test and the D values of the five kinds of distribution modes are summarized in Table 2-19. The hypothesis on the assumed distributional form is rejected if the test statistic D is greater than the critical value $D_{0.05}$.

$$D_{0.05} = \frac{1.36}{\sqrt{n}}$$
(2-19)

Table 2-19   K-S Test Results for Candidate Distributions

Temporal/Spatial	Critical value $D_{0.05}$	D value of K-S test		
		Log-normal	Weibull	Gamma
Before 10:00	0.1984	0.0907*	0.0998	0.1008
10:00-17:00	0.0969	0.0658*	0.1221	0.1158
After 17:00	0.1014	0.0697*	0.1217	0.1057
GZS-SG	0.1279	0.0938*	0.1231	0.1115
SG-HYE	0.1314	0.0907*	0.1359	0.1348
HYE-CSS	0.1442	0.0659*	0.1235	0.1117
CSS-CBN	0.1334	0.0506*	0.1022	0.0901

*the smallest deviations

In Table 2-19, the D values of Log-normal are smaller than $D_{0.05}$, we, therefore, cannot reject H_0, whereas we do not have enough evidence to accept H_0 assumptions when assuming the Weibull and Gamma distributional forms. According to the Kolmogorov-Smirnov test results, the D values of Weibull and Gamma distributions are greater than $D_{0.05}$ on the time periods of "10-00-17:00" and "After 17:00", and the segment of "SG-HYE". Consequently, in what follows we fit the frequency of the primary delay duration, using the Log-normal, Weibull, and Gamma distributions to determine which one provides a better fit. Further comparison of the "D value of K-S test" confirms that for each period and segment, the Log-normal distribution has the smallest deviation among the candidates, which is an indication of better fitness. Therefore, we can say that the Log-normal distribution can better approximate the temporal and spatial distributions of PDs. By replacing the values of μ and σ in equation (2-14) with that in Table 2-19, the temporal and spatial distribution models of PDs on W-G HSR can be obtained.

2.3.4.3   Validating of the temporal and spatial distribution models

Validating Models with Testing Data

The data from March 1st, 2016 to November 20th, 2016 was used as the test dataset to verify the goodness-of-fit of different candidate models. The K-S tests of the three candidate models were carried out on the TD and the entire data that combines MD and TD, whose results shown in Table 2-20 and Table 2-21.

Table 2-20   The K-S Test Results of the Candidate Models on Testing Data

Temporal/Spatial	Critical value $D_{0.05}$	D value of K-Stest			Sample size
		Log-normal	Weibull	Gamma	
Before 10:00	0.1904	0.0714*	0.100	0.1004	51
10:00-17:00	0.1179	0.0755	0.0736	0.0590*	133
After 17:00	0.1458	0.0833*	0.1211	0.1123	87

Temporal/Spatial	Critical value $D_{0.05}$	D value of K-Stest			Sample size
		Log-normal	Weibull	Gamma	
GZS-SG	0.1418	0.0973*	0.1224	0.1165	91
SG-HYE	0.1713	0.1086*	0.1293	0.1214	62
HYE-CSS	0.1771	0.0707	0.0556	0.0506*	58
CSS-CBN	0.1851	0.0827	0.0728	0.0673*	54

*the smallest deviations

Table 2-21　The K-S Test Results of the Candidate Models on Entire Data

Temporal/Spatial	Critical value $D_{0.05}$	D value of K-S test			Sample size
		Log-normal	Weibull	Gamma	
Before 10:00	0.1374	0.0489*	0.0890	0.0787	98
10:00-17:00	0.0757	0.0515*	0.0994	0.0837	323
After 17:00	0.0839	0.0520*	0.1043	0.0920	263
GZS-SG	0.0950	0.0655*	0.1081	0.1128	204
SG-HYE	0.1043	0.0859*	0.1339	0.1290	169
HYE-CSS	0.1118	0.0468*	0.0724	0.0590	147
CSS-CBN	0.1082	0.0490*	0.0907	0.0740	158

*the smallest deviation.

According to Table 2-20, the K-S test results show that all the candidate models can meet the deviation requirements and pass the test in each period and segment. In detail, comparing the "D value of K-S test" of each model, for the temporal distribution model tests, the Gamma distribution has the best goodness-of-fit on the period "10:00-17:00" while the Log-normal distribution has the best goodness-of-fit on the other two periods. However, for the spatial distribution model, the Gamma distribution has the best goodness-of-fit on the segments "HYE-CSS" and "CSS-CBN", and the Log-normal distribution has the best goodness-of-fit on the other two periods. In general, the Log-normal distribution has the best performances when fitting the temporal and spatial distributions on *TD*. The results in Table VI show that the Log-normal distribution model has the best goodness-of-fit on all of the periods and segments, which affirms that the deviations of Log-normal distribution model will be reduced as more data become available, increasing the accuracy of the model.

Two Sample Identically Distributed Test:

A K-S test sampling two identically distributed values is a common hypothesis test, and is mainly used to test whether the two samples come from the same population, or to test whether the two samples are identically distributed. If the variation of the two identically distributed samples is smaller than the critical value of the K-S two sample test, then the model can be said to have a good fit, and can be used to predict the distribution of new samples. The hypothesis is as follows:

$\overline{H}_0$: The two samples have the same distribution

$\overline{H}_a$: The two samples do not follow the same distribution

The cumulative distribution function of the test is shown in the formulation (2-20):

$$\overline{D} = \max \left| \overline{F}(x) - \overline{G}(x) \right| \tag{2-20}$$

where $\overline{F}(x)$ and $\overline{G}(x)$ are the empirical distribution functions of the first and the second sample respectively, and $\overline{D}$ is the statistic value of the K-S two sample. By calculating the differences between the cumulative distribution function of the two samples, it is possible to obtain the probability p under the assumption that the two samples follow the same distribution. The smaller the p-value is, the larger the deviation between the two samples will be, and the two samples do not follow the same distribution when p is less than the critical value assuming a significance of $\alpha=0.05$.

In this study, $\overline{G}(x)$ represents the cumulative probability distribution function based on the entire data, while $\overline{F}(x)$ represents the cumulative probability distribution function based on MD and TD respectively. We carried out the K-S two sample identically distributed tests between the Log-normal distributions based on entire data and that based on MD and TD respectively. The p values of the K-S two sample identically distributed tests are summarized in Table 2-22.

Table 2-22　The K-S Two Sample Identically Distributed Test Results

Temporal/Spatial	p-value	
	Entire dada and MD	Entire dada and TD
Before 10:00	0.9848	0.8733
10:00-17:00	0.9488	0.9356
After 17:00	0.4792	0.3259
GZS-SG	0.7277	0.4238
SG-HYE	0.9317	0.2374
HYE-CSS	0.8054	0.4049
CSS-CBN	0.8662	0.3665

The K-S two sample test results, shown in Table 2-22, confirm that the Log-normal distribution models can pass the test. We, therefore, assume that the Log-normal distribution models can well-approximate the temporal and spatial distribution of PDs in W-G HSR and that it can be used for delay distribution prediction in our future work.

2.3.5　Conclusions

This study has presented the results of an investigation aiming at developing statistical models for capturing the temporal and spatial distribution of primary delays on a high-speed rail line. A case study using two years of historical train operation data from theW-G HSR was conducted, and the results confirmed the needs to account for the spatial and temporal variation of delays. Both spatial and temporal patterns of the primary delay distributions were investigated. The temporal distribution is captured by time-dependent models while the spatial distribution by segment-specific models. The K-S test results show that all the candidate models can fit the PD distribution well while the Log-normal distribution yielded the best fitness. Furthermore, the validation of the temporal and spatial distribution models was carried out using both the testing data and the entire data set (training data plus testing data). The K-S test confirmed that all the candidate models could meet the deviation requirements and pass the test in each period and segment. Again, the Log-normal distribution has the best fitness performance.

Delay distribution will be the fundamental of train dispatching practice and research. The data-driven models in this study can be used for railway traffic control. More explicitly, the HSR dispatchers can use probabilities of PDs in each period and segment to infer or estimate the occurrence and the severity of certain PDs. With the distribution models, the dispatchers obtain the real-time and future status of the trains under certain train operation circumstance. The delay patterns can be derived from the data to assist the dispatchers to make decisions. This can support the rescheduling and adjusting the train operation strategies.The contributions of investigating of PDs distributions also can be used as input in data-driven simulation studies, especially as delay generation distributional functions in predictive models for delay propagation. By considering the disturbances, estimating the running times and the potential conflicts, and predicting the delay occurrence, the dispatching decisions can be made from the following aspects.

(1) The temporal and spatial distributional models of PDscan be used as a predictive tool by the dispatchers to assess the delay occurrence distributions, given certain operation time and location. The PDs temporal and spatial distributional models can be updated continuously when new train operation data comes. With the fruitful data, it is possible to assist the dispatchers to carry out predictive dispatching.

(2) The presented data-driven models can also be used in simulating train operations for railway traffic management, to replace the incumbent models that have been widely used so far. These models, used as the delay generation rules in the delay simulation module, can reflect the real situation of train operations. Moreover, it will be of profound theoretical as well as practical contribution to use the developed PDs models as a basis for knock-on delays models to establish delay recovery models.

(3) As an extension, models that combine the occurrence time, occurrence location, and delay causes will be much more precise and representative of the actual operation when used for delay management practices.

In this work, we just modeled the temporal and spatialdistributions separately, aiming to provide a basic data-driven method to model the Chinese HSR PDs based on limited data. There is still much work to do using the data-driven methods to tackle the operation problems of HSR in China. In our ongoing work, we will develop the integrated models of temporal, spatial, and cause-specific distribution models of delays using more delay records under longer time periods to establish more precise models. Then, we will investigate the delay propagation owning to different operation periods, segments, and delay causes.

This study was a part of the research had been carried on the temporal and spatial distribution of PDs, aimed to establish a predictive dispatching decision support tool to help dispatchers in managing HSR train operations. A train operation simulation system will be developed in our future work, beginning with delay generating simulation based on PDs distributions.

Chapter 3

Data-driven delay propagation mechanism on horizontal

3.1 Cause-specific Investigation of Primary Delays of Wuhan–Guangzhou HSR

This chapter presents the results of a case study on the causes and effects of typical service disruptions in a High-speed rail (HSR) system in China—Wuhan—Guangzhou High-speed railway (W-G HSR) – a 1096-kilometer HSR line, using its wealth of train operation records, for improved train operations. With a cause-specific approach, seven delay causalities are identified, and the properties and consequences of each PD factor is derived. The comparison of candidate distributional forms shows that the Log-normal distribution model can approximate better the length of all identified PD. For each PD cause, the distribution of delay duration is estimated and tuned. Next, cause-specific distributional models for PDs severity are discussed. The models for the number of affected trains are presented in the form of inverse regression models with specific domains. Then, comparing five different kinds of candidate models, the results show that the Cubic is the best to approximate the distributions of total affected time. The results show that bad weather factor has the highest impact in terms of delay duration time and the number of involved trains, and the primary delays due to failures in train control system or track are shorter with fewer aftermath impacts on train operations. This chapter proposes a framework to establish a decision support tool, aimed to help dispatchers on managing train operations and improving the reliability of HSR services.

3.1.1 Introduction

As a fast and low pollution mode of transportation, HSR has been developed in many counties. HSR can be used to solve the road and airport congestion, promote the growth and of regional economy[214]. Ever since the operation of first HSR line in China in 2008, it has been expanded very fast and become more popular in the passenger transport market during the following years. Currently, the total length of the lines exceeds 22,000 km, operating 4,665 electronic multiple units (EMU) HSR trains every day, which counts about 65.3% of the passenger trains on the HSR network. All of these indicate that large-scale operation of high-speed railways, in China, have achieved an outstanding performance in improving the network scale and service quality to cope with the shortage of transport capacity while considering the quality of rail transport services. Train operation necessities the integration of several sub-systems, such as railway infrastructure, rolling stock, timetable, human behavior, as to why many unavoidable disturbances can happen during train operation [103]. The uncertainties arise from these sub-systems can conspire to unexpected events and disturbances and eventually lead to delays and displacements in train operation. According to the analysis conducted on delay factors on passenger railways, the delay causes can be associated with train operators, infrastructure authorities, and external factors, see [215] and [29]. Generally, a PD is a type of delay that does not result from another delayed train or another delay to the same train during preceding operations. To assess the offered services, train punctuality is one of the indices used by passengers, and by train operating companies as criteria of efficiency in railway operations. In fact, PDs are known as one of the most important factors that lead to poor performances of railways due to which the punctuality of the railways in several countries is quite low. For instance, in China, the average original departure punctuality of conventional railway is 88%, and estimated as high as 98.8% for HSR in 2015. However, due to the disturbances in the operation process, the average operation punctuality of HSR is reported less than 90% [216].

Delay occurrences are highly dependent on operational conditions and factors that only come true meanwhile the operation of trains. This necessitates to incorporate train operations data and data-driven models in analytical and simulation approaches of studying delay issues. Data-driven approaches of studying PD, and cause and effect analysis of contributing factors can help control the railway operations by taking proactive and retroactive actions to manage delay. For instance, the estimates of primary delay duration can is used as a basis for evaluating the effectiveness of different conflict resolution strategies [217], and the ability of a timetable to absorb delays is used as timetable resilience measure [218]. This study builds on [29], and presents a detailed statistical modelling of PDs in W-G HSR, and its stimuli, relying on data on train operations from the specified line.

In this study, given the train operation data from W-G HSR, we study different causes contributing to PDs, and provide results on the consequences of each of them. To this end, seven types of causes are identified and the distribution model for duration of each PD cause is estimated using the Log-normal distribution model. Next, the distribution models of the number of affected trains and the PD duration times (severity) of each PD cause is established. The contributions of this work mainly include: 1) developing PD cause-specific models to support decision-making inrailway traffic control, 2) presenting models for estimating affected number of trains and affected time models to help the operators in estimating the propagation of the delays, 3) providing data-driven results that can be used in further researches in HSR operation optimization.

The remainder of this study is organized as follows. Section 3.1.2 briefly reviews the existing studies on causes and effects ofPDs literature. The structure of the data obtained from

W-G HSRand the delay causes are presented in section 3.1.3. Modelling of HSR PD distributions for each of the identified causes is carried out in section 3.1.4. Section 3.1.5 presents the cause-specific distribution models of affected trains and time respectively. Section 3.1.6 concludes and highlights future research directions.

3.1.2 Literature review

Delay management requires short-term adjustments to the timetable (delay recovery) to limit delay propagation [219]. A delayed train can cause delays to other trains over a large area and time period. For instance, once a train arrives late to a station because of some exogenous delay it may transfer a part of its delay to other trains that share same infrastructure [1]. Even worse, PD of trains may propagate to other trains and cause a whole cascade of secondary delays over the railway network [220], and other delays can be caused by these primary delays due to train interactions [36]. According to the analysis of the railway in Great Britain, the impact of delays on passenger railways, with particular reference to the national rail network in Great Britain, is examined. Causes of delay can be associated with train operators, infrastructure authorities, and external factors [215]. Using train operation records of W-G HSR, key delay reasons are examined in [29]. Exogenous factors, such as natural disasters, and bad weather conditions,and endogenous factors, such as operation interference resulted from equipment failure, man-made faults, erroneous communication between trains and control center, railway construction,temporary speed limitations, defective braking systems, signal and interlocking failures, and excessive passenger demand can contribute, alone or together, to primary delay [132, 221, 222]. Also, the running and waiting times, if increase due to unexpected disturbances, can result in knock-on delays and delays for other trains [196]. The experience from the Taiwan High-speed Rail shows that shortening the maintenance cycle can effectively alleviate the problem of train delay caused by signal failures [223]. Serious disruptions such as switch or signal failures, if not managed effectively, can result in queuing of trains with a chain of delayed trains.

There are two types of data: 1) simulation data from train operation simulator tool, and 2) real data from command system of monitoring train operation. Usually, simulation data is more accessible than real data, since it is easier to obtain, though with many restrictive assumptions. In this regard, automatic calibration of disturbance parameters, which are used to generate stochastic disturbances in simulation tools, is developed with the support of the reinforcement learning technique [88]. A data-mining approach was used for analyzing rail transport delay chains, with data from passenger train traffic on the Finnish rail network, but the data from the train running process limited one month's data[22]. Aggregation of train operation data on track circuit is obtained based on limited real-world data too [224]. Delay dependencies due to resource conflicts and train connections are analyzed from the macroscopic perspective [225]. R. M. PGoverde and I. Hansen are among the pioneers in analyzing daily train operation data using a tool named TNV-Prepare. TNV-Prepare derives detailed information of event times associated to train services data obtained from the Dutch train describer systems[16]. The data of each train event contains signaling and interlocking information of entire traffic control area were used, including train description steps, section entries and clearances, signals, and point switches [139].

Some studies have made contributions on distributions of delay and the respective fitness models. The Weibull distribution, Gamma distribution, and Log-normal distributions have been adopted in several studies [80, 201]. It shows that the distributional form of primary delays, and the affected number of trains can be well-approximated by classical methods such as Log-normal distribution and line regression models [29]. A q-exponential function is used to demonstrate the distribution of train delays on the British railway network [79]. Using spatial and temporal resolution transport data from the UK road and rail networks, and the intense storms of 28 June 2012 as a case study, a novel exploration of the impacts of an extreme event has been carried out in [23]. Given the HSR operation data, maximum likelihood estimation was used to determine the probability distribution of the different disruption source, and the distributions of affected trains, however, the models of primary delay consequences have not been established in detail [61]. Probabilistic distribution functions of both train arrival and departure delays at the individual station were derived in general based on the data from Beijing-Shanghai HSR [226]. Van der Meer et al. mined peak hours, rolling stock, weather data and developed a predictive model involving the mining of track occupation data for delays estimations [196].

In the literature, a few studies have been identified focusing on the modeling of PDs, and cause-and-effect analysis of consequences, especially in HSR operations. It is more crucial for HSR operating companies to predict and reduce dispositions in train operations, and operate as much close as possible according to the announced planned to the passengers. In particular, they need to identify the different source of delays that can cause severe delays or interruptions, and decrease delay propagations and aggravations through effective design of timetables or real-time scheduling. This study aims to fill this gap by conducting a detailed cause-specific analysis on primary delay based on empirical from W-G HSR.

3.1.3 Data Description

We collected train operation records of the W-G HSR line, which is shown in Fig. 3-1. This line connects Wuhan (Hubei province) to Guangzhou (Guangdong province) that is a 1096-kilometre double-track HSR line with18 stations. However, only the data on 15 stations and 14 sections from GZS to CBN are obtained from the Guangzhou Railway Bureau, as the remaining parts are operated by the Wuhan Railway Bureau. Chinese HSR train operations are fully under the supervision of the Centralized Traffic Control (CTC) system, which can record all the real-time events on a second by second intervals. As a train moves around the network, it is continuously monitored by remote controls via the track occupancy reports that are logically linked to the train number. When a train passes a station signal, this event is recorded by a remote control and simultaneously transmitted to the CTC system. The CTC records and displays the data with its exact time. The data gathered from CTC includes the arrival and departure times, which describes the overall running process of the trains. There are numerous records in graph and table formats. Table 3-1 shows a sample of train operation records that we used to obtained information about the W-G HSR, such as nominal timetable, train classes and speeds, each train's realized running and dwell times to figure out the spatial and temporal occurrence of any unexpected disturbance or disruption.

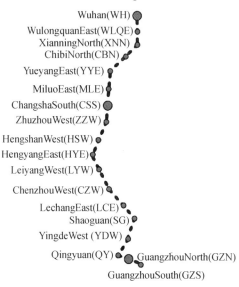

Fig. 3-1   Map of Wuhan-Guangzhou HSR

Table 3-1   Train running records in a database

Train NO	Date	Station	Scheduled arrival time	Scheduled departure time	Arrival time	Departure time
G634	2015-2-24	GZS	17:26:00	17:26:00	17:28:00	17:28:00
G6152	2015-2-24	QY	17:16:00	17:18:00	17:18:00	17:20:00
G9694	2015-2-24	YDW	19:00:00	19:02:00	19:00:00	19:03:00
G548	2015-2-24	SG	17:26:00	17:29:00	17:25:00	17:29:00

In gathering and processing of data, we considered the following two points: 1) the required data type and 2) how the collected data should be processed. To explain more, we only considered the train movements in one direction, from GZS to WH. And the data collected from February 24, 2015 to November 30, 2015, that includes 29662 HSR train records in total. These data include primary delays, secondary delays and normal operating data (on-time train data).In data cleaning step, records with more than 90 minutes primary delay were excluded. Ultimately, data of 1249 primary delayed trains are left and used in our analysis on primary delay.

3.1.4 Time Duration Distributional Models of PDs

According to delay source, we classified the reasons for HSR train delays into seven categories. The description of these categories and their abbreviations are provided in Table 3-2. To see how disturbance instances are spread, we looked at the histogram and the theoretical densities and CDFs of all the primary delaysdurations different in Figure 3-2, represents. Fig. 3-2(a), the primary delay Duration scatter diagram, whose horizontal axis is the sequence number of the delayed train in the database, and the vertical axis is the delay duration of the respective train. It can describe the primary delay distribution in different time intervals roughly. For example, we can know that mostly primary delays duration are less than 20 min and fewer primary delays duration are more than 60 min. In Figure 3-2(b), the horizontal axis is the primary delay duration in a 5 minutes intervals, and the vertical axis is the frequency of each duration interval.

Table 3-2　Description, abbreviations, and samples of each delay causes

Factor categories	Abbreviation	Samples
Failure of ATP: it refers to the failure of Chines train control system, mainly appears as failure of automatic train control system (ATP)	FA	197
Failure of track: it refers to the failure of tracks, switches, bridges, and tunnels	FT	84
Failure of rolling stock:　it refers to broken or mechanical failure of rolling stock	FRS	259
Failure of Pantograph and Signal and Catenary: it refers to the failure of pantograph, catenary of electronic multiple units, and signal system	FPSC	217
Failure of foreign material: it refers to factors that animals or foreign matters entering the track	FFM	156
Fault of weather: it refers to the severe weather, such as torrential rains and snow, frost, hurricane, flood.	FW	201
Other factors: it refers the factors that are not listed above	FO	135

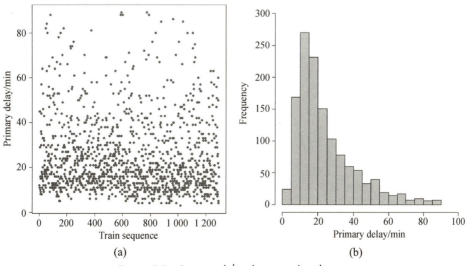

Figure 3-2　Primary delay duration distribution

Our calculations show that over 73% of the delays are less than 30 minutes and the average duration of delays is about 25 minutes. Considering the shape of Fig. 3-2(b), we tested the fitness performances of the Normal distribution, Log-normal distribution, Weibull distribution, Chi-square Distribution, and Gamma Distribution using the Kolmogorov-Smirnov (K-S) test as provided in the Equation (3-1). The K-S teststatistic, for a given cumulative distribution function $F(x)$, quantifies the distance between the empirical distribution function derived from the sample and the cumulative distribution function of the assumed distribution. The hypothesis of the test is as follows:

H_0: The data follow the specified distribution

H_a: The data do not follow the specified distribution

$$D = \max |F'(x) - F(x)|, \qquad (3-1)$$

where $F'(x)$ is the cumulative distributions of candidate distribution models which are Log-normal distribution, Weibull distribution and Gamma distribution applied in this study. Log-normal distribution and Weibull distribution. The smaller the value of D is, the better the goodness of fit will be, i.e., the empirical distribution fits the primary delay better. The critical value of Dat 0.05 significance level is derived according to the Equation (3-2), where n is the sample size. The critical value of K-S test and the D values of the five kinds of distribution modes are summarized in Table 3-3, where TD denotes all the identified cause types from the entire data. The hypothesis on the assumed distributional form is rejected if the test statistic D is greater than the critical value $D_{0.05}$.

$$D_{0.05} = \frac{1.36}{\sqrt{n}}. \qquad (3-2)$$

Table 3-3　Test results for candidate distributions

Delay Cause	Critical Value $D_{0.05}$	D				
		Normal	Chi-square	Log-normal	Weibull	Gamma
TD	0.0378	0.1387	0.1900	0.0352	0.0826	0.0724
FA	0.0964	0.1406	0.1607	0.0386	0.0930	0.0758
FT	0.1426	0.1302	0.1980	0.0463	0.0882	0.0763
FRS	0.0835	0.1629	0.2091	0.0491	0.0988	0.0795
FPSC	0.0913	0.1356	0.2266	0.0477	0.0841	0.0754
FW	0.0941	0.1861	0.2676	0.0867	0.1238	0.1265
FFM	0.1065	0.1437	0.1444	0.0586	0.0959	0.0834
FO	0.1137	0.1766	0.1756	0.0497	0.1079	0.0924

According to Table 3-3, only the values of D of Log-normal are smaller than $D_{0.05}$, we therefore cannot reject H_0, whereas we do not have enough evidence to accept H_0 assumptions when testing Weibull distribution and Gamma distributional forms, asthe D values of Weibull distribution are greater than $D_{0.05}$ on FRS and FW and that of Gamma distribution is greater than $D_{0.05}$ on FW. What is worse, is that both the Weibull distribution and Gamma distribution cannot pass the test on the total causes of entire data, and the Normal distribution and Chi-square distribution cannot pass the test for any kind of delay cause. Consequently, in what follows we fit the frequency of the primary delay duration, for each of the identified factors, using Log-normal, Weibull, and Gamma distributions to determine which one provides a better fit. In probability theory, a positive random variable x is Log-normally distributed if the logarithm of x is normally distributed. Given a log-normally distributed random variable x with the mean parameter μ, and the shape parameter σ, it has a probability density function as follows:

$$f(x;\mu,\sigma)=\frac{1}{x\sigma\sqrt{2\pi}}e^{-\frac{(\ln x-\mu)^2}{2\sigma^2}}. \tag{3-3}$$

where μ and σ are also called the location and the scale parameters, respectively. Also, the probability density function of a Weibull random variable x with, respectively, positive shape and scale parameters k, and $\lambda > 0$ is defined as:

$$f(x;\lambda,k)=\begin{cases}\frac{k}{\lambda}\left(\frac{x}{\lambda}\right)^{k-1}e^{-(x/\lambda)^k} & x\geq 0 \\ 0 & x<0\end{cases}. \tag{3-4}$$

The probability density function ofGamma distribution with a shape parameter α, and an inverse scale parameter β is:

$$f(x;\alpha,\beta)=\begin{cases}\frac{\beta^\alpha}{\Gamma(\alpha)}x^{\alpha-1}e^{-\beta x}, & x\geq 0 \\ 0 & x<0\end{cases} \tag{3-5}$$

Where $\Gamma(x)$ is a complete Gamma function. The Gamma function for all complex numbers except the non-positive integers is defined as:

$$\Gamma(x)=\int_0^{+\infty}t^{x-1}e^{-t}dt \tag{3-6}$$

We estimated the parameters of the Log-normal distribution, Weibull distribution, and Gamma distribution using the maximum-likelihood method in R-project, and provided the results in Table 3-4. The cause-specific histograms and the delay duration distributions are depicted in Fig. 3-3. We can see that for each of the cause types, the Log-normal distribution has the smallest deviation among the candidates, which is the indication of better fitness performance. Therefore, we can say that the Log-normal distribution can approximate the duration of primary delay distributions better for all types of the identified delay causes.

These figures show that the duration of primary delays due to FA tends to be shorter than other types of primary delays. On the contrary, the primary delay distribution due to FW has a longer tail on the right-hand side, meaning that delays are expected to last longer due to bad weather conditions. This means that when a bad weather condition is forecasted, there should be especial attention on the flexible and time supplements to reduce the unexpected delays due to a case of terrible weather.

Table 3-4 Parameters estimation of PD distributions

Delay Cause	Parameters of Log-normal		Parameters of Weibull		Gamma distribution	
	μ	σ	k	λ	α	β
TD	2.99747504	0.63855183	1.61221606	27.63021607	2.6132	0.1064
FA	2.84706222	0.56817337	1.85387583	22.86780993	3.3235	0.1646
FT	3.1692923	0.57613649	1.8201887	31.688372	3.2337	0.1155
FRS	3.0590007	0.65832801	1.60916097	29.59315027	2.5198	0.0957
FPSC	3.06389894	0.64017584	1.64199668	29.48479863	2.6411	0.1009
FW	2.98934404	0.71910327	1.42406861	28.67830308	2.0560	0.0796
FFM	2.96730581	0.56105448	1.786322	25.8225979	3.2897	0.1443
FO	2.92658934	0.63187645	1.61547917	25.61936577	2.6740	0.1175

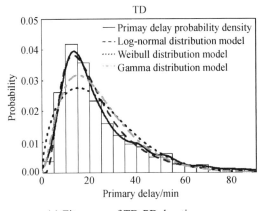

(a) Fit curves of TD-PD duration

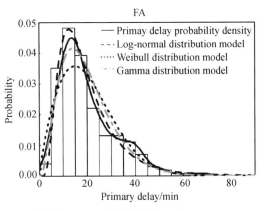

(b) Fit curves of FA-PD duration

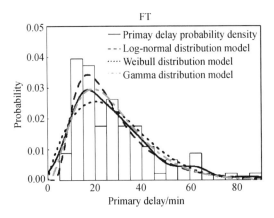

(c) Fit curves of FT-PD duration

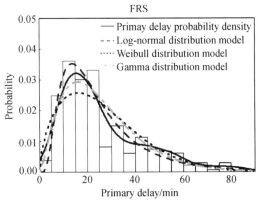

(d) Fit curves of FRS-PD duration

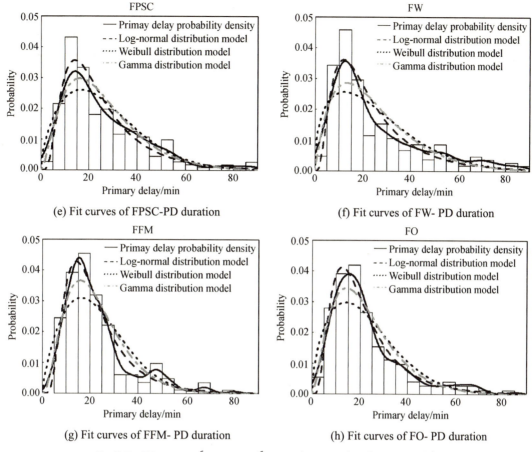

Fig.3-3　Fit curves of cause-specific time duration distribution models

3.1.5　Cause-specific Distributional Models for PDs severity

To evaluate the severity of each PD cause, and see how trains are involved in the case of a PD occurrence, we studied the affected number of trains and durations of delays for each incident class. Following a primary delay incident, usually, the number of affected trains is used to as an upper bound for the possible number trains may be involved or delayed. Indeed, it is similar to the spatial distribution of the PD as the trains will be delayed at different stations and sections because of the knock-on effect. Also, the influenced time refers to the sum of the delay time of all the delayed trains owing to a PD.

3.1.5.1　Cause-specific Distribution Models of Affected Trains

Each instance of disturbance may have a unique effect on the operation of all the trains, as to why the number of affected trains can differ in each case. To check this, we looked at the scattergram and histogram of the affected number of trains, as depicted in Fig. 3-4. In Fig. 3-4(a), the horizontal axis is the sequence number of the delayed train in the database and the vertical axis is the trains affected by each primary delay. In Fig. 3-4(b), the horizontal axis shows the number of affected trains with a class interval of two trains and the vertical axis represents the frequency at which trains are affected. We can see that these two parameters are highly dependent on each delay instances such that the number of affected trains can reach up to 60. Also in about 80% of cases the number of affected trains, other than the incurred train, is less than 10.

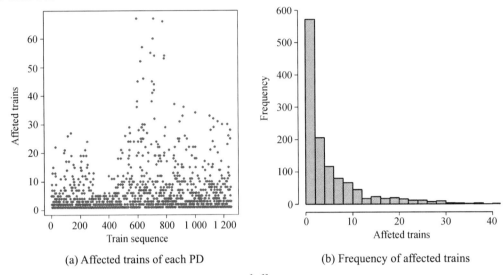

(a) Affected trains of each PD   (b) Frequency of affected trains

Fig. 3-4　Distributions of affected trains owing to PD

Considering the skewness in the histogram of a number of affected trains, we fit the affected delayed trains' distribution with a linear model, Logarithmic model, Inverse model, Quadratic model, and Cubic model respectively. The R-Square of different models, see Table 3-5, the Inverse model can fit the affected number of trains distribution well for all type of causes (TD), with very high R-square for each delay cause. Therefore, the Inverse model is proposed to model the affected trains' distribution of different PD types. Given a random variable x and two parameters β_1, and β_2, the probability density function of the inverse model is as follows:

$$y = \beta_1 \frac{1}{x_t} + \beta_2, \tag{3-7}$$

where x_t is the number of affected trains, and y is the probability of affecting a certain number of trains. The cause-specific distributions of a number of affected trains are sufficiently well-approximated, as the lowest R-square of FW is 0.866 and the highest R-square of TD is 0.996. The coefficients and test results are summarized in Table 3-6. The fit curves using the inverse model are presented in Fig.3-5, where the scatter diagrams are the distributions of the affected trains due to each cause.

Table 3-5　R-Square of affected trains' distribution of different models

Delay Cause	Linear model	Logarithmic model	Inverse model	Quadratic model	Cubic model
TD	0.246	0.616	0.996	0.482	0.657
FA	0.501	0.786	0.971	0.784	0.892

continued

Delay Cause	Linear model	Logarithmic model	Inverse model	Quadratic model	Cubic model
FT	0.513	0.813	0.967	0.800	0.898
FRS	0.402	0.749	0.986	0.676	0.845
FPSC	0.458	0.811	0.912	0.744	0.878
FW	0.380	0.758	0.866	0.658	0.801
FFM	0.457	0.803	0.946	0.755	0.855
FO	0.281	0.591	0.935	0.504	0.661

For all of the delay causes, the scatter diagrams look heterogeneous to some extent, owing to the diversity of the number of samples. For instance, the curve of the FRS could fit better than that of the FW, as the diversity of the cause of FW is higher. According to Fig.3-5, the affected trains' probability has a descending trend when the number of affected trains increases. We can infer that there will be a very little probability when the number of affected trains is larger than a certain number, as the statistical results for a long-run period reflect this situation well. These models may work and perform well for a given range of the independent variables. The cumulative probability is used to illustrate the range of affected trains, and the critical value K_t is used to represent the affected trains threshold when the cumulative probability is closest to 1.

Table 3-6   Coefficients and test results of the inverse model

Delay Cause	β_1	β_2	p-value
TD	0.3106	−0.0073	0
FA	0.5158	−0.0493	0
FT	0.3692	−0.0159	0
FRS	0.3500	−0.0134	0
FPSC	0.2507	−0.0014	0
FW	0.1836	0.0018	0
FFM	0.2520	−0.0009	0
FO	0.3708	−0.0162	0

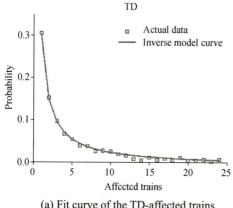

(a) Fit curve of the TD-affected trains

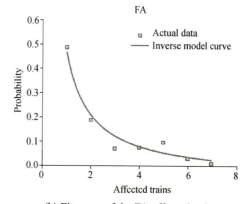

(b) Fit curve of the FA-affected trains

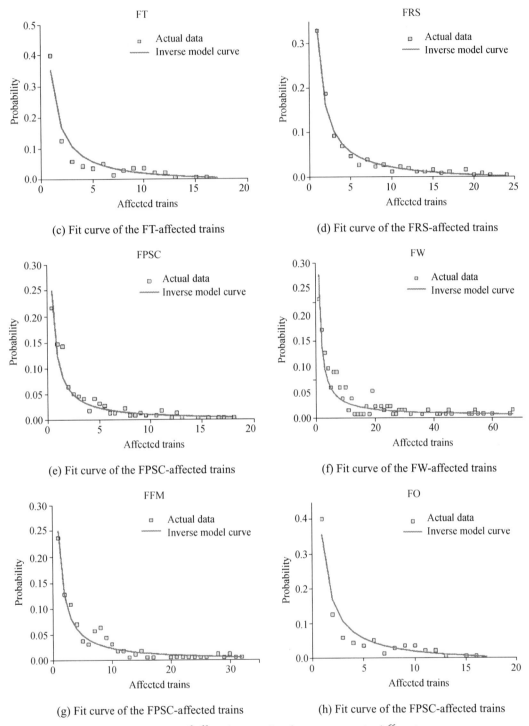

Fig.3-5　Fit curves of affected trains' distributions owing to different causes

For the probability distribution of TD-affected trains, the plot of the cumulative probability was shown in Fig. 6(a), and there is the probability mass function (PMF):

$$\begin{cases} P(x_{t1}=K_{t1}) = 0.3106 \Big/ x_{t1} - 0.0073 \\ \sum P(x_{t1} > K_{t1}) = 2.4\text{E-03} \end{cases} \quad x_{t1} = 1,2,\ldots,24 \quad K_{t1} = 24 \quad (3\text{-}8)$$

For the case of $k_1 > 24$ we have a cumulative probability of 2.4E-03. That is to say, when a case of delay happens, there will be a very small chance that more than 24 trains to be affected. The cumulative distributions of affected trains under each cause type are shown in Figure 3-6. We used the index of "Ed_i" to represent the accuracy of the proposed model, when the cumulative probability is closest to 1, that is:

$$Ed_i = \frac{S_i}{SZ_i} \quad (3\text{-}9)$$

Where, S_i is the number of the cases under cause type i that are covered when $x_{ti} \leq K_i$, while SZ_i is the samples size of cause type i. For instance, 189 cases can be covered by the model of FA-affected trains when $x_{t2} \leq 7$, taking up 95.9% of all the 197 samples. And that is to say, the accuracy of the model of FA-Affected trains reaches 95.9%. The critical value of K and the explanation degree of each model are summarized in Table 3-7. In this formula, K distinguishes variability in the affected number of trains due to the respective cause, i.e., the larger the value of K is, the more uncertainty is attributed to the corresponding factors. From Table 3-7, we can see that the failure of FT affects the least number of trains for a particular event due to the high stability of the ATP. It means that there is a very low probability that more than 17 trains are affected in case of FT. On the contrary, the factor of FW affects the highest number of trains because of the high uncertainty in weather condition, for which there is a significant probability that more than 60 trains may be affected due to a case of terrible weather.

Table 3-7　Maximum value K and the explanation degree of affected trains model for each cause type

Cause	SZ_i	S_i	K	Ed_i
TD	1249	1193	24	95.5%
FA	197	189	7	95.9%
FT	84	84	17	100%
FRS	259	257	24	99.2%
FPSC	217	216	36	99.5%
FFM	156	155	32	99.3%
FW	201	201	67	100%
FO	135	122	17	90.4

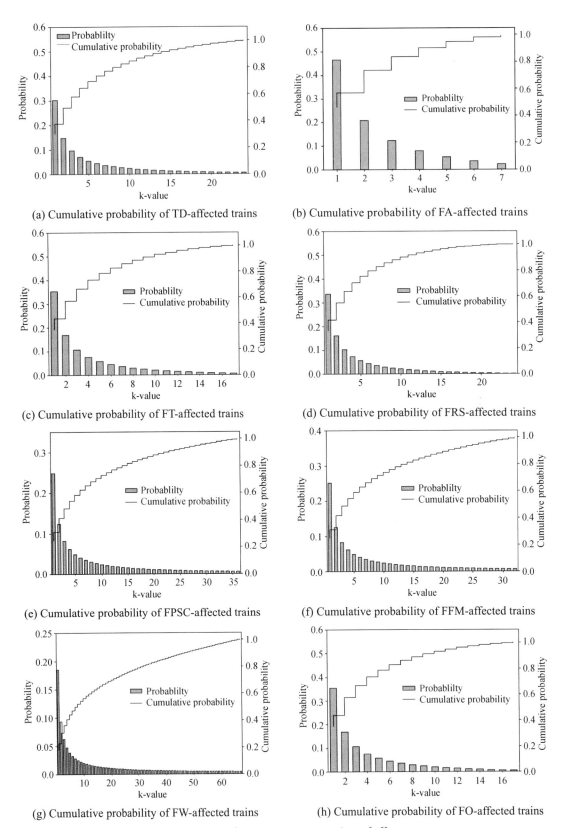

(a) Cumulative probability of TD-affected trains

(b) Cumulative probability of FA-affected trains

(c) Cumulative probability of FT-affected trains

(d) Cumulative probability of FRS-affected trains

(e) Cumulative probability of FPSC-affected trains

(f) Cumulative probability of FFM-affected trains

(g) Cumulative probability of FW-affected trains

(h) Cumulative probability of FO-affected trains

Fig.3-6　Cause-specific cumulative probability of affected trains

We obtained all of the cause-specific PMF for affected number of trains as follows:

PMF of FA-affected trains:

$$\begin{cases} P(x_{t2}{=}K_{t2}) = 0.5158\!\Big/\!x_{t2} - 0.0493 \\ \sum P(x_{t2} > K_{t2}) = 7.70E-03 \end{cases} \qquad x_{t2} = 1,2,\cdots,7 \quad K_{t2} = 7 \qquad (3\text{-}10)$$

PMF of FT-affected trains:

$$\begin{cases} P(x_{t3}{=}K_{t3}) = 0.3692\!\Big/\!x_{t3} - 0.0159 \\ \sum P(x_{t3} > K_{t3}) = 4.17E-04 \end{cases} \qquad x_{t3} = 1,2,\cdots,17 \quad K_{t3} = 17 \qquad (3\text{-}11)$$

PMF of FRS-affected trains:

$$\begin{cases} P(x_{t4}{=}K_{t4}) = 0.35\!\Big/\!x_{t4} - 0.0134 \\ \sum P(x_{t4} > K_{t4}) = 1.46E-05 \end{cases} \qquad x_{t4} = 1,2,\cdots,24 \quad K_{t4} = 24 \qquad (3\text{-}12)$$

PMF of FPSC-affected trains:

$$\begin{cases} P(x_{t5}{=}K_{t5}) = 0.2507\!\Big/\!x_{t5} - 0.0014 \\ \sum P(x_{t5} > K_{t5}) = 3.84E-03 \end{cases} \qquad x_{t5} = 1,2,\ldots,36 \quad K_{t5} = 36 \qquad (3\text{-}13)$$

PMF of FW-affected trains:

$$\begin{cases} P(x_{t6}{=}K_{t6}) = 0.1836\!\Big/\!x_{t6} + 0.0018 \\ \sum P(x_{t6} > K_{t6}) = 7.49E-05 \end{cases} \qquad x_{t6} = 1,2,\ldots,67 \quad K_{t6} = 67 \qquad (3\text{-}14)$$

PMF of FFM-affected trains:

$$\begin{cases} P(x_{t7}{=}K_{t7}) = 0.252\!\Big/\!x_{t7} - 0.0009 \\ \sum P(x_{t7} > K_{t7}) = 6.06E-03 \end{cases} \qquad x_{t7} = 1,2,\cdots,32 \quad K_{t7} = 32 \qquad (3\text{-}15)$$

PMF of FO-affected trains:

$$\begin{cases} P(x_{t8}{=}K_{t8}) = 0.3708\!\Big/\!x_{t8} - 0.0162 \\ \sum P(x_{t8} > K_{t8}) = 1.39E-05 \end{cases} \qquad x_{t8} = 1,2,\cdots,17 \quad K_{t8} = 17 \qquad (3\text{-}16)$$

3.1.5.2　Cause-specific Distribution Models of Affected Time

Boxplots in Fig. 3-7 illustrate the influence of each PD, in which each point denotes the value of the total delay time of all the delayed trains affected by a particular PD. After excluding the singularity points, using SPSS, we obtain the descriptive statistics of the total delay due to each type of factors shown in Table 3-8, including the mean, confidence interval, variance, maximum, and a minimum of delay.

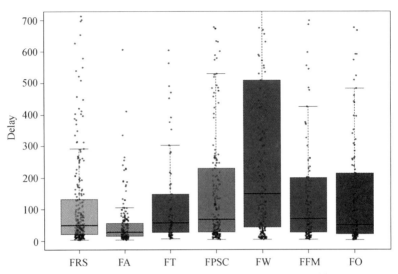

Fig.3-7 Total delay distributions of each disturbance of factors

Table 3-8 Descriptive statistics of the total delay due to each type of cause (minute)

Delay reason	Mean	Confidence Interval		Variance	Minimum	Maximum
		Lower Bound	Upper Bound			
FA	35.2	30.2	40.2	1156.3	4	265
FT	79.6	59.0	100.3	8472.3	7	490
FRS	90.1	75.1	105.1	14291.3	4	782
FPSC	128.1	106.1	150.0	25032.3	5	819
FFM	137.6	102.9	172.3	44799.0	5	1097
FW	333.4	246.6	420.3	366147.9	5	3965
FO	99.7	77.9	121.6	15618.0	4	676

From the results of Table 3-8, we can infer some approximation about the PD due to different types of causes. Firstly, the PD that affected by FW has the most severe effect on railway operation because of the high uncertainty of weather. Actually, the mean of total delay of all the trains reaches 333 minutes, and the maximum total delay is up to 3965 minutes in case of FW. Secondly, the primary delay that affected by FA has the least effect on railway operation because of the high stability of the ATP, the mean and the maximum total delays are 35 and 265 minutes, respectively. Each PD type can spread over a very wide range, from less than 10 to thousands minutes. To build the cause-specific distributional models of affected time, we divided the samples into 5 minutes intervals. The Linear model, Logarithmic model, Inverse model, Quadratic model, and Cubic model are used to fit the case-specific distributions, respectively, and the goodness-of-fit of all the models are presented in Table 3-9.

Table 3-9　Different model's R-Square of affected time distribution

	Linear model	Logarithmic model	Inverse model	Quadratic model	Cubic model
TD	0.5005	0.8233	0.6444	0.7599	0.8725
FA	0.6910	0.8200	0.6011	0.8780	0.8810
FT	0.4268	0.4507	0.1684	0.5313	0.5313
FRS	0.5365	0.7805	0.5594	0.7570	0.7940
FPSC	0.4160	0.5692	0.3456	0.5830	0.6064
FW	0.2114	0.3309	0.3720	0.2522	0.3938
FFM	0.5672	0.7764	0.5548	0.7674	0.8005
FO	0.2909	0.4630	0.2276	0.5316	0.5774

According to Table 3-9 the Cubic model can fit better all the causes. Given a random variable x and coefficients $a, b, c,$ and d, the PMF formulation of the Cubic model is as follows:

$$y = ax_{\mathrm{v}}^3 + bx_{\mathrm{v}}^2 + cx_{\mathrm{v}} + d \tag{3-17}$$

Where x_{v} is the number of the influenced time interval, for instance, when $x_{\mathrm{v}} = 1$, it means that the influenced time interval of $(0, 5]$. And y is theprobability corresponding to x_{v}. Only about 80% samples of each cause are selected for modelling, as the rest of the samples were recognized as an anomaly and deleted automatically from the estimation process. The coefficients and test results of the models were summarized in Table 3-10.

Table 3-10　Coefficients of Cubic models owing to different causes

	a	b	c	d
TD	−9.94E-07	1.29E-04	−5.29E-03	7.45E-02
FA	−1.10E-06	1.42E-04	−5.96E-03	8.75E-02
FT	−2.13E-05	1.44E-03	−2.89E-02	1.94E-01
FRS	1.15E-07	8.95E-05	−5.55E-03	8.81E-02
FPSC	−1.55E-06	1.65E-04	−5.73E-03	7.54E-02
FFM	−8.52E-07	9.08E-05	−3.15E-03	5.06E-02
FW	−1.30E-06	1.38E-04	−4.81E-03	6.38E-02
FO	−1.25E-06	1.60E-04	−6.41E-03	8.49E-02

The fit curves using the Cubic models are presented in Fig.3-8, where the scatter diagrams are the distributions of the affected time interval in sequence due to each cause.

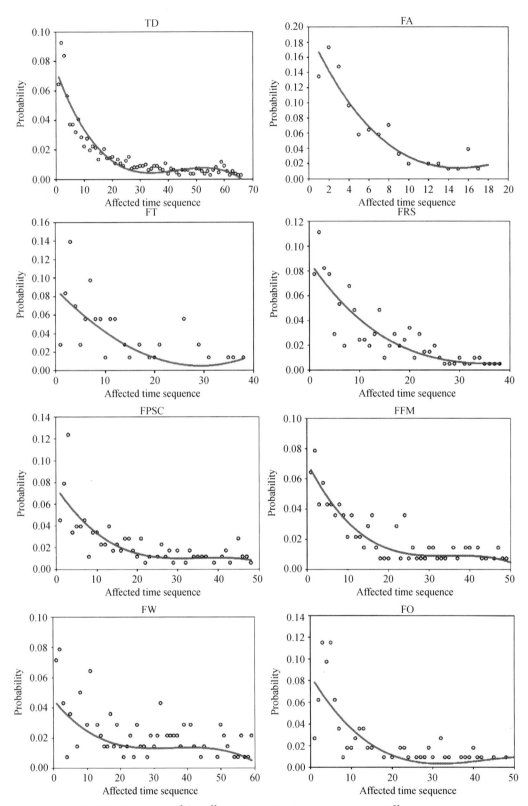

Fig.3-8　Fit curves of the affected time distributions owing to different causes

According to Figure 3-8, the probability of affected time has a descending trend when the affected time increases. We can infer that there is a very little probability when the affected time is larger than a certain value, as the statistical results for a long-run period can reflect the real situation well. Similarly, with the affected trains, the cumulative probability is used to illustrate the range of affected time as well, and the critical value K_{vi} is used to represent the sequence number of affected time interval when the cumulative probability is closest to 1. The model of PMF of TD-affected time follows as formula (3-18), and the plot of the cumulative probability is shown in Figure 3-9(a).

$$\begin{cases} P(x_{v1} \leqslant K_{v1}) = -9.94 \times 10^{-7} x_{v1}^3 + 1.29 \times 10^{-4} x_{v1}^2 - 5.29 \times 10^{-3} x_{v1} + 0.0745 & x_{v1} = 1, 2, \cdots, 63 \\ \sum P(x_{v1} > K_{v1}) = 0.0016 & K_{v1} = 63 \end{cases} \quad (3\text{-}18)$$

In the cases of $x_{v1} > 63$, the affected time is more than 316 minutes with a total residual probability of 0.16%. That is to say, when a case of delay happens, there is 0.16% probability that more than 335 train-minutes wasted. The cause-specific cumulative probabilities are shown in Fig.3-9.

Similarly, the critical value of K and the explanation degree of each model are summarized in Table 3-11. About 90.8% of samples are used for modelling, since the sample percentages of other causes were different due to the distribution decentralization, which results in differences between the samples of TD and the sum samples of each cause.

Table 3-11　Maximum value of K and the explanation degree of affected time for each cause type

Causes	SZ_i	S_i	K	Ed_i
TD	1135	1118	63	98.50%
FA	156	156	19	100.00%
FT	72	71	37	98.61%
FRS	207	207	37	100.00%
FPSC	178	177	46	98.31%
FFM	140	136	56	97.14%
FW	156	136	48	87.20%
FO	113	113	62	100.00%

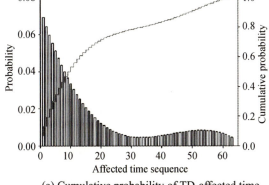

(a) Cumulative probability of TD-affected time

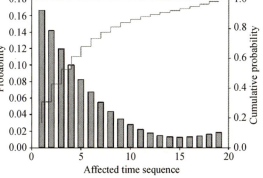

(b) Cumulative probability of FA-affected time

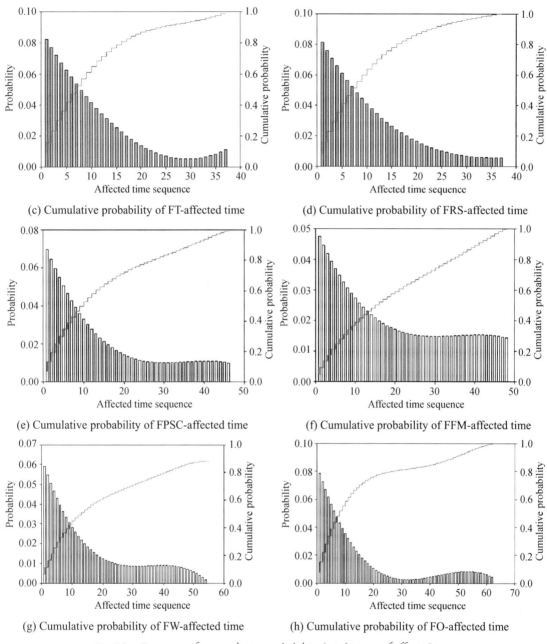

(c) Cumulative probability of FT-affected time

(d) Cumulative probability of FRS-affected time

(e) Cumulative probability of FPSC-affected time

(f) Cumulative probability of FFM-affected time

(g) Cumulative probability of FW-affected time

(h) Cumulative probability of FO-affected time

Fig.3-9　Cause-specific cumulative probability distribution of affected time

The FA case has a small range of affected time, which is in accordance with the character of the affected trains. However, the FW case has a wide range of affected time with a very low explanation degree comparing to other delay causes. The results in Table 3-11 supports the facts that the FA has the lowest uncertainty, the FW has the highest uncertainty. We obtained all the PMFs of affected time as follows:

PMFof FA-affected time:

$$\begin{cases} P(x_{v2}=K_{v2}) = -2.13\times10^{-5} x_{v2}^{3} + 1.44\times10^{-3} x_{v2}^{2} - 2.89\times10^{-2} x_{v2} + 0.0194 & x_{v2}=1,2,\cdots,19 \\ \sum P(x_{v2}>K_{v2})=0.0171 \quad K_{v2}=19 \end{cases} \quad (3\text{-}19)$$

PMF of FT-affected time:

$$\begin{cases} P(x_{v3}=K_{v3}) = 1.15\times10^{-7} x_{v3}^{3} + 8.95\times10^{-5} x_{v3}^{2} - 5.55\times10^{-3} x_{v3} + 0.0881 & x_{v3}=1,2,\cdots,37 \\ \sum P(x_{v3}>K_{v3})=0.0122 \quad K_{v3}=37 \end{cases} \quad (3\text{-}20)$$

PMFof FRS-affected time:

$$\begin{cases} P(x_{v4}=K_{v4}) = -1.1\times10^{-6} x_{v4}^{3} + 1.42\times10^{-4} x_{v4}^{2} - 5.96\times10^{-3} x_{v4} + 0.0875 & x_{v4}=1,2,\cdots,37 \\ \sum P(x_{v4}>K_{v4})=0.0004 \quad K_{v4}=37 \end{cases} \quad (3\text{-}21)$$

PMF of FPSC-affected time:

$$\begin{cases} P(x_{v5}=K_{v5}) = -1.55\times10^{-6} x_{v5}^{3} + 1.65\times10^{-4} x_{v5}^{2} - 5.73\times10^{-3} x_{v5} + 0.0754 & x_{v5}=1,2,\cdots,46 \\ \sum P(x_{v5}>K_{v5})=0.0077 \quad K_{v5}=46 \end{cases} \quad (3\text{-}22)$$

PMF of FFM-affected time:

$$\begin{cases} P(x_{v6}=K_{v6}) = -8.52\times10^{-7} x_{v6}^{3} + 9.08\times10^{-5} x_{v6}^{2} - 3.15\times10^{-3} x_{v6} + 0.0506 & x_{v6}=1,2,\cdots,48 \\ \sum P(x_{v6}>K_{v6})=0.0013 \quad K_{v6}=48 \end{cases} \quad (3\text{-}23)$$

PMFof FW-affected time:

$$\begin{cases} P(x_{v7}=K_{v7}) = -1.3\times10^{-6} x_{v7}^{3} + 1.38\times10^{-4} x_{v7}^{3} - 4.81\times10^{-3} x_{v7} + 0.0638 & x_{v7}=1,2,\cdots,56 \\ \sum P(x_{v7}>K_{v7})=0.118 \quad K_{v7}=56 \end{cases} \quad (3\text{-}24)$$

PMFof FO-affected time:

$$\begin{cases} P(x_{v8}=K_{v8}) = -1.25\times10^{-6} x_{v8}^{3} + 1.6\times10^{-4} x_{v8}^{3} - 6.41\times10^{-3} x_{v8} + 0.0849 & x_{v8}=1,2,\cdots,62 \\ \sum P(x_{v8}>K_{v8})=0.0027 \quad K_{v8}=62 \end{cases} \quad (3\text{-}25)$$

3.1.6 Conclusions

This work shared some of the findings from studying the primary delay issue on Wuhan-Guangzhou HSR operation in China, using ten months of train operation records. After classifying different causes of PD, models for delay duration and delay influence due to each cause factor is established. It was found that the Log-normal probability distribution model can approximate better the empirical distribution of delay duration under each cause. Then, for each cause factor, the parameters of the PD duration distribution were estimated. Next, an inverse model was proposed to fit the distributions of the number of affected trains under different causes. It was shown that the affected trains' probability has a descending behavior when the number of affected trains increase. The cumulative probability was used to determine the domain of the functions and obtain the threshold values of each cause type. Moreover, cause-specific models of the affected time distributions were developed using a Cubic model. Eight models of the cause-specific time distributions in the format of the Cubic model were acquired, with the domain of the functions determined by the cumulative probability. This study provides insightful findings that help to understand primary delays in HSR operation and conduct further research. Built upon a comprehensive analysis of HSR operation data, this study has contributed to the following theoretical practical directions.

(1) The models established in this study can be used for railway traffic control. More explicitly, the HSR dispatchers can use probabilities of PD under different situations to infer or estimate the occurrence and the severity of certain PDs. This can support the rescheduling and adjusting the train operation strategies.

(2) The distributions of PD can be used as input in data-driven simulation studies, especially as delay generation distributional functions in predictive models for delay propagation. By considering the disturbances, estimating the running times and the potential conflicts, and predicting the delay occurrence, the dispatching decisions can be made from the following aspects.

- The cause-specific distributional model of PDscan be used as a predictive tool by the dispatchers to assess the delay duration and their influences, given certain operation circumstances. With new train operation data, the PD distribution models can be updated via a dynamic or Bayesian predicting system for HSR delays.

- The presented data-driven models can also be used in simulating train operations for delay management, to replace the incumbent models that have been widely used so far. Moreover, it will be of profound theoretical as well as practical contribution to use the developed PDs models as a basis in knock-on delays models to establish delay recovery models.

Obviously, more precise cause-specific results and models of PD would have been obtained if more temporal and spatial data were available. In our ongoing work, we will develop temporal and spatial distribution models of delays using more delay records under longer time periods to establish more precise models. We will investigate how a PD affects engaging trains at each station and section, and model the relationship between the PD and knock-on delay. We will establish cause-specific delay chains for each delayed train, and predict delay propagation based on the delay chain to support dispatching decisions in railway traffic management and control. This study was a part of the work aimed to establish a predictive dispatching decision support tool to help dispatchers in managing HSR train operations. Fig.3-10 depicts the framework of dispatching tool and the overall picture of our practical and theoretical works in continuation.

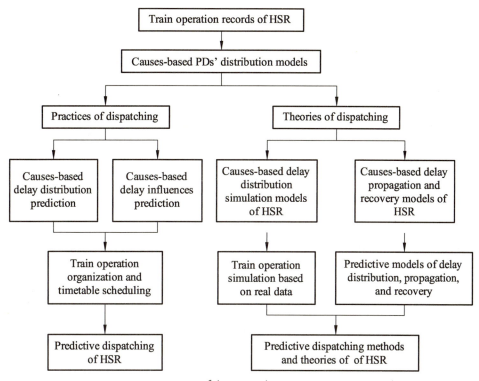

Fig.3-10　Framework of the dispatching decision support tool

3.2　Modelling of Effects of Primary Delays Using High-speed Train Operation Records

Primary delays are the driving force of delay propagation, and predicting the number of affected trains (NAT) and the total time of affected trains (TTAT) due to primary delay (PD) can provide reliable decision supports for real-time train dispatching. In this chapter, based on the real operation data from 2015 to 2016 at part of stations in Wuhan-Guangzhou high-speed railway (HSR), the NAT and TTAT influence factors were determined after analysing the primary delay propagate mechanism, XGBOOST algorithm was used to establish NAT predictive model and several machine learning methods were compared. Then, the TTAT predictive model using SVR algorithm were established on the basis of the NAT predictive model. The results indicate that: XGBOOST algorithm has a good performance on the NAT predictive model. While SVR is the optimal model for TTAT prediction under the verification index which is the ratio of the difference between the actual and the predicted value is less than 5 min. The real operation data in 2018 were used to test the applicability over time of NAT and TTAT model, and the results indicate that NAT and TTAT models on the basis of XGBOOST and SVR respectively have a good applicability over time.

3.2.1 Introduction

Compared with other modes of transportation, with the advantages of high-speed, high-safety, and high-density, high-speed railways (HSR) are becoming more and more popular all over the world. In China, HSR train has become one of the main ways for people to travel. The high punctuality of HSR is not only an important goal pursued by railway companies, but also a vital factor in attracting passengers[80]. However, during the operation of HSR trains, they are inevitably influenced by the bad weather, mechanical failure of the systems, or organization strategies, these factors could lead to delay. On the one hand, delay will disturb the order of railway operation, cause disorder of transportation organization, on the other hand, delay will increase travel time of passengers, reduce the passenger travel experience and the reliability of HSR.

Delay can be divided into primary delay (PD) and knock-on delay(secondary delay), primary delay is caused by some uncertain events directly while knock-on delay is attributed to the propagation of PD. Primary delays are the driving force of delay propagation. At present, the operation adjustment mainly depends on the experience of train dispatchers when a PD occurs, so the quality of adjustment strategy mainly depends on the ability and skill of the train dispatcher. There is no scientific theory and method to support the strategy. The number of affected trains (NAT) and the total time of affected trains (TTAT) due to PD can forecast the PD influence scope and identify the severity of delay accurately. Therefore, establish the NAT and the TTAT predictive model at station can assist the train dispatcher in estimating the train operation state, provide the theoretical basis for the rescheduling strategy, help the train dispatcher to make more scientific and reliable rescheduling decisions and adjustment of the station work plan[83]. Meanwhile, the NAT and the TTAT predictive models at station are also a vital foundation for realizing the train automated operation and intelligent dispatching of HSR

In this study, analysing the mechanism of the PD propagation at station, we determined the influencing factors composition of the NAT and TTAT predictive models. Based on the real data from part of Wuhan-Guangzhou HSR station managed by Guangzhou Railway Bureau, the data from March 2015 to November 2016 were using to establish the NAT and TTAT predictive models. Compared with some commonly used machine learning classification and regression algorithms, the results indicated that the XGBOOST algorithm is optimal for NAT predictive model while the SVR algorithm has the best predictive precision for the TTAT predictive model in station. Then, the 2018 data was used to test the applicability of the NAT and TTAT predictive models over time, the results show that the predictive models established at station have a good prediction effect and has a good applicability to time.

3.2.2 Literature review

PD may be caused by exogenous events or irregularities in internal system, such as natural environment, or vehicle fault, accidents, facility failures [227] etc. Delay probability distribution model is an analytic method to measure the delay severity,[228] assumed the primary delaycorresponded to exponential distribution and predicted the secondary delays in different traffic scenarios.[93]used a phase-type distribution to obtain knock-on delay distribution from PD distributions.[229] found the Weibull distributions can fit the PD distribution by using empirical data. [230] indicated that Log-normal distribution can be well-approximated for PD duration while line regression models can be used to approximate the NAT distribution. Studies on delay predictive models were mostly based on traditional mathematical optimization method. Queuing model [78] and petri net model [28] were used to estimate train delays. [231] proposed an online model by using timed event graphs to predict running time and arrive times.[232] presented a timed event graph with dynamic arc weights model to predict train event times accurately. [233] establish a delay propagation model by using max-plus algebra theory.

Data-driven studies are increasingly being used in delay/disruption management.[227] explained the systematic delay propagation and employed a robust linear regression to investigate the correlation between arrival delays by using the train delays in the Eindhoven Station. [106] described dynamics of a train delay over time and space as a stochastic process and modelled uncertainty of train delays based on a Markov stochastic process. [26] described train operation process as a Markov chain and the train states at certain event timesteps can be determined by transition probability matrices. [234] presented an online Bayesian network to forecast train delay over time by using historical data in Sweden, while [235] established a hybrid Bayesian network to estimate the arrive delay and departure delays based on real data in China. Artificial neural networks (ANN) was used to predict delays of passenger trains widely[115, 117, 236]. [118]indicated that support vector regression has a better fitness in predicting passenger train arrival delays using the data of Serbian Railways compared with ANN algorithm.[237]uncover the relationship among causes of the delay, duration time of a PD, NAT and TTAT by using support vector regression, however, the NAT is unknown when a PD occur that will lead to the model cannot predict online.

3.2.3 Problem statement and data description

3.2.3.1 Problem statement

In the operation process of the HSR train, the headway between two trains consists of the minimum interval time and the timetable supplement time at station. In this study, if a train delayed when it arrived station and the train preceding the delay train is not delayed or the headway between the preceding train actual arrive time and the delayed train scheduled arrive time keep a minimum threshold (5min in Wuhan-Guangzhou HSR) with the delayed train, the delayed train is defined as a PD delay train at station. The PD train take up the transportation resources of the subsequent train, that lead to the subsequent train will be delayed by the PD train, the subsequent train occur knock-on delay. Then, the same process takes place among the trains after. When the PD duration is less than 5minutes, there is a little influence to the subsequent trains and it is no necessary to reschedule. So only the PD duration more than 5 minutes would be considered in this study. Meanwhile, delays will be absorbed by timetable supplement time until delays return to zero. Thus, there is a PD influence sequence. In this sequence, the count of PD train and knock-on delay train is marked the number of affected train (NAT), the sum of the PD time and knock-on delay time is called total time of affected train (TTAT).

An example of a PD delay propagation at station is shown in figure 3-11. Station A and Station B are two stations on the Wuhan-Guangzhou HSR, and the red lines are actual train lines while the black lines are scheduled train lines. The train in front of Train 1 was not delayed or kept a minimum interval with Train 1, so Train 1 is a PD train with a delay duration of t_1, Train 2 is delayed because the interval between the actual arrival time of train 1 and the scheduled arrival time of train 2 is less than 5min. Train 3 and Train 4 occur delay for the same reason. Because of the supplement time t_{sup}^i, the PD delay propagates until Train 4, and Train 5 returns to normal operation. The delayed train (Train 1 to Train4) form a PD sequence. In this PD influence sequence, the number of affected trains (NAT) is 4 and the total time affected trains (TTAT) is $\sum_{i=1}^{4} t_i$.

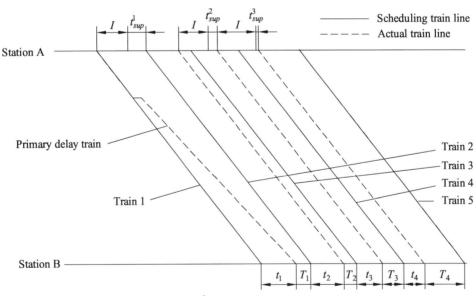

Figure 3-11　PD delay propagation process at station

In a PD influence sequence, if the train actual arrival sequence is not same with the scheduled arrival sequence, that is to say there is an overtaking. This sequence is a result of rescheduling, the propagation process is complex and too much influence factors need to considered. So, these sequences are eliminated in this study.

3.2.3.2 Data description

The data used in this section was obtained from the W-G HSR. Table 3-12 shows a sample raw data at station.

Table 3-12　Raw data from Guangzhou Station

Train NO	Date	Station	Scheduled arrive time	Scheduled departure time	Actual arrive time	Actual departure time
G280	2015/3/24	GuangzhouNorth	7:00:00	7:00:00	7:01:00	7:01:00
G636	2015/3/24	GuangzhouNorth	7:07:00	7:07:00	7:07:00	7:07:00
G1102	2015/3/24	GuangzhouNorth	7:13:00	7:13:00	7:14:00	7:14:00
G6102	2015/3/24	GuangzhouNorth	7:20:00	7:20:00	7:20:00	7:20:00

The data used to establish the primary influence predictive model is obtained by preprocessing. The preprocessing process for raw data is summarized as follows:.

➤ Step 1: Gather the data from database, eliminate abnormal data, including: duplicate items, error items, invalid data.

➤ Step 2: Sort data by actual arrive time in station.

➤ Step 3: Select the primary delay train, obtain the primary delay influence sequences which not overtaking.

➤ Step 4: Extract the influencing factor features and calculate the NAT and TTAT based on the primary delay influence sequences.

Analysing the mechanism of the PD propagation, the feature set of influence factors of NAT and TTAT were obtained, these influence factors are shown as follows:

D:Primary delay duration

I: Scheduled interval between the PD train and its following adjacent train

B:0-1 variable, it equals to 0 when the PD train does not stop at the station, otherwise it equals to 1

T: Period of a PD occurs

N:The number of affected trains if supplement times were fully utilized.

Table 3-13 shows a sample data after preprocessing at station：

Table 3-13　A sample of modeling data

D	I	B	T	N	NAT	TTAT
5	6	0	8:00-9:00	2	2	9
6	7	0	16:00-17:00	3	3	12
5	8	1	8:00-9:00	3	2	7
6	6	0	9:00-10:00	3	5	28
6	7	0	17:00-18:00	2	2	11

In this study, D presents the primary delay train delay duration; I record the schedule headway between the PD train and the first train subsequently; B is a 0-1 variable and it equals to 0 when the PD train does not stop at the station, otherwise it equals to 1; Classify the period by hour andmarked T as the period of PD occurs. N indicates the number of affected trains when the supplement times were fully utilized. All of the factors above can be obtained according to the real-time timetable structure when the PD occurs. So, if the NAT and TTAT predictive models can be investigated using these factors, it is possible to make real-time rescheduling.

The data from March 2015 to November 2016 was used to establish the NAT and TTAT predictive model. In order to prevent overfitting, 70% of the data was used as the training data while the rest was used as the validation data for the model. Finally, the data in 2018 was used as test data to test the application of the NAT and TTAT predictive model

3.2.4 Predictive model of NAT and TTAT

3.2.4.1 The predictive model of NAT

The heatmap and 3D histogram can show the PD influence intensity distribution over time. To some extent, they can assist train dispatchers to carry out risk warnings. In this study, PD duration and the period of PD occur was used as the horizontal and vertical coordinates respectively, using the GZN station as a sample, the NAT heatmap and 3D histogram are shown in Fig.3-12.

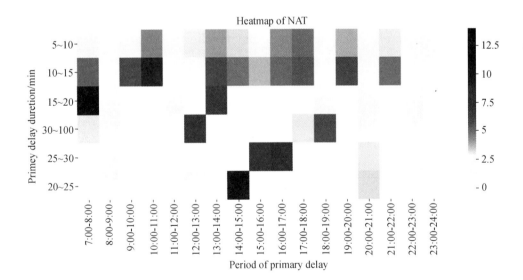

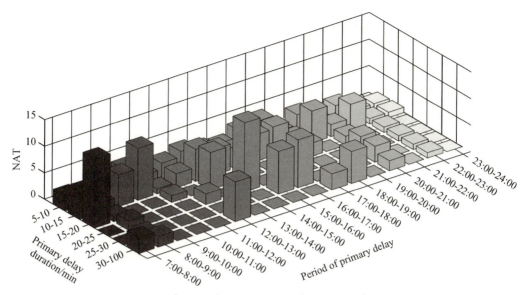

Figure 3-12　The NAT heatmap and 3D histogram of GZN station

Based on the analysis of the PD propagation process in section 3.2.3.2, it is determined that the influence factors of NAT including D, B, I, T, N. NAT is a discrete random variable and its prediction is a classification problem. The NAT is set to S as the output of the model, and the influencing factor feature set of NAT is set to G as the input of the model. G consists of D, B, I, T, N and the function between S and G can be described as follow:

$$S = \Phi(D, B, T, I, N) \tag{3-26}$$

Φ is the classification algorithm. In the data of this study, when the NAT value is more than 5, the sample size corresponding to each value is small and the value distribution is discrete. Therefore, the NAT values more than 5 were classified as 6 and more. Finally, NAT is divided into six categories (1 / 2 / 3 / 4 / 5 / 6 and more).

XGBOOST is used as the classification algorithm for NAT predictive model. There is a brief introduction to the XGBOOST algorithm: XGBOOST (eXtreme Gradient Boosting) is an improved algorithm based on the gradient boosting decision tree. It can be used for regression and classification problems highly efficient and flexible. For a given data set with n examples and m features, define $\hat{y}_i$ as the result given by an ensemble represented by the model as follows:

$$D = \{(x, y) : i = 1, 2, \cdots n, x_i \in R^m, y_i \in R\} \tag{3-27}$$

$$\hat{y}_i = \phi(x_i) = \sum_{k=1}^{K} f_k(x_i), f_k \in F \tag{3-28}$$

$$F = \{f(X) = w_{q(x)}\}(q : R^m \longrightarrow T, w \in R^T) \tag{3-29}$$

In the formulas above, f_k is a regression tree (also known as CART) and

$f_k(x_i)$ represents the score given by the k-th tree to the i-th sample in the data. Each f_k corresponds to an independent tree structure q and leaf weights w. q represents the structure of each tree that maps an example to the corresponding leaf index. T is the number of leaves in the tree.

Minimize the following regularized function as the objective function:

$$\ell(\phi) = \sum_i l(\hat{y}_i, y_i) + \sum_k \Omega(f_k) \tag{3-30}$$

l is the loss function and Ω is the penalty term that used to prevent over-fitting and too large complexity of the model. Where Ω is shown as follow:

$$\Omega(f) = \gamma T + \frac{1}{2}\lambda \|w\|^2 \tag{3-31}$$

The parameter γ and λ control penalty for the number of leaves T and magnitude of leaf weights w respectively.

In order to minimize the objective function an iterative method was used. The objective function that minimized in t-th iterative we want to add is

$$\ell^{(t)} = \sum_{i=1}^{n} l(y_i, \hat{y}_i^{(t-1)} + f_t(x_i)) + \Omega(f_t) \tag{3-32}$$

Using the Taylor expansion, the formula (7) can be derived for loss reduction after the tree split from given node:

$$\ell_{split} = \frac{1}{2}\left[\frac{(\sum_{i \in I_L} g_i)^2}{\sum_{i \in I_L} h_i + \lambda} + \frac{(\sum_{i \in I_R} g_i)^2}{\sum_{i \in I_R} h_i + \lambda} - \frac{(\sum_{i \in I} g_i)^2}{\sum_{i \in I} h_i + \lambda}\right] - \gamma \tag{3-33}$$

Where

$$g_i = \frac{\partial L(y_i, \hat{y}_i^{(t-1)})}{\partial \hat{y}_i^{(t-1)}}, h_i = \frac{\partial^2 L(y_i, \hat{y}_i^{(t-1)})}{\partial \hat{y}_i^{(t-1)}} \tag{3-34}$$

Where I is a subset of the available observations in the current node and I_R, I_L are subsets of the available observations in the left and right node after the split. The best split can be found from the formula ℓ_{split} at any given node. This formula is determined by the regularisation parameter λ and the loss function.

The detail derivation procedures are presented in [238].

In order to evaluate the prediction accuracy of XGBOOST algorithm, other classification algorithms commonly used are selected as evaluation criteria, including Random Forest (RF), Support Vector Machine (SVM), Logistics regression (LR) and K-Nearest Neighbor (KNN) algorithm. Hyperparametric search was used to calculate the optimal parameter value of each algorithm. ACCURACY was used as the standard to measure the predictive precision of the model, the calculation method of accuracy is as follows:

$$ACCURACY = \frac{N_c}{N_a}$$

N_c: The sample size of classify correctly

N_a: All sample size.

The ACCURACY value of each classification algorithm at different stations using the validation data are shown as table 3-14 and figure 3-13.

Table 3-14　NAT predictive accuracy using different classification algorithm

	RF	XGBOOST	SVM	LR	KNN
GZN	0.7711	0.7766*	0.7520	0.6676	0.7084
QY	0.7105	0.8005*	0.6972	0.5642	0.7864
YDW	0.7200	0.7200*	0.7200	0.6400	0.6933
SG	0.6453	0.6816*	0.6065	0.5375	0.6271
LCE	0.7573	0.7908*	0.7414	0.6837	0.7774
CZW	0.7239	0.7692*	0.6916	0.6099	0.7652
LYW	0.7173	0.7589*	0.6922	0.6182	0.7543
HYE	0.7544	0.7424*	0.6393	0.5773	0.7246
HSW	0.7316	0.7677*	0.6677	0.6098	0.7231
ZZW	0.6799	0.7266*	0.6173	0.6072	0.7165
CSS	0.6805	0.7427*	0.6473	0.6017	0.6390

*indicate the best predictive accuracy

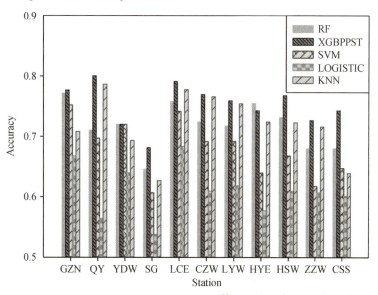

Fig 3-13　NAT predictive accuracy using different classification algorithm

The following conclusions can be drawn from tables 3-13 and 3-14, (1) the XGBOOST algorithm has the highest accuracy value in all stations compared with other classification algorithms; (2) The ACCURACY value of XGBOOST algorithm has maintained a high level in all stations which can reach up to 0.7 except SG. It proves that NAT predictive established based on XGBOOST algorithm has a good predictive precision.

The timetable structure and infrastructure from 2015 to 2016 of the Wuhan-Guangzhou HSR do not change greatly compared with 2018. Hence, it can be considered that the train operation data can be used as test data to test the predictive precision of the model established based on the data from 2015 to 2016. The data from March to July 2018 is used as a test data to test the application over time, its ACCURACY values of NAT at different stations are shown as Fig 3-14.

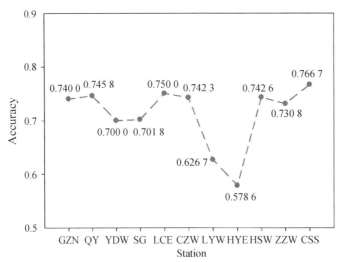

Fig 3-14　XGBOOST algorithm predictive accuracy of NAT in 2018

As the Fig 3-14 shows, most of the NAT predictive models based on XGBOOST algorithm have a good predictive precision in Wuhan-Guangzhou HSR station. The ACCURACY value can reach up to 0.7 except LYW and HYE station. Combined with the ACCURACY values of the validation data, the results indicate that the NAT predictive model based on the XGBOOST algorithm can accurately predict the number of affected trains by PD at Wuhan-Guangzhou HSR station.

3.2.4.2　The predictive model of TTAT

TTAT is another indicator to measure the severity of the PD influence. After predicting TTAT, combined with the NAT already occurred and its accumulated time, subsequent influence scope can be calculated. The specific derivation process can be expressed as follows:

Assume there in a PD influence sequence, the TTAT is T_{td} and the NAT is N_1 obtained by the predictive model, the delay duration of i-th train is T_{at}^i. Then there is a discriminant relation:

IF　$i = 1$; THEN, the TTAT of the PD sequence is T_{td}　while NAT is N_1.

IF　$1 < i \leqslant N_1$; THEN, the subsequent TTAT of the PD sequence is $T_{td} - \sum_{i=1}^{N_1} t_{at}^i$, while NAT is

$N_1 - i$.

Same as NAT predictive model, GZN Station was taken as an example, the heatmap and 3D histogram of the TTAT are drawn as Fig.3-15.

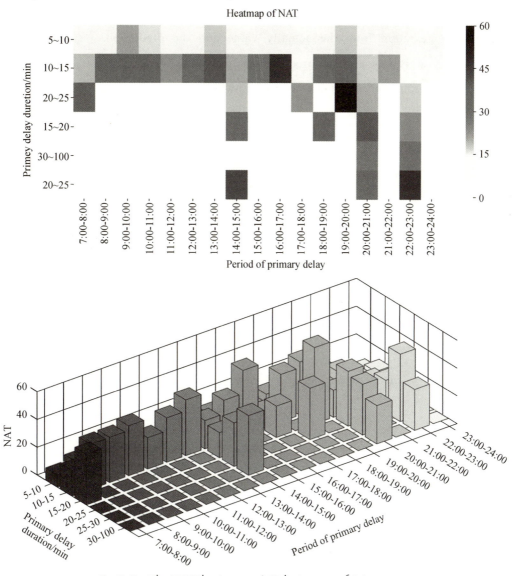

Fig.3-15   The TTAT heatmap and 3D histogram of GZN station

Considering that TTAT strongly depends on the NAT, we establish the predictive model on the basis of the model of NAT. This study set the prediction of NAT as S' and the TTAT as Y. TTAT predictive model can be described as follows,

$$Y = \varphi(D, B, T, I, N, S') \tag{3-15}$$

TTAT is a continuous variable, so φ should be a regression algorithm. In this study, Support Vector Regression (SVR) was used to establish the TTAT predictive model, while several commonly used algorithms are considered to compare with SVR, including: Random

Forest (RF), XGBOOST, Ridge regression (Ridge) and Lasso regression (LASSO)

The introduction of the SVR algorithm is as follows:

Assume there is a data set, $D = \{(x_i, y_i) : i = 1, 2, \cdots n, x_i \in R^m, y_i \in R\}$, x_i denotes the input while y_i represent the output of the sample. The goal of SVR is to find a function $f(x)$ that has at most ε deviation from the actually value and the prediction. $f(x)$ is defined as $f(x) = w^T x + b$, w is a hyperplane direction and b is an offset scalar.

The objective function can be denoted as follows:

$$
\begin{aligned}
&\min_{w, b, \xi_i, \xi_i^*} = \frac{1}{2}\|w\|^2 + C\sum_{i=1}^m \left(\xi_i + \xi_i^*\right) \\
&\text{s.t.} \begin{cases} -\varepsilon - \xi_i^* \leqslant f(\mathbf{x}_i) - y_i \leqslant \varepsilon + \xi_i \\ \xi_i^*, \xi_i \geqslant 0, i = 1, 2, \cdots, m \end{cases}
\end{aligned}
\tag{3-36}
$$

C is a penalty factor which determines the trade-off between the flatness of f and the amount up to which deviations larger than ε are tolerated. ε-insensitive loss function $|\xi|_\varepsilon$ described by

$$
|\xi|_\varepsilon := \begin{cases} 0, & if\ |\xi| \leqslant \varepsilon; \\ |\xi| - \varepsilon, & otherwise. \end{cases}
\tag{3-37}
$$

Utilizing Lagrange multipliers and the formula can be described as follows:

$$
\begin{aligned}
L(w, b, \alpha, \alpha^*, \xi_i, \xi_i^*, u, u^*) &= \frac{1}{2}\|w\|^2 + C\sum_{i=1}^m \left(\xi_i + \xi_i^*\right) - \sum_{i=1}^m u_i \xi_i - \sum_{i=1}^m u_i^* \xi_i^* \\
&+ \sum_{i=1}^m \alpha_i (f(\mathbf{x}_i) - y_i - \varepsilon - \xi_i) + \sum_{i=1}^m \alpha_i^* (f(\mathbf{x}_i) - y_i - \varepsilon - \xi_i^*)
\end{aligned}
\tag{3-38}
$$

The optimal solution can be obtained by solving formula (13), the optimal solution for SVR is

$$
\begin{aligned}
&f(\mathbf{x}) = \sum_{i=1}^m (\alpha_i^* - \alpha_i)\mathbf{x}_i^T \mathbf{x} + b \\
&b = y_i + \varepsilon - \sum_{i=1}^m (\alpha_i^* - \alpha_i)\mathbf{x}_i^T \mathbf{x} + b
\end{aligned}
\tag{3-39}
$$

The detail derivation procedures are presented in [239].Lessthan5 is defined as a new variable to evaluate the model. The definition of Lessthan5 is as follows:

$$
Lessthan5 = \frac{N_d}{N_a}.
$$

N_d: The sample size that the absolute value of the difference between the actual value and the predicted value is less than 5 minutes.

N_a: All sample size.

Hyperparametric search was used to calculate the optimal parameter value of each algorithm. Then based on the optimal parameter the less than 5 value of each algorithm was calculated and they are shown as in Table 3-15 and Fig.3-16:

Table 3-15   TTAT Less than 5 value using different algorithm

	RF	XGBOOST	SVR	Ridge	LASSO
GZN	81.638	81.638	85.311*	79.096	80.508
QY	77.526	77.526	78.739*	76.395	77.850
YDW	70.000	70.000	74.286*	70.000	71.429
SG	74.444	74.444	76.173*	73.827	74.321
LCE	83.761	83.761	84.444*	78.291	79.915
CZW	76.590	76.590	77.009*	72.676	72.467
LYW	76.410	76.410	77.098*	72.765	73.040
HYE	73.829	73.829	74.582*	72.324	71.739
HSW	74.917	74.917	75.116*	69.927	69.661
ZZW	76.362	76.362	76.510*	72.680	71.355
CSS	80.090	80.090	81.900*	78.281	78.281

*indicate the maximum Less than 5 value in different regression algorithm

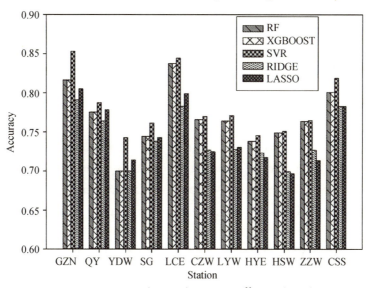

Fig 3-16   TTAT Lessthan5 value using different algorithm

The table 3-15 and Fig 3-16 indicate that: (1) The SVR algorithm has the maximum Less-than-5 value at the Wuhan-Guangzhou HSR station Compared with other four algorithms. It proved that the SVR algorithm is the most suitable algorithm for the TTAT predictive model at Wuhan-Guangzhou HSR stations. (2) The TTAT predictive accuracy (evaluated by Less-than-5 value) of SVR algorithm at all stations is reach up to 0.74, which proves that SVR algorithm has a good predictive accuracy.

As with the NAT applicability analysis, the 2018 data was used as the test data to test the applicability of the TTAT model in time. The Less-than-5 value on the test data for Wuhan-Guangzhou HSR stations is as shown in Fig 3-17.

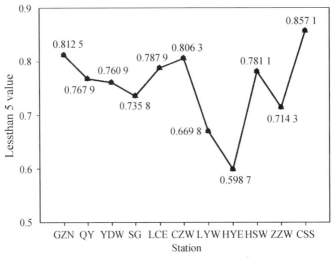

Fig 3-17   SVR algorithm predictive accuracy of TTAT in 2018

As is shown in figure 7, there is a good predictive accuracy of the TTAT predictive models at most Wuhan-Guangzhou HSR station by using test data. With the exception of LYW and HYE, the less-than-5 value of other stations have reached up to 0.71. Because of the low precision of NAT predictive model in LYW and HYE stations, that has a significant influence for the low precision of TTAT predictive model.

3.2.5 Conclusion and future study

Primary delays are the driving force of delay propagation and the prediction of the PD influence severity at station can assist the train dispatcher to make the rescheduling strategy and adjust the work plan of the station. Analysing of the mechanism of PD delay propagation process, the NAT and TTAT influence factors are determined. These factors were used as the model input, then the NAT and TAT predictive models were established compared with several algorithm. Based on the data from March 2015 to November 2016, the NAT and TTAT modes were established, and then the applicability over time of the models was tested with the data in 2018. The main conclusions are as follows:

(1) There is a good predictive accuracy when the XGBOOST algorithm was used to establish the NAT predictive model at Wuhan-Guangzhou HSR station. The data in 2018 was used as test data, and the results in test data also showed the NAT predictive model has a good applicability over time.

(2) The NAT prediction result was also used as the input of the TTAT prediction model, the TTAT predictive model was establish by using SVR algorithms compared with other regression algorithm. Then, 2018 data was used as test data to test the time applicability of TTAT model under SVR algorithm, the result also indicates that the TTAT predictive model

also has a predictive accuracy in time dimension.

(3) When a PD occurs, using the established NAT and TTAT predictive models of each station, it is possible to predict the influence scope accurately. That will provide a theoretical support for the dispatcher to make the rescheduling strategy and adjust the station work plan.

3.3 Modelling the influence of disturbances for real-time train dispatching

Accurately forecasting the influence of disturbances in High-Speed Railways (HSR) has great significance for improving real-time train dispatching and operation management. In this study, we show how to use historical train operation records to estimate the influence of high-speed train disturbances (HSTD), including the number of affected trains (NAT) and total delayed time (TDT), considering the timetable and disturbance characteristics. We first extracted data about the disturbances and their affected train groups from historical train operation records of Wuhan-Guangzhou (W-G) HSR in China. Then, in order to clarify the concatenation and differences of disturbances, we used a K-Means clustering algorithm to classify them into four categories. Next, parametric and non-parametric density estimation approaches were applied to fit the distributions of NAT and TDT of each clustered category, and the goodness-of-fit testing results showed that Log-normal and Gamma distribution probability densities are the best functions to approximate the distribution of NAT and TDT of different disturbance clusters. Specifically, the validation results show that the proposed models accurately revealed the characteristics of HSTD and that these models can be used in real-time dispatch to predict the NAT and TDT once the basic features of disturbances are known.

3.3.1 Introduction

An operating train may encounter various unexpected disturbances such as bad weather, power outage, facility failures, and so on [25], which can lead to considerable losses for both railway managers and travelers. For example, in the Dutch railway network, statistics show that there are approximately 22 infrastructure-related delays per day, lasting on average for 1.7 hours [159]. According to the statistics of the China Railway Corporation, the average departure punctuality in origin stations for China's 23,000km high-speed rail (HSR) network was as high as 98.8% in 2016. However, due to various disturbances during the trip, the average punctuality at final destination stations was less than 90%, even though delays smaller than five minutes are considered punctual[240].

When disturbances occur, dispatchers need to anticipate the potential influences of a specific delay. They need to estimate the number of affected trains (NAT) and total delayed time (TDT) before rescheduling the timetable. Modeling the high-speed train disturbances

(HSTD) will be helpful and of great significance, although it is extremely challenging due to the following two aspects:

(1) Various influencing factors. The influence of railway disturbances is related to various factors, for example, timetable structure, facility conditions, and experience and preference of dispatchers which makes it difficult for these factors to be interpreted through functional relationships.

(2) Complex train interactions. Due to resources occupation conflicts and the continuity of train operation, trains are interactive, which makes mathematical model incapable of modeling train interaction.

In practice, some skilled dispatchers usually predict HSTD empirically, which leads to differences in dispatching even for the same dispatcher when working in different situations. Data-driven approaches have recently gained more attention due to their better understanding of train delay concatenation and the fact they are more supportive of robust timetables and real-time dispatching [241]. In addition to the availability of train operation records, advanced data-mining techniques enable us to address these problems from a data-analysis perspective. Train operation records are therefore assumed to be the interactive consequences of all influencing factors. Therefore, mining train operation records provides us with a brand-new way of examining train interactions arising from heterogeneous factors.

To bridge the gap between the empirical and mathematical models, this study aims to establish data-driven models of the NAT and TDT caused by different types of disturbances using the train operation data of Wuhan-Guangzhou (W-G) HSR in China. To this end, we used a K-Means algorithm to categorize the extracted disturbances according to their influencing factors. Next, we applied five widely-used probability density models and two kernel functions to fit the distributions of NAT and TDT. We then selected the best models for each cluster based on goodness-of-fit testing. Finally, the test data from the operation records from nine months were used to validate the generalization of the fitted models, which showed that these models could be applied to estimate the NAT and TDT of future disturbances.

3.3.2 Literature review

Since the 1970s, there has been active research on disturbance management in train dispatching [2]. Most recently, the topic of the INFORMS 2018 Railroad Problem Solving Competition was "Predicting Near-Term Train Schedule Performance and Delay" using operational records. A large number of methods and algorithms have been proposed to improve rail operations, but due to unavailable or insufficient historical data, research was mainly based on simulation and mathematical delay propagation models.

Many approaches have been uncovered and proposed to manage railway disturbances. Exogenous factors, such as natural disasters, and bad weather conditions,and endogenous factors, such as operation interference resulted from equipment failure, man-made faults, railway construction,temporary speed limitations, defective braking systems, signal and interlocking failures, and excessive passenger demand can contribute, alone or together, to the primary delay [132, 221, 242]. Also, if the running and dwell times increase due to unexpected disturbances, it can result in knock-on delays and delays for other trains [196]. Serious disruptions such as switch or signal failures, if not managed effectively, can result in queuing of trains creating a chain of delayed trains. The experience from the Taiwan High-speed Rail shows that shortening the maintenance cycle can effectively alleviate the problem of train delay caused by signal failures [60]. Some studies have made contributions on statistical models of delay and the respective fitness models. The Weibull, Gamma, and Log-normal distributions have been adopted in several studies [80, 201]. It was shown that the distributional form of primary delays, and the affected number of trains could be well-approximated by classical methods such as Log-normal distribution and linear regression models [29]. A q-exponential function is used to demonstrate the distribution of train delays on the British railway network [212]. Using spatial and temporal resolution transport data from the UK road and rail networks, and the intense storms of 28 June 2012 as a case study, a novel exploration of the impacts of an extreme event has been carried out in [242]. Given the HSR operation data, the maximum likelihood estimation method was used to determine the probability distribution of the different disturbances factors, and the distributions of affected trains, however, the models of primary delay consequences have not been established in detail [61]. Probabilistic distribution functions of both train arrival and departure delays at the individual station were derived in general based on the data from Beijing-Shanghai HSR [243].

Data-driven research studies proposed for delay/disruption management mainly focused on using regression or distribution approaches to fit delay data. Van der Meer et al. mined data from peak hours, including rolling stock, and weather data, and developed a predictive model involving the mining of track occupation data for delay estimations [196]. A data-mining approach was used for analyzing rail transport delay chains, with data from passenger train traffic on the Finnish rail network, but the data from the train running process was limited to one month [22]. Murali et al. reported a delay regression-based estimation technique that models delay as a function of train mix and network topology [96]. A statistical analysis of train delays in the Eindhoven Station in the Netherlands was used to explain systematic delay propagation based on the use of a robust linear regression model to uncover the correlations between arrival delays [227]. Recently, Kecman and Goverde developed separate predictive models for the estimation of running and dwell times by collecting data on the respective process types from a training set [99]. Javad et al. examined different distribution models for running times of individual sections in an HSR system and showed that the log-logistic probability density function is the best distributional form to approximate the empirical distribution of running times on the specified line[240]. A hybrid Bayesian network model is also established to predict arrival and departure delays for Wuhan-Guangzhou HSR [235].

A review of the literature reveals that only a few studies focus on the modeling of the NAT and TDT of disturbances, especially in HSR operations. It is crucial for HSR operating companies to predict and reduce disruptions in train operations and to operate as closely as possible to published timetables. It is therefore important that they identify the severity of displacements or interruptions to train services. This can help dispatchers reduce delay propagation and the possibility of aggravation through effective designing of timetables or real-time dispatching decisions. This study aims to fill this gap by conducting a detailed factor-specific analysis of delays based on empirical data from W-G HSR.

3.3.3 Train operation data and problem description

3.3.3.1 Train operation data

The data, which were collected from W-G HSR line, include 57,796 trains in the GZS-HYE section and 64,547 HSR trains in the HYE-CSS section. The data contain operational records covering the period from March 24, 2015 to November 10, 2016, comprising scheduled/actual arrival/departure records for each train at each station, train numbers, dates, and information on occupied tracks in a time format precise to 1 min, as shown in Table 3-16.

3.3.3.2 Problem description

In both practice and research, train delays and disturbances are always classified according to their causes. However, this method seems to have a drawback, as some disturbances with different causes sometimes have the same influencing mechanism on train operation. For example, track failure in sections and power supply fault in sections are different causes, but they have the same effect on train operation, because in both conditions, trains have to wait for the availability of the section. In other words, from the perspective of railway management, it is significant to classify disturbances according to their impacts on train operation. Besides, other cases like signal fault and turnout fault, speed limitation for bad weather and speed limitation for construction, they both have the same effect on train operation. In this research, weintend to classify the disturbances focusing on some key factors that influence their effects on train operation.

Table 3-16　Train operation data format in database

Train	Station	Date	Actual arrival	Actual departure	Scheduled arrival	Scheduled departure	Occupied track*
G280	GZN	2015/3/24	7:02	7:02	7:01	7:01	II
G548	SG	2015/8/27	17:26	17:30	17:26	17:29	4
G1118	HYE	2015/10/2	13:37	13:40	13:38	13:40	8
G6025	HSW	2015/11/28	20:57	20:57	20:58	20:58	I

*The passage tracks at the station are labeled with Roman characters, while the dwelling tracks are labeled with numbers.

3.3.4 Clustering model for disturbances

3.3.4.1 Influencing factors

In order to meet passenger demand, train services tend to vary across different periods and segments even on the same HSR line. Train interval is a key factor in delay propagation, as a disturbance tends to cause more severe effects in smaller interval periods and segments, and smaller effects in larger interval periods and segments. Figure 3-18(a) and (b) reveal theNAT and TDT of disturbancesat GZN and HSW. It clearly shows that the NAT and TDT of W-G HSR differ significantly across time periods and segments. In addition, the disturbance length will directly influence their consequences; the longer the disturbance, the more delayed trains and total delays it will cause. Based on the analysis, the following featuresforclustering models and indexes to measure the influence of disturbances were ascertained:

- Train interval (I): the average scheduled train interval when a disturbance occurs (minute);
- Occurrence time (T): the time when a disturbance starts (in the railway operation, it can be indicated by the scheduled arrival time of the first delayed train in its affected trains group);
- Disturbances length (L): the time span from starting time to ending time of the disturbance (it can be indicated by the delay times of the first train in the affected train group (minute).
- NAT and TDT indexes are used to measure their influence.

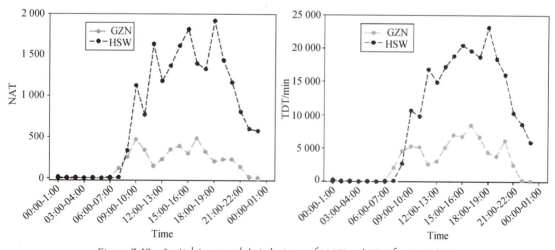

Figure 3-18   Spatial-temporal distribution of NAT and TDT for W-G HSR.

Based on the indexes, data on 6006 disturbances and their consequences on train operations were extracted from the raw data; five cases are shown in Table 3-17. In order to validate the proposed model, the extracted data were split into a training dataset, which included 3154 disturbances in the preceding 12 months, and a validation dataset, which contained 2852 disturbances over the following nine months. We extracted only those disturbances with a disturbance longer than 4 minutes according to the standard set by the Chinese Railway Company. Shorter disturbances, which can be assimilated by the time supplements distributed in timetables, tend not to cause delay propagation and are therefore eliminated from the dataset.

Table 3-17　Examples of disturbances and their influences for modeling

Train	Date	Station	Occurrence time	Length (min)	Train interval (min)	NAT	TDT (min)
G1406	2015/9/2	LYW	19:55	9	6.5	2	17
G6020	2015/9/6	ZZW	17:16	17	7.5	8	93
G1102	2016/6/24	HSW	9:07	21	10.0	1	21
G1032	2016/9/14	GZN	13:26	46	7.9	17	183
G6486	2016/10/29	LCE	10:33	30	8.1	31	173

3.3.4.2　K-Means clustering

A K-Means cluster is a typical and popular algorithm that has strong robustness on high-dimensional and multi-collinear datasets in unsupervised learning. For the given dataset $D = \{\vec{x}_1, \vec{x}_2, \cdots, \vec{x}_N\}$, assuming that the clustering centers $C = \{C_1, C_2, \cdots, C_K\}$ are initialized, the object of K-Means is to minimize the mean squared error (MSE):

$$Min(MSE) = \sum_{k=1}^{K} \sum_{\vec{x}_i \in C_k} \| \vec{x}_i - \vec{u}_k \|^2 \tag{3-40}$$

where $\vec{u}_k = \dfrac{1}{|C_k|} \sum_{\vec{x}_i \in C_k} \vec{x}_i$ is the mean vector of C_k. Equation (1) indicates the nearness between samples in a cluster and their mean vector.

The core principle of the K-Means cluster is to choose K points in space as centers and assign the samples to their nearest cluster. By iteratively updating their centers, the objective is to minimize until the stopping condition is satisfied. The K-Means clustering algorithm can be concluded as following and more details are shown in literature[244].

K-Means algorithm：

Input: dataset $D = \{\vec{x}_1, \vec{x}_2, \cdots, \vec{x}_N\}$, and initial centers K;

Output: categories of every sample $C = \{C_1, C_2, \cdots, C_K\}$

Initialization：Randomly classify samples as K categories, and calculate the initial center of each category;

Repeating the following step until stopping condition is satisfied:

● Calculating the sign (λ_i) of sample $\vec{x}_i$, $\lambda_i = \arg(\min |\vec{x}_i - \vec{u}_k|)$

● Classifying $\vec{x}_i$ into its nearest cluster, $C_{\lambda_i} = C_{\lambda_i} \cup \{\vec{x}_i\}$

● Updating the mean vector, $\vec{u}_k = \dfrac{1}{|C_k|} \sum_{\vec{x}_i \in C_k} \vec{x}_i$

● Stopping condition：mean vectors do not change, thus: $\hat{\vec{u}}_k = \vec{u}_k$

3.3.4.3 Model performance

The performance of clustering models is commonly evaluated from two perspectives: 1) the tightness of the samples in the cluster and 2) the distances between clusters. The widely used evaluation indexes are distance and covariance [245, 246], both of which require smaller values among samples in the same cluster and larger values among samples in different clusters. To systematically evaluate the clustering models, we simultaneously chose distance- and covariance-based indexes, namely, the Silhouette Coefficient (SC) and Calinski-Harabasz Score (CHS) as shown in equation (3-41) and (3-42), respectively.

$$SC(i) = \frac{b(i) - a(i)}{max\{a(i), b(i)\}} \tag{3-41}$$

where $a(i)$ is the average distance between $\vec{x}_i$ and other samples in a cluster; $b(i)$ is the average distance between $\vec{x}_i$ and samples in other clusters; notifying: the range of SC is [-1,1].

$$CHS(k) = \frac{tr(B_k)}{tr(W_k)} \frac{m-k}{k-1} \tag{3-42}$$

where m is the number of samples, k is the number of clusters, B_k is the covariance matrix among samples in the same cluster, while W_k is the covariance matrix among samples in different clusters, and $tr(g)$ is the trace of the matrix. According to equations (3-41) and (3-42), better clustering results require larger SC and CHS.

To obtain reasonable clustering results, we also applied other clustering algorithms including the BIRTH, Gauss Mixture, and Agglomerative models and investigated the number of clusters (K) of each model from 2 to 20 in order to categorize the disturbances. The result is shown in Figure 3-19 in which the SC index of each model decreases with the growth of clusters (K) and the CHS index of the K-Means algorithm reaches its maximum value when $K=4$. Therefore, to ensure that the proposed clustering algorithm has the best performance regarding distance and covariance, we finally chose a K-Means algorithm that has four clusters as the clustering model for HSR disturbances.

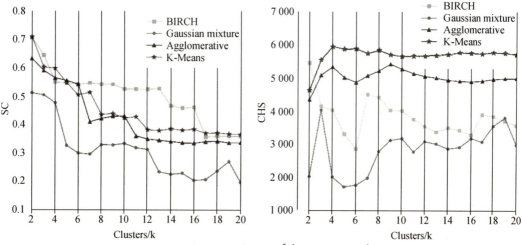

Figure 3-19 SC and CHS of clustering models.

Finally, HSR disturbances were classified into four categories using the K-Means clustering algorithm, as shown in Figure 3-20. According to the distribution of each cluster, we can define them as follows:

● Cluster A: disturbances occurred between 7:00 am and 23:30 pm; train intervals range from 3 to 13 minutes; lengths range from 5 to 14 minutes.

● Cluster B: disturbances occurred between 7:30 am and 23:30 pm; train intervals range from 5 to 25 minutes; lengths range from 14 to 31 minutes.

● Cluster C: disturbances occurred between 7:30 am and 23:30 pm; train intervals range from 4 to 30 minutes; lengths are longer than 31 minutes.

● Cluster D: disturbances occurred between 10:30 am and 23:30 pm; train intervals range from 13 to 30 minutes; lengths range from 5 to 22 minutes.

The statistics of NAT and TDT of each cluster are shown in Table 3-18.

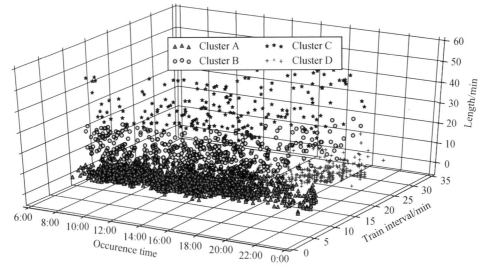

Figure 3-20 Spatial distribution of each disturbance cluster.

Table 3-18 Statistics of NAT and TDT.

Cluster	Sample size	NAT				TDT			
		Min	Mean	Max	SD	Min	Mean	Max	SD
A	2200	1	8.46	40	7.98	5	36.57	266	36.77
B	462	1	12.54	40	9.71	15	101.66	300	65.56
C	197	1	11.77	40	8.59	33	136.50	292	69.99
D	295	1	6.13	31	5.38	5	32.50	142	27.13

3.3.5 Estimating models of NAT and TDT

3.3.5.1 Candidate models

In order to reveal the rules of disturbance influences, we first investigated the histogram of NAT and TDT, as shown in Figure 5, which indicates that both NAT and TDT appear to have right-skewed distributions. Since the locations and shapes of the histograms are very different, we fitted the data using five common right-skewed distribution models and two kernel functions as the candidate models. The distribution models including the Log-Normal, Weibull, Gamma, Exponential, and Logistic and kernel functions, including Gaussian and Epanechnikov kernels were employed to fit the data from parametric and non-parametric perspectives. The probability distribution models and kernel functions of these models are as follows[247]:

- Log-Normal distribution:

$$f(x;\mu,\sigma) = \frac{1}{x\sigma\sqrt{2\pi}} e^{-\frac{(\ln x - \mu)^2}{2\sigma^2}} \tag{3-43}$$

where σ is the shape parameter and μ is the location parameter.

- Weibull distribution:

$$f(x;\lambda,k) = \begin{cases} \frac{k}{\lambda}\left(\frac{x}{\lambda}\right)^{k-1} e^{-(x/\lambda)^k} & x \geq 0 \\ 0 & x < 0 \end{cases} \tag{3-44}$$

where $\lambda > 0$ is the scale parameter and $k > 0$ is the shape parameter.

- Gamma distribution:

$$f(x;\alpha,\beta) = \begin{cases} \frac{\beta^\alpha}{\Gamma(\alpha)} x^{\alpha-1} e^{-\beta x} & x \geq 0 \\ 0 & x < 0 \end{cases}$$

$$\Gamma(z) = \int_0^\infty t^{z-1} e^{-t} dt \tag{3-45}$$

where α is the shape parameter and β is the scale parameter.

- Exponential distribution:

$$f(x,\lambda) = \begin{cases} \lambda e^{-\lambda x} & x \geq 0 \\ 0 & x \leq 0 \end{cases} \tag{3-46}$$

where λ is the shape parameter.

- Logistic distribution:

$$f(x;u,s) = \frac{1}{s\left(e^{\frac{x-u}{2s}} + e^{-\frac{x-u}{2s}}\right)^2} \tag{3-47}$$

Where u is the location parameter and s is the scale parameter.

- Gaussian kernel

$$k(\mu) = \frac{1}{\sqrt{2\pi}} e^{-\frac{1}{2}u^2} \tag{3-48}$$

- Epanechnikov kernel

$$k(\mu) = \begin{cases} \dfrac{3}{4}\left(1 - u^2\right) & \text{if } |u| \leqslant 1 \\ 0 & \text{else} \end{cases} \tag{3-49}$$

The parameters were estimated using maximum likelihood and are shown in Table 3-19, and the fitting results of the distribution models are shown in Figure 3-21 and 3-22. These figures clearly show that all the candidate probability density models mimic the shape of the non-parametric estimation using Gaussian and Epanechnikov kernels, which enables us to choose the best model from the parametric candidates as the estimating model of disturbance influences.

Table 3-19　Fitted parameters of NAT and TDT.

Cluster		Log-normal		Weibull		Gamma		Exponential	Logistic	
		μ	σ	k	λ	α	β	λ	u	s
NAT	A	1.754	0.884	1.176	9.003	1.455	0.172	0.118	7.016	3.912
	B	2.175	0.932	1.308	13.616	1.557	0.124	0.079	11.229	5.380
	C	2.155	0.874	1.406	12.943	1.760	0.149	0.085	10.771	4.650
	D	1.506	0.781	1.288	6.688	1.773	0.289	0.163	5.120	2.557
TDT	A	3.233	0.861	1.146	38.660	1.439	0.039	0.027	29.683	17.195
	B	4.386	0.728	1.616	113.677	2.273	0.022	0.010	95.280	37.595
	C	4.769	0.567	2.086	154.544	3.560	0.026	0.007	131.530	41.077
	D	3.188	0.764	1.334	35.677	1.859	0.057	0.031	27.779	13.421

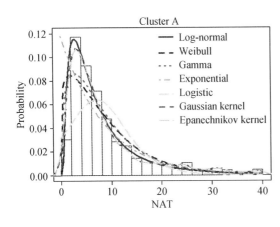
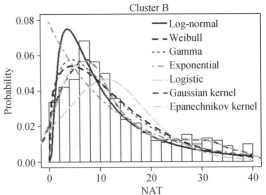

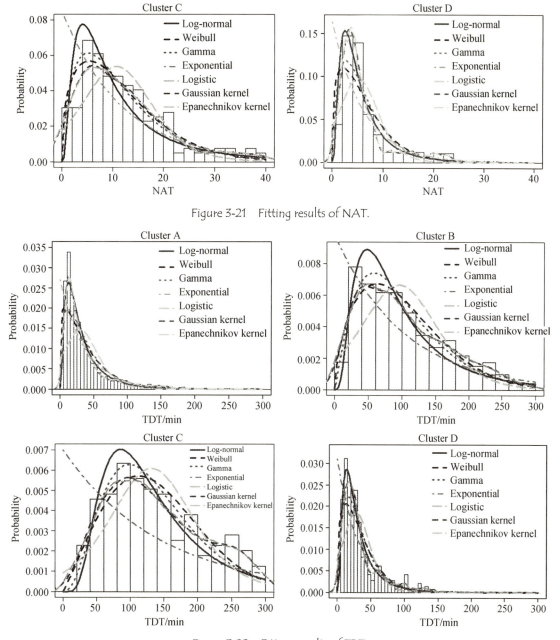

Figure 3-21　Fitting results of NAT.

Figure 3-22　Fitting results of TDT.

3.3.5.2　Goodness-of-fit test

In this section, we evaluated the goodness-of-fit of the distribution models using the Kolmogorov-Smirnov (K-S) method [248] and selected the optimal distribution model for each category.

K-S testing is proposed to test whether a group of data follows a theoretical distribution model; its null hypothesis is that the dataset follows a theoretical distribution. Its testing statistics are the largest difference between the cumulative distribution function of the data and the theoretical distribution, as shown in equation 12. Because the number of trains is the integer, and the historical train operation data were recorded in the minimum unit of one minute, we inserted some random numbers that follow uniform distribution in order to meet the continuity requirement of the K-S method.

$$D = \max \left| F'(x) - F(x) \right| \tag{3-50}$$

where $F'(x)$ is the cumulative distribution function of the samples, which are the NAT and TDT; $F(x)$ is the cumulative distribution function of the theoretical distribution models, which are the five alternative distribution models. We chose the significance level $\alpha=0.05$; when the sample size is large enough (over 50), the critical value of D should be:

$$D_{0.05} = \frac{1.36}{\sqrt{n}} \tag{3-51}$$

where n is the sample size.

According to the rules of the K-S test, if $D<D_{0.05}$, the null hypothesis is accepted and the samples are considered as following the theoretical distribution. The smaller D is, the closer the sample is to the theoretical distribution. The K-S testing results of all the models are shown in Table 3-20.

Table 3-20   Goodness-of-fit testing of NAT and TDT.

Cluster		Log-normal		Weibull		Gamma		Exponential		Logistic		$D_{0.05}$
		D	Pass?	D	Pass?	D	Pass?	D	Pass?	D	Pass?	
NAT	A	0.025*	Yes	0.055	No	0.037	No	0.104	No	0.159	No	0.030
	B	0.077	No	0.046	Yes	0.044*	Yes	0.117	No	0.121	No	0.063
	C	0.088	No	0.045	Yes	0.038*	Yes	0.139	No	0.104	No	0.097
	D	0.042*	Yes	0.066	Yes	0.043	Yes	0.165	No	0.135	No	0.079
TDT	A	0.026*	Yes	0.082	No	0.058	No	0.116	No	0.187	No	0.030
	B	0.057	Yes	0.038	Yes	0.037*	Yes	0.146	No	0.105	No	0.063
	C	0.059	Yes	0.060	Yes	0.049*	Yes	0.208	No	0.083	Yes	0.097
	D	0.037*	Yes	0.064	Yes	0.041	Yes	0.156	No	0.151	No	0.079

Superscript "*" indicates the best models;

Finally, we chose the model that passes the K-S test and has the smallest D as the distribution model of each disturbance cluster. The parameters of distribution models for NAT and TDT of each cluster are shown in Table 3-21.

Table 3-21　Parameters of the best distribution models.

Cluster	NAT		TDT	
	Model	Parameters	Model	Parameters
A	Log-normal (μ, σ)	(1.754, 0.884)	Log-normal (μ, σ)	(3.233, 0.861)
B	Gamma (α, β)	(1.557, 0.124)	Gamma (α, β)	(2.273, 0.022)
C	Gamma (α, β)	(1.760, 0.149)	Gamma (α, β)	(3.560, 0.026)
D	Log-normal (μ, σ)	(1.506, 0.781)	Log-normal (μ, σ)	(3.188, 0.764)

3.3.5.3　Generalization test

In order to investigate the generalization of the fitted distribution models, we used the disturbances in the following nine months of W-G HSR line to validate the models. We first fed the disturbances into the proposed K-Means clustering algorithm and obtained the clustering labels of each sample. The clusters that have the same labels as the training dataset are used to validate the fitted models. The fitting results are shown in Figure 3-23 and 3-24, and the descriptive statistics and their K-S testing results are shown in Table 3-22.

The testing results indicate that all the fitted models pass the goodness-of-fit and generalization testing. The fitted models can therefore accurately reveal the distributive disciplines of NAT and TDT and are of great significance to real-time train dispatching.

Table 3-22　Statistics and the testing result of NAT and TDT.

Cluster		Samples size	Min	Mean	Max	SD	D_value	Pass?	$D_{0.05}$
NAT	A	1757	1	8.06	40	7.51	0.007	Yes	0.032
	B	357	1	12.61	40	9.58	0.055	Yes	0.072
	C	195	1	12.28	39	8.86	0.056	Yes	0.097
	D	273	1	6.31	24	5.11	0.069	Yes	0.082
TDT	A	1757	5	35.13	238	34.73	0.023	Yes	0.032
	B	357	15	99.18	294	64.13	0.027	Yes	0.072
	C	195	32	135.90	299	66.85	0.046	Yes	0.097
	D	273	5	32.61	162	26.29	0.067	Yes	0.082

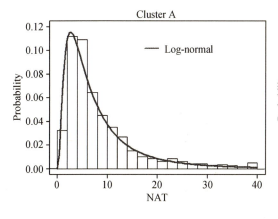
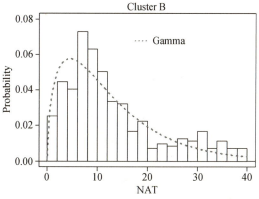

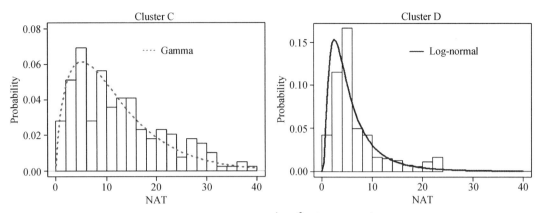

Figure 3-23　Fitting results of NAT on test data.

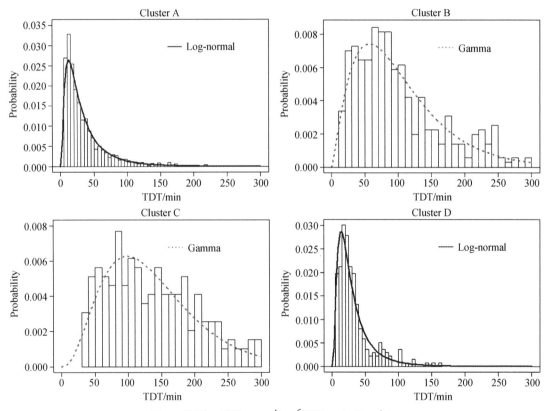

Figure 3-24　Fitting results of TDT on testing data.

3.3.6　Conclusion

This study is the first study to cluster railway disturbances according to their characteristics and timetable structure in order to estimate NAT and TDT resulting from HSR operation disturbances. We first extracted data on the delayed train groups caused by disturbances, from which the NAT and TDT were obtained. The disturbances were then classified into four clusters using a K-Means algorithm according to the time of occurrence, disturbance length, and train interval. Next, we applied five different distribution modelsand two kernel functions to fit the NAT and TDT of these four clusters and selected the most reasonable models based on goodness-of-fit testing. Finally, disturbances in the following nine months were used to validate the model generation; the performance of the test data indicated that the fitted models can accurately reveal the distributive disciplines of NAT and TDT of HSR. The proposed clustering algorithm, which fully takes the disturbance characteristics and timetable structure into consideration, compensates the shortage of existing models in railway disturbance classification. In real-time operation, once a disturbance happens, its features are therefore known (including train interval, length and occurrence time of disturbance), which can be fed into the trained K-means clustering algorithm, and its classifying label can be outputted. Then, according to the label, the specific distribution model can be chosen to help dispatchers predict the NAT and TDT.

The established distribution models are general models for W-G and X-S HSR lines. However, train services and infrastructure could both vary at different stations, leading to differences in distribution model parameters. Therefore, our future work will focus on establishing models for each station on the HSR network.

Chapter 4

Data-driven delay propagation mechanism on vertical

4.1 A hybrid model to improve the train running time prediction ability during high-speed railway disruptions

This chapter presents a hybrid model comprising support vector regression (SVR) and a Kalman filter (KF) to improve the train running time prediction accuracy of machine learning models during disruptions. SVR is trained using offline data, whereas the KF updates the SVR prediction using real-time information. Thus, the hybrid model mitigates the time-consuming online training of machine learning models and their incapability to reflect real-time information when using offline training. To obtain a high-performance prediction model, four key SVR parameters were first optimized based on cross-validation. Then, the SVR prediction was evaluated using the mean absolute error and mean absolute percentage error on testing datasets and considering trains which suffered disruptions. The results from this evaluation show that SVR notably outperforms other benchmark models but cannot provide satisfactory predictions under unexpected situations. Next, we applied the KF to update the SVR prediction using real-time information and conducted a model performance evaluation on the prediction from the hybrid model. The corresponding results show that the KF greatly improves the accuracy of SVR prediction under unexpected disruption situations. Furthermore, the computation time substantially reduces by using offline training along with the KF instead of online training.

4.1.1 Introduction

Risk handling ability has become essential for transportation operators to improve service quality and meet passenger expectations. Nevertheless, railway operations are inevitably affected by unpredictable factors such as facility failures, bad weather, and human error. Such operation disruptions can lead to train delays and cancellations, which undermine punctuality and impose a bottleneck that limits the service quality of railway transportation. According to the reports from the China Railway Corporation, the average punctuality of China's 25,000 km high-speed railway network at destination stations is below 90%, with punctuality comprising delays up to 5 minutes [240]. In Norway, the best-performing routes have a punctuality rate of 94% and the worst-performing routes have low rates reaching 80% [249]. Train operation conflicts are the potential results of the delays due to disruptions and they may lead to the propagation of the delays [250]. In order to minimize the effects of the conflicts and to adjust scheduling as well as to improve train punctuality, the delay prediction and the train running time estimation are studied during timetable rescheduling [251].

However, the train operation is a dynamic process as the unexpected disruptions and the delay propagation may influence the operation of trains in sections and/or at stations. It is quite hard to capture the rules of train running time in certain sections with many uncertainties due to disruptions and train operation conflicts. The great development of artificial intelligence has led to the ever-increasing use of machine learning (ML) models, which consider few mathematical assumptions and provide outstanding performance, to address railway problems. In fact, ML models are considered suitable for determining nonlinear relationships between outcomes and their influential factors and capable of handling high-dimensional and noisy data, thus being applicable for railway data modeling given the interactions among trains and facilities. ML-based approaches can provide a deeper understanding of train event concatenation and be used to develop more robust timetables and provide more accurate decisional support [241]. However, ML models present drawbacks when applied to real-time prediction, as they learn information from large-scale datasets, thus making their training time usually unacceptable. On the other hand, if models are trained using offline data, the resulting prediction may fail to capture real-time variations, thus undermining prediction under unexpected situations. To address these problems, we propose a hybrid model comprising support vector regression (SVR) [252] and a Kalman filter (KF) [253]. In the proposed model, the ML component (SVR) is trained using offline data to be applicable in real-time dispatching, whereas the KF uses real-time information to update and correct the SVR prediction. Therefore, the proposed model satisfies both timeliness and real-time learning requirements.

The remainder of this study is organized as follows. In Section 4.1.2, we present a survey of related work. In Section 4.1.3, we briefly introduce SVR and KF, and formulate the proposed hybrid model. Then, we describe the train operation data and SVR training. In Section 4.1.4, we report the performance evaluation of SVR and the hybrid model on testing datasets and trains which suffered disruptions. Finally, we discuss our findings and draw conclusions in Section 4.1.5.

4.1.2 Related work

Generally, railway disruptions can be caused by exogenous factors, such as natural disasters, and bad weather conditionsand endogenous factors, such as operation interference resulted from equipment failure, man-made faults, railway construction,temporary speed limitations, defective braking systems, signal and interlocking failures, and excessive passenger demand [132, 221, 242]. To manage these disruptions, train operation simulation systems such as LUKS [254], RailSys [255], and OpenTrack [46] have been developed to improve the train operation process. However, the disruptions or delay parameters in these systems mainly depend on hypothetical and theoretical models.

For decades, statistical models are widely used for railway disruptions management. These methods usually arise from two aspects: 1) predicting the occurrence or length of disruptions; or 2) predicting the train-event deviations (arrival, departure, running, and dwelling) caused by disruptions. [110] used a Copula Bayesian Network model to predict the railway disruption length in Dutch railway network. [96] introduced a delay-regression-based estimation that models delay as a function of the train mix and network topology. [86] focused on a statistical analysis of train running times among stations to improve the prediction accuracy of delay propagation in railway systems. The analysis retrieved a strong correlation between arrival delays and dwell times, whereas the correlation between running times and departure delays was found to be much weaker. [240] developed a statistical method to estimate the arrival delay distribution according to the previous departure delay and running time distributions. [49] proposed an analytical stochastic model to estimate train delay propagation, with the Stieltjes convolution of individual independent distributions being the essential and most challenging modeling problem.[235] developed a hybrid Bayesian network model taking the arrival and departure events from origin to destination stations of every train in the network as network nodes to predict train delays, which shows that the proposed model had small errors under disruptions.

Along with the rapid development of big data and artificial intelligence, ML models are being increasingly applied to railway research. For instance, some common ML models such as decision trees, artificial neural networks (ANNs), support vector machines, and k-nearest neighbors are used to predict train events. [68] proposed a method based on decision tree to estimate the key factors in knock-on delays, where operation prediction is performed by overtaking and behaviors, which are classified and analyzed to observe the chain of delay propagations in detail. [115]applied moving average and k-nearest neighbors models for real-time train travel time estimation. Their models notably improved baseline models by choosing a proper moving window span and number of neighbors. [116] applied ANNs to process available delays abstracted from known railway operation data to generate delay predictions for depending trains up to a near horizon. [117] introduced an accurate ANN to predict delays of passenger trains in Iranian railways using three different inputs, namely, normalized real numbers, binary coding, and binary set encoding. The comparison between this ANN, decision trees, and multinomial logistic regression models confirmed the high accuracy, low training time, and good solution qualities of the proposed ANN. A pioneering study applied SVR for prediction of passenger train arrival delays [118]. Data associated with the influences of infrastructure along different routes on train arrival delays were collected from the Serbian railways. The SVR outperformed the ANN by retrieving a higher R-squared than the ANN on test data, thus suggesting a new direction for applying ML models to analyze and predict train delays. Based on train location data, three different models, namely, the least squares method, support vector machine, and least-squares support vector machine, have been applied to predict train locations [120] and both improve the positioning accuracy of high-speed railway trains and reduce the number of balises while maintaining positioning accuracy. [52] investigated the accuracy of linear regression, ANNs, SVR, and random forest (ensemble decision trees) on the prediction of train delay recovery time, finding that random forest slightly outperformed the other models.

Reviewing the existing studies, …….

4.1.3　Methods

4.1.3.1　SVR

SVR can be regarded as a function approximation problem that finds the narrowest tube centered around a surface while minimizing the prediction error, i.e., the distance between the predicted and desired outputs [256]. Taking a one-dimensional input as example, Fig. 1 shows the constraint to minimize the error between the predicted value of the function for a given input and the real output. SVR adopts an ε-insensitive loss function, penalizing predictions that are farther than ε from the desired output. The value of ε determines the width of the tube, with a smaller value indicating a lower error tolerance and affecting the number of support vectors and, consequently, the solution sparsity.

Adopting a soft-margin approach, slack variables ξ and ξ^* can be added to guard against outliers. These variables determine the number of points that can be tolerated outside the tube (Fig. 4-1). The objective and constraint of SVR optimization are given by

$$min \frac{1}{2}\|w\|^2 + C\sum_{i=1}^{N}(\xi + \xi^*) \tag{4-1}$$

subject to

$$y_i - w^\mathrm{T}x_i \leqslant \varepsilon + \xi^*,$$

$$w^\mathrm{T}x_i - y_i \leqslant \varepsilon + \xi,$$

$$\xi \geqslant 0, \xi^* \geqslant 0, i = 1, 2, \cdots, N,$$

$$\begin{aligned} L(w,\xi^*,\xi,\lambda,\lambda^*,\alpha,\widehat{\alpha}_i) &= \frac{1}{2}\|w\|^2 + C\sum_{i=1}^{N}(\xi + \xi^*) + \sum_{i=1}^{N}\widehat{\alpha}_i(y_i - w^\mathrm{T}x_i - \varepsilon - \xi^*) \\ &+ \sum_{i=1}^{N}a_i(w^\mathrm{T}x_i - y_i - \varepsilon - \xi^*) - \sum_{i=1}^{N}\lambda_i\xi_i - \sum_{i=1}^{N}\lambda_i^*\xi_i^* \end{aligned} \tag{4-2}$$

where C is a coefficient of error regularization, which represents a tunable parameter where larger values increase the weight to minimize flatness, for this multi-objective optimization problem. This constrained quadratic optimization problem can be solved by finding the Lagrangian (see (4-2)). The Lagrange multipliers, or dual variables, are nonnegative real numbers λ, λ^*, α, and $\hat{\alpha}$.

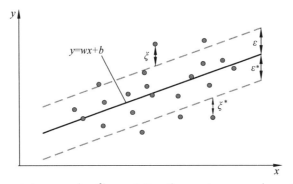

Fig. 4-1   Example of linear SVR with one-dimensional input.

The minimum of (4-2) can be found by taking its partial derivatives with respect to the variables and setting them equal to zero based on the Karush–Kuhn–Tucker (KKT) conditions, which state that the product of Lagrange multipliers and constraints equals zero. The primary problem can be written as

$$\max \frac{1}{2}\sum_{i=1}^{N}\sum_{j=1}^{N}(\hat{\alpha}_i - \alpha_i)(\hat{\alpha}_j - \alpha_j)x_i^T x_j - \sum_{i=1}^{N}\left[y_i(\hat{\alpha}_i - \alpha_i) - \varepsilon(\hat{\alpha}_i + \alpha_i) \right] \tag{4-3}$$

subject to

$$\sum_{i=1}^{N}(\hat{\alpha}_i - \alpha_i) = 0 \,.$$

$$\alpha_i \geqslant 0, \alpha_i^* \geqslant 0 \,.$$

with KKT conditions being

$$KKT\begin{cases} a_i(w^T x_i - y_i - \varepsilon - \xi_i) = 0 \\ \hat{\alpha}_i(y_i - w^T x_i - \varepsilon - \xi_i) = 0 \\ \lambda_i \xi_i = 0 \\ \lambda_i^* \xi_i^* = 0 \\ (C - \alpha_i)\xi_i = 0 \\ (C - \hat{\alpha}_i)\xi_i^* = 0 \end{cases} .$$

Let $\alpha^* = (\alpha_1^*, \alpha_2^*, \cdots, \alpha_N^*)$ be a solution. The optimization problem can be written as

$$b^* = y_j + \varepsilon - \sum_{i=1}^{N}(\hat{\alpha}_i - \alpha_j^*)x_i^T x_j \,, \tag{4-4}$$

$$y = \sum_{i=1}^{N}(\hat{\alpha}_i - \alpha_i^*)x_i^T x_j + b^* \,. \tag{4-5}$$

If a nonlinear function (kernel function) $K(x_i, x)$ is needed, the SVR is given by

$$y = \sum_{i=1}^{N} (\hat{\alpha}_i - \alpha_i) \mathrm{K}(x_i, x) + \mathrm{b}. \qquad (4\text{-}6)$$

4.1.3.2 KF

The KF addresses the general problem of estimating state $x \in \mathbb{R}^m$ of a discrete-time controlled process governed by linear stochastic difference equations. Hence, the filter estimates the process state at some time and then considers feedback from (noisy) measurements [253]. Consequently, the KF equations can be divided into two groups: time and measurement update equations. The time update equations are responsible for projecting forward (in time) the current state and error covariance estimates to obtain *a priori* estimates for the next timestep. The measurement update equations are responsible for the feedback, i.e., incorporating a new measurement into the *a priori* estimate to improve the *a posteriori* estimate. The time and measurement update equations can be considered as predictor and corrector equations, respectively.

1. Time update

The KF first predicts the process state at timestep k according to the optimal estimation at timestep $k-1$:

$$\hat{x}_k^- = A\hat{x}_{k-1} + w_{k-1}. \qquad (4\text{-}7)$$

Then, it calculates the new error according to the error and process noise of the last timestep:

$$\mathrm{P}_k^- = AP_{k-1}A^\mathrm{T} + Q, \qquad (4\text{-}8)$$

where $\hat{x}_k^-$ is the *a priori* estimation at timestep k, $\hat{x}_{k-1}$ is the optimal estimation at timestep $k-1$, A is transform coefficient from timestep $k-1$ to timestep k, w_{k-1} is process noise with Gaussian distribution $p(w) \sim N(0, Q)$, P_{k-1} is the covariance at timestep k, and P_k^- is the *apriori* covariance at timestep k. At timestep k, the system state has measurement z_k given by

$$z_k = H\hat{x}_k^- + v_k, \qquad (4\text{-}9)$$

where v_k is measurement noise with Gaussian distribution $p(v) \sim N(0, R)$.

2. Measurement update

After time update, the Kalman gain is calculated based on the process noise and measurement noise:

$$K_k = P_k^- H^T (HP_k^- H^T + R)^{-1}. \qquad (4\text{-}10)$$

Next, the estimation is updated to retrieve the optimal estimation at timestep k based on the predicted state and measurement:

$$\hat{x}_k = \hat{x}_k^- + (z_k + H\hat{x}_k^-). \tag{4-11}$$

Finally, the error at timestep k is calculated for the update at timestep $k + 1$:

$$P_k = (I - K_k H)P_k^-, \tag{4-12}$$

where K_k is the Kalman gain, $\hat{x}_k$ is the optimal/posterior estimation at timestep k, and I is the identity matrix.

4.1.3.3 Prediction model

ML models can present low performance when applied for prediction of real-time train events because information should be learned from large-scale data, thus making the training time usually prohibitive for this application. In contrast, offline training may impede to accurately predict unexpected situations. We propose the combination of SVR, a ML model, and KF, a state-space model, to improve the prediction performance. SVR is trained using offline data for application to real-time train dispatching, whereas the KF aims to utilize the latest information for updating the SVR prediction. The proposed hybrid model, therefore, can simultaneously satisfy both timeliness and real-time learning requirements.

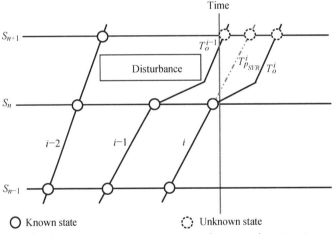

Fig. 4-2　Diagram of real-time delay prediction in time (horizontal axis) and space (vertical axis).

Fig. 2 illustrates real-time train running time prediction, where train i arrives at station S_n (at the red vertical line), and the next section, S_n–S_{n+1}, is blocked due to an unexpected fault. The dispatcher should estimate the running time of train i in section S_n–S_{n+1} to reschedule the timetable. Therefore, we consider SVR prediction $T_{P_{SVR}}^i$ as the process state in (4-7), and treat the observed running time (T_o^{i-1}) of the previous train in this section as the measurement in (4-9). To consider noise in $T_{P_{SVR}}^i$ and T_o^{i-1}, the Kalman gain is calculated according to the variance of the historical running times of trains i and $i - 1$, with Q in (4-8) and R in (4-10) being the variance of the historical running times of trains i and $i - 1$, respectively. Specifically, we calculate the Kalman gain based on the variance of historical running times from both the SVR predictions and the observed values from train $i - 1$ that do not represent the actual running times of train i. As a result, a more reliable prediction is obtained by considering real-time information and instantaneous predictions are provided by the proposed hybrid model. We summarize the prediction process combining SVR and KF in Algorithm 4-1.

Algorithm 4-1 Hybrid model prediction of train running times combining SVR and KF.

Input: 1) influential factors on running time, 2) historical running times of each train

Output: 1) SVR prediction, 2) optimal estimation of running time

To predict running time of train i, the optimal estimation of every section is obtained by repeating the following steps:

1) Train and validate SVR using offline data to obtain prediction $T_{p_{\mathrm{SVR}}}^{i}$

2) Calculate the running time variance of train i: $Q = var(T_{o_1}^{i}, T_{o_2}^{i}, \cdots)$

3) Identify running time of preceding train $i - 1$ (T_o^{i-1}), and calculate the historical running time variance of train $i - 1$: $R = var(T_{o_1}^{i-1}, T_{o_2}^{i-1}, \cdots)$

4) Calculate Kalman gain K according to (10);

5) Update the SVR prediction using measurement from train $i - 1$ and obtain optimal estimation for train i: $T_p^{i} = T_{p_{\mathrm{SVR}}}^{i} + K(T_o^{i-1} - T_{p_{\mathrm{SVR}}}^{i})$

4.1.3.4 SVR training

1. Train operation data and analysis

In this study, we established and calibrated our model with real-world train operation data from Wuhan-Guagnzhou HSR, which is 1096 km long and is one of the busiest passenger railway lines in China. It connects to the Guangzhou-Shenzhen HSR line at GZS station, the Hengyang-Liuzhou HSR line at HYE station, and the Shanghai-Kunming HSR line at CSS station, respectively. All the trains operating on this line are equipped with the Chinese Train Control System (CTCS), which allows a maximum speed of 350 km/h and the Automatic Train Supervision system that records the movements of all trains. We considered data from trains in the northbound direction comprising the segment from Guangzhou South (GZS) to Hengyang East (HYE), as shown in Fig. 4-3. The collected data contain 57,796 train records in the selected segment comprising information about train operations from March 24, 2015 to November 10, 2016. The scheduled/actual arrival/departure records of each train and station, the number of trains, dates, occupied tracks, and section length were collected to construct a database with data recorded every minute.

Given unexpected disruptions, the train running times are sometimes longer than the prearranged running times per section. Fig.4-4(a) and (b) show the scheduled and observed train running times per section, respectively, clearly indicating that the scheduled running times have centralized distributions, whereas the observed running times, due to disruptions, have long-tailed distributions. To verify the superior performance of the proposed hybrid model, we compared the performance of SVR and that of the hybrid model on regular and widely distributed running times, as reported in Section 4.1.4.

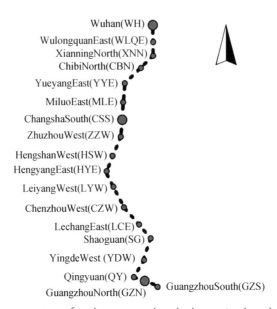

Fig. 4-3 Map of Wuhan-Guangzhou high-speed railway line.

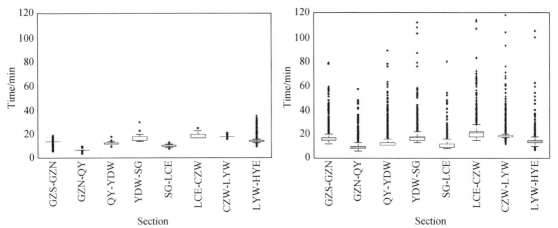

Fig. 4-4 Scheduled and observed train running time distributions per railway section.

2. SVR parameters

Several parameters can be adjusted for SVR. However, to prevent a very high computation time, we optimized the following four essential parameters:

(1) insensitive loss function coefficient ε, which determines the width of the approximation tube.

(2) regularization coefficient C to minimize flatness or the error in the objective function.

(3) kernel function $K(x_i, x)$ that maps data into a higher-dimensional space before solving the ML task as a convex optimization problem. It should be chosen according to different nonlinear relationships in the training data.

(4) Kernel function parameter γ.

We chose ε from (0.001, 0.005, 0.01, 0,05, 0.1}, C from (0.25, 0.5, 1, 2, 4, 8}, kernel function from {linear kernel $K(x,z) = x \cdot z$, polynomial kernel $K(x,z) = (\gamma(x \cdot z+1) + r)^p$,

Gaussian kernel $K(x,z) = \exp(-\gamma\|x-z\|^2)$, sigmoid kernel $K(x,z) = \tanh(\gamma(x \cdot z)+r)$}, and γ from (1, 4, 16, 64, 256}. Then, we optimized these four parameters based on cross-validation, obtaining the best parameters for running time prediction by considering those retrieving the highest goodness of fit calculated by (4-13). After running the SVR with each candidate value, we recorded its goodness-of-fit score on a testing dataset, as shown in Fig. 4-5. According to the cross-validation results, we obtained the best SVR parameters as being $\varepsilon = 0.01$, $C = 1$, Gaussian kernel function, and $\gamma = 64$.

$$score = 1 - \frac{\sum_{T_{test}} (y_i - \hat{y}_i)^2}{(y_i - \bar{y})^2} \tag{4-13}$$

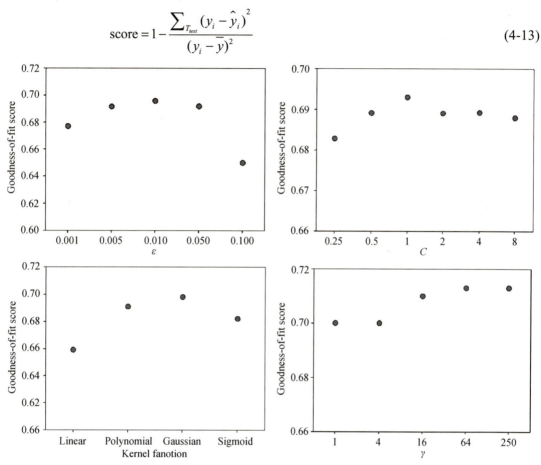

Fig. 4-5 Cross-validation for determining coefficients ε and C, kernel function K, and parameter γ.

4.1.4 Prediction and performance results

4.1.4.1 SVR

We evaluated the SVR prediction accuracy compared to observed values of train running times. Fig. 4-6 shows the comparison of the actual and predicted running times, clearly indicating that the predicted running times, like the scheduled running times, have a centralized distribution mainly because the SVR cannot accurately predict times that are much larger than the schedules due to disruptions.

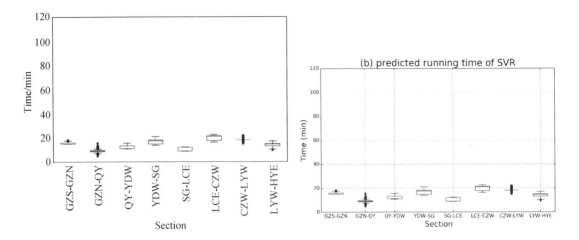

Fig. 4-6　Actual and predicted train running time distributions per railway section.

Then, we evaluated three widely used ML models, namely, random forest, k-nearest neighbors, and ANN as benchmarks to determine the SVR performance. These benchmarks have the following main characteristics:

(1) Random forest is an ML method based on the bagging technique [257] and uses an ensemble of decision trees $\{h(X, \beta_k), k = 1, ...\}$ for mapping vectors of predictor and dependent variables, where X is the input vector and β_k is an independent stochastic variable that decides the growth of every tree. Each tree is a decision tree without pruning and established according to the classification and regression tree principal and bootstrap sampling techniques. For regression, the result of random forest is the average among trees.

(2) The k-nearest neighbors algorithm is based on feature similarity with accuracy determined by the closeness of out-of-sample features resembling the training set. The algorithm first calculates the distance of eigenvalues between input and training data, and then chooses the k nearest neighbors to conduct classification or regression [258]. When used for regression, the output is the value for the object (predicts continuous values) corresponding to the mean (or median) of the values from the k neighbors.

(3) In the ANN, neurons between adjacent layers are fully connected and information flows from the input to the output layer [259]. By comparing the fitted with the observed values, a loss function is obtained and error is backpropagated from the output to the input layer to optimize the weights and remove bias of each neuron [260].

To understand the predictions of SVR and the comparison models, we determined the residual (i.e., difference between observed and predicted values) distribution of each model, as shown in Fig. 4-7. SVR retrieves the narrowest residual distribution around zero, thus indicating its highest accuracy among the evaluated methods. Still, the residuals of the four models have long-tailed distributions, indicating their incapability to accurately predict unexpected situations.

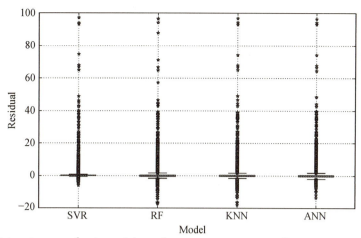

Fig. 4-7 Residual distribution of each model on all sections. (RF, random forest, KNN, k-nearest neighbors)

To quantitatively evaluate model performance, we used an absolute error metric, the mean absolute error (MAE), and a relative error metric, the mean absolute percentage error (MAPE), given by formulas (4-14) and (4-15), respectively. The prediction MAE and MAPE of each model on testing data are shown in Fig. 4-8 and 4-9, where it is clear that SVR retrieves the smallest error among the evaluated methods. The MAE and MAPE of SVR are very low, 0.55 min and 3.7%, respectively, thus confirming the high SVR accuracy that outperforms the other ML models as predictor for real-time train running time estimation.

$$MAE = \frac{1}{N}\sum_{k=1}^{N}\left|\hat{y}_k - y_k\right| \tag{4-14}$$

$$MAPE = \frac{100}{N}\sum_{k=1}^{N}\left|\frac{\hat{y}_k - y_k}{y_k}\right| \tag{4-15}$$

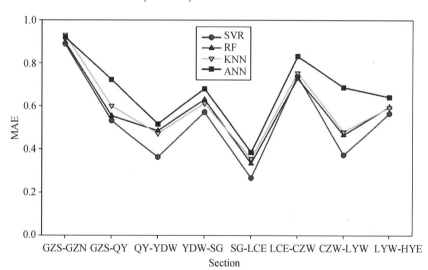

Fig. 4-8 Prediction MAE of SVR and benchmark models.

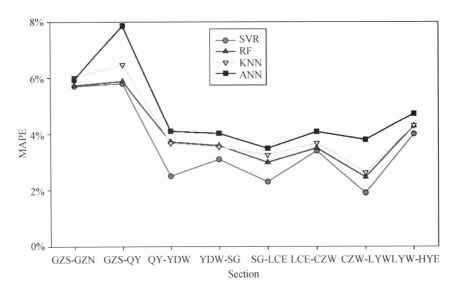

Fig. 4-9　Prediction MAPE of SVR and benchmark models.

Finally, to quantitatively evaluate the SVR performance on outliers, we first identified data from trains which suffered disruptions by considering samples with running times longer than the schedules. Then, we calculated the MAE and MAPE of SVR prediction both on testing data and outliers, as shown in Fig. 4-10 and 4-11. The prediction errors of SVR on outliers are much larger than those on the testing data, with high MAE and MAPE of 9.6 min and 35.0%, respectively. These results confirm that SVR alone is incapable of predicting unexpected situations during real-time train dispatching, being consistent with our assumption and making necessary the KF correction.

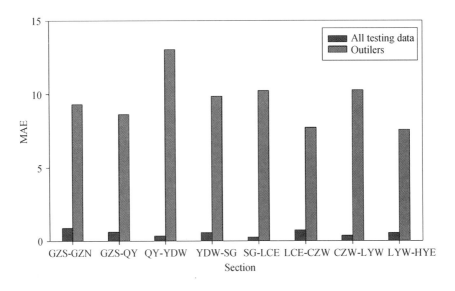

Fig. 4-10　Prediction MAE of SVR on testing data and outliers.

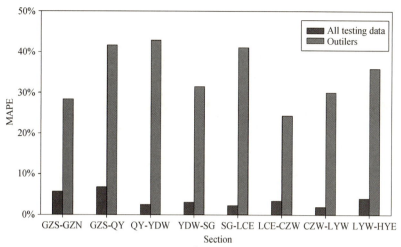

Fig. 4-11   Prediction MAPE of SVR on testing data and outliers.

4.1.4.2   Hybrid model combining SVR and KF

As ML models can be incapable of predicting unexpected situations, we implemented the proposed hybrid model to predict the train running time under any situation. The predicted values of the hybrid model were obtained using the KF on the SVR prediction. To evaluate the hybrid model, we only corrected the predictions on the outliers identified in Section 4.1, whereas the prediction of the other samples within schedule were obtained only from SVR for comparison. We obtained the MAE and MAPE of the hybrid model on outliers and of SVR on regular samples as shown in Fig. 4-12 and 4-13. Applying the KF on the hybrid model greatly reduces the prediction MAE and MAPE from 9.6 to 5.7 min (40.6% improvement), and from 35.0% to 20.7% (40.9% improvement), respectively. Furthermore, the computation time was also substantially reduced, as the online SVR training required an average of 258.7 s per run, whereas only 0.9 s were required using the offline-trained SVR combined with the KF to predict the outliers on a computer endowed with an Intel Core i5-8250U processor.

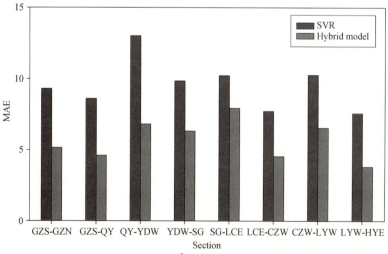

Fig. 4-12   Prediction MAE of SVR and hybrid model on outliers.

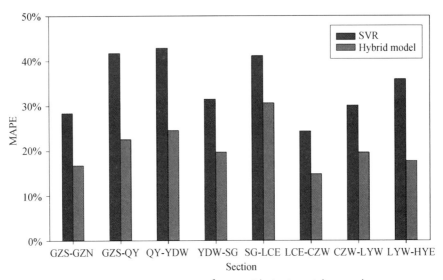

Fig. 4-13 Prediction MAPE of SVR and hybrid model on outliers.

4.1.5 Discussion and conclusion

We propose a hybrid model comprising SVR and KF to improve the disruption handling ability in real-time train dispatching. First, we verified that SVR retrieves small prediction errors and the best performance under normal situations compared to other widely used ML models, namely, random forest, k-nearest neighbors, and ANN, thus suggesting the suitability of SVR for running time prediction. Then, we evaluated the SVR performance on trains which suffered disruptions by unexpected situations, showing that SVR cannot accurately predict the running time in real-time train dispatching under such situations. Therefore, we applied a KF to improve the predicting ability of the ML model. Comparing SVR to the hybrid model confirmed that the KF improves the prediction accuracy under unexpected situations. Furthermore, compared against online training, the computation time was greatly reduced by combining offline-trained SVR and the KF.

In real-time train running time prediction, timeliness and accuracy are essential factors for dispatchers to consider the retrieved information as adequate. The proposed hybrid model simultaneously meets these two requirements. The proposed method is both accurate and efficient for real-time implementation in train dispatching, which can support the decision-making of railway operators and improve the logistics and scheduling of trains within a railway network. Therefore, the proposed model is valuable for railway operations and has been designed considering the real-time requirements that are encountered in practice.

In future research, we will aim to further improve the ML model, as SVR may not be the best-performing model for running time prediction. In addition, as SVR prediction is only for trains within expected schedules, prediction should be updated using the KF under unexpected situations, making the result of the hybrid model dominantly influenced by the latest estimation. This aspect and its effects on the prediction accuracy should be also addressed in future developments.

4.2 A Deep Learning Model for Train Delay Prediction in High-speed Railway Systems

Train delay prediction is one the kernel issues that dispatchers care about, and it is essential for dispatchers to command the train operations. However, inter-train interaction and the heterogeneity of delay influencing factors (including time-series and non-time-series features), make most of the existing predictive models hard to accurately estimate the future status of trains. To address these problems, we developed a deep learning (DL) architecture, which combines long short-term memory (LSTM) and fully-connected (FC) neural network, named LSTM-FC, to consider the influencing factors with different formats separately. In this structure, the non-time-series factors are fed into the FC, while the time-series related factors are fed into the LSTM units to capture the interactions embedded in train groups. To obtain a well-performed model, we firstly optimized the model parameters and compared the losses of model under different involved trains. The Cross-validation of the model training shows that, in a certain range, the larger the train group is, the smaller the final loss and the more stable of the model would be. The predicting results based on testing dataset indicate that LSTM-FC apparently outperforms other classical train delay prediction models on three model evaluation metrics: root mean squared error (RMSE), mean absolute error (MAE) and mean absolute percentage error (MAPE). Then, the model generalization results on two different HSR lines demonstrated that LSTM-FC model could be well applied into HSR lines with different operation features. Finally, the sensitivity analysis clarified the quantitative impacts of each influencing factor on LSTM-FC, which demonstrates that the inter-train interaction is one of the most significant factors that should be considered in the delay prediction work.

4.2.1 Introduction

Despite the availability of advanced communication and control technologies, trains could still be delayed subjecting to various unexpected disruptions, such as bad weather, power outage, and facility failures [25]. In China, according to the statistics of the China Railway Corporation, the average departure punctuality in origination stations for China's 22,000 km High-speed rail (HSR) network is as high as 98.8% in 2016. However, due to various disturbances during their operations, the average punctuality at the final destination stations is less than 90%, though the delays smaller than 5 minutes are considered punctual [240].

After trains are delayed, dispatchers need to estimate the future states of the trains when rescheduling the timetable. Passengers also tend to know the delay information as soon as possible to determine whether they need to change their itineraries. Accurately forecasting train delays can facilitate both the effectiveness of train dispatching and the qualities of services to passengers. Developing advanced techniques to accurately predict train delays is thus of great significance in managing railway operation.

Traditional models on trains' delay propagation, such as event-driven models (i.e., activity-graph and network models) and statistical models (i.e., distribution models and regression models), either simplify the procedures of train operation or set too many mathematical assumptions, which makes this kind of models can hardly reflect the practical operations accurately. The train operation is usually modeled as Markov process, since many researchers believe that the current state of a train subjects to its last state. Şahin establishes a Markov chain model to illustrate the delay propagation and recovery, using the observed historical data collected from a single track line in Turkish State Railways [26]. When data-driven status transition matrix is available, it will be possible to predict train states at certain event time steps and to estimate steady-state delay probabilities. However, data used for modeling in this paper was 6-h and 18-station train-graphs of 7 days on 14-20 July of 2002, and just 6 delay classes that distinguish delay states are used. Supposing the probability of a state change depends on the moment of transition, train delay predictions are modeled by a non-stationary Markov chain [106]. But in a practical situation, dispatchers will think over the adjacent trains and they will also make decisions according to the effects of historical decisions. It is essential to establish models that can imitate the decisions of dispatchers. Thanks to the application of Automatic Train Supervision system in HSR in China, historical data of train operations are available now. And the development of Artificial Intelligence (AI) has provided us with advanced approaches to process and make use of high-dimension and non-linear data, which enables us to establish better-performed models for train delay prediction from the Big-Data perspective. One of the most successfully used AI approaches is Neural Networks (NN), and many variants of NNs have been proposed and applied in different applications scenarios, such as Convolutional Neural Network (CNN) in image processing [174] and Recurrent Neural Network (RNN) in sequence/timeseries analysis [176]. The RNN, with strong feedback abilities, is capable of using the past information, and this feature provides a brand-now idea for recognizing the potential train interaction from vehicle operation data. As so far as our knowledge, RNN-based models have been already successfully applied into travel time estimation in highway [178] and air transport [179], and all these researches verified that the RNN-based models outperform other ML predictors due to their feedback mechinism, but there have been no applications in train delay/travel time prediction. Therefore, in this paper, based on an improved RNN model, named Long Short-Term Memory (LSTM), we developed a DL architecture to capture temporal dependences in train operation data. This architecture, called LSTM-FC which combines the LSTM and Fully-Connected (FC) neural network, was proposed considering the different data format of delay influencing factors, where time-series variables are fed into LSTM, and non-time-series variables are fed into FC. The function of this architecture is two folds:

1) Factors with different formats were fed into different NNs: the attribute of delay influencing

factor is heterogeneous (timeseries format and non-timeseries format), but traditional predictors all treat them as non-timeseries features, which makes them neglect much potential information embedded in timeseries data.

2) Capturing train interaction: the timeseries features of a train group are fed into LSTM-FC whose LSTM units have feedback mechanism to capture the train interaction.

To the best knowledge of the authors, this paper is the first attempt to predict train delays using deep learning models, also considering the interaction among trains in a group. We conducted a large quantity of experiments and analyses to develop a reasonable LSTM-FC model to investigate the effectiveness of train delay prediction.

4.2.2 Literature review

Train delay management is challenging for both field researchers and practitioners. It has been a subject undergoing intense research for decades and a host of delay prediction models and algorithms have been proposed to improve rail operations [2]. Most recently, the 2018 Railroad Problem Solving Competition launched by INFORMS has created the topic "Predicting Near-Term Train Schedule Performance and Delay" using operation records [268]. In general, there are two types of train delay prediction models, namely mathematical model-driven methods and data-driven models. The former tries to estimate the train arrival/departure time by applying interpretable formulations correspondingto the train events, such as track and signal occupation. The latter tends to mine train operation data to come up with solutions for delay prediction, such as statistical models, computational intelligence, and ML models.

4.2.2.1 Mathematical model-driven methods

Model-fitting approaches use time-event graphs [269], event-activity graphs[82], and phase-type distributions to calculate secondary delays and establish delay propagation models [93]. Carey and Kwieciński proposed simple stochastic approximations to derive knock-on delays and simulate the interactions between trains [75]; based on the approximations, the authors developed and assessed a simulation model to predict knock-on delays at the stations [270]. Yuan and Hansen proposed an analytical stochastic model of delay propagation that could realistically estimate knock-on delays caused by route conflicts and late transfer connections[49]. A review of the previous literature reveals that it is hard to find generalizableor even specific railway traffic control system models that can handle train operation dynamics in real time[7, 8]. Most of the proposed models are for abstracted problems that obtain solutions based on simplifying assumptions, predetermined rules, sets of contingency plans, intuition, and personal experience. In practice, however, dispatchers must potentially integrate all of these along with supporting data to obtain structured and unstructured information in order to make necessary decisions.

4.2.2.2　Data-driven methods

1. Computational intelligence models.

Kecman and Goverde employed a timed-event graph with dynamic arc weights to develop a microscopic model for the accurate prediction of train event times[232]. Using operational constraints and the actual headway times between adjacent trains, their system could model train interactions with high accuracy. Sahin generated a transition matrix of state-to-state transition probabilities using actual records of train movements[26]; however, the data used for modeling was comprised of 6-h, 18-station train-graphs covering 7 d (14-20 July, 2002) and employed only six delay classes for distinguishing the delay states. A fuzzy Petri net (FPN) model for estimating train delays that uses expert knowledge to define the fuzzy sets and rules to transform the expertise into a model to calculate train delays was proposed in [271]. An adaptive network fuzzy inference system (ANFIS) model based on historical data of train delays in the Serbian Railways system was set up in[28]. An HSR running state model based on triangular fuzzy number workflow nets of fuzzy train activity times was generated using data for 21–24 June 2012 from five stations between Beijing South and Dezhou East in the Beijing-Shanghai HSR system [109]. Using the ability of Bayesian networks to update the train running statuses in a timely manner based on new operational data, Zilko et al. attempted to use a non-parametric Bayesian network for predicting the disruption length to develop a Copula Bayesian networks model to assess the factors influencing the lengths of disruptions [110]. In [235], the authors applied a hybrid Bayesian network model to predict HSR delays using the operational records of the Wuhan-Guangzhou HSR; the proposed hybrid model was able to obtain about 80% accuracy for the prediction over a 60-min horizon.

2. ML models.

ML models learn information from input data and map it to outputs using activation functions. Such models are powerful tools for fitting nonlinear and high-dimensional data, however, less straightforwardly interpretable than statistical models. As noted by Wallander and Mäkitalo, data mining approaches can be used to obtain a better understanding of train delay concatenation and developmore robust timetables and powerful support systems for real-time dispatching[263]. The most widely used conventional ML approaches in train delay prediction are ANNs [272, 273], although such networks have been outperformed in train delay prediction by support vector regression (SVR) systems[118]. Other ML applications for train delay prediction include the use of the k-nearest neighbor (KNN) approaches to estimate dwell times at shortstops during real-time scheduling of Dutch railway traffic [274]. In another study by the authors, the accuracy of predicting delay recoveries using multiple linear regression, SVR, ANN, and random forest regression (RFR) are compared and it was shown that when the prediction tolerance is less than 1 minute, the RFR model outperforms the other models with a prediction accuracy of up to 80.4% [52]. ML approaches are found superior to computational intelligence for handling train operational data owing to their reliance on fewer internal and mathematical restrictive assumptions. In all ML applications of train delay estimation, the input data on all individual trains are required; however, the train interactions have not been taken into account. Furthermore, because none of the existing ML models use a time-series-based approach, none of them is capable of incorporating diverseinput data. These are serious drawbacks in a train delay prediction process because train delays are influenced by both time-series and non-time-series features. Moreover, train interactions are another part of challenges caused by the interlocking and continuity of train operations. It is, therefore, important to take train interactions into account through the application of appropriate techniques in conjunction with historical train operation data.

Motivated by the successful applications of LSTM and the drawbacks of existing train delay prediction models, we decided to establish train delay predicting models based on LSTM and FC neurons and treat input timeseries factors as a sequence to capture the potential train interaction. The most important advantages of our work includ: 1) features in different formats are fed into different units to better recognize the influences; and 2) for the prediction of each train delay, the input of our model has several adjacent trains which are regarded as sequences to recognize the cumulative interaction carried by time series data.

4.2.3 Preliminaries

4.2.3.1 Delay-influencing factors

Trains are interactive since they are interlocked by tracks, signals, dispatching system and so on. In particular, when disturbances occur, these interactions are more remarkable, due to the resource occupation conflicts. Figure 4-14 shows a disturbance case of Wuhan-Guangzhou HSR in China, where a disturbance happened in section YDW-SG. Apparently, due to this disturbance, a number of trains were delayed, called knock-on delay. Due to the interlock constraints, the future delays of succeeding trains are highly related to the delays of their preceding trains when a delayed preceding train occupies the routes of the succeeding trains. And we can see that the delay propagated. Figure 4-14 shows the train delay interactive relations, where we can see that each time-event point is spatiotemporally related to its previous points. As far as we know, all existing train delay prediction models just take a single train's features as input, without considering the interaction between trains. To address the drawbacks of existing models, in this research, we propose LSTM-FC model which takes the features of multiple trains at their all past stations/sections as inputs and treats these trains as a sequence to capture the rules of train interaction. For example, in Figure 1 (b) if we want to predict the delay time of train i at s_{n+k} (point P), then, the inputs of our model include the known features of train $i, i-1, \cdots$ at the previous stations/section $s_n, s_{n-1}, \cdots, s_1$ ..

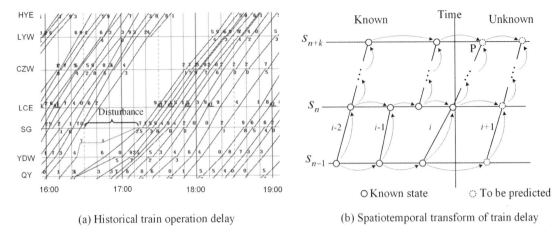

(a) Historical train operation delay   (b) Spatiotemporal transform of train delay

Figure 4-14   Real-time dispatching scenario (horizontal axis represents time; vertical axis represents space).

In addition, trains delays are also related to other timetable, infrastructure, weather, and other operational-related factors. To better understand the influence of the timetable- and infrastructure-related factors, we obtained train operation data from the HSR in the territory of the Guangzhou railway corporation. The obtained records include the scheduled, practical timetable and the infrastructure data. We ultimately selected 10 parameters that are more likely to have impacts on train delays, including:

The factors that are related to the scheduled timetable:

(1) T, scheduled travel time in each preceding section

(2) W, scheduled dwelling time at each previous station

(3) I, scheduled interval with preceding train at each previous station

(4) S, scheduled stops at two previous adjacent stations

The factors related to the practical timetable:

(5) D, delays at each previous station (including arrival delays and departure delays)

(6) T', practical traveled time in each preceding section

(7) I', practical interval with preceding train at each preceding station

(8) W', practical dwelling time at each preceding station

Lastly, the factors that are related to the infrastructure:

(9) L, section length

(10) N, occupiedtrack at the station.

4.2.3.2   Train Operation Data

In this study, we established and calibrated our DL model with real-world train operation data from two HSR lines in China,namely, the W-G HSR and the X-S HSR. The former one is 1096 km that is one of the busiest passenger railway lines. It joins to the Guangzhou-Shenzhen HSR line at GZS station, the Hengyang-Liuzhou HSR line at HYE station, and the Shanghai-Kunming HSR line at CSS station, respectively. All the trains operating on this line are equipped with the Chinese Train Control System (CTCS) which allows a maximum speed of

350 km/h and the Automatic Train Supervision [255] system that records the movements of all trains. The latter one (X-S HSR) is 514 km and the maximum speed of the trains is 250 km/h. In this study, trains in the upstream direction of these lines from GZS to HYE are located in the southern part of the W-G HSR line and trains from SZ to PN are located in the southern part of the X-S HSR line. As shown in Figure 4-15, the stations GZS and HYE on the W-G HSR line and SZ on the X-S HSR line are intersection stations where trains originate, terminate, turn around, and cross lines.

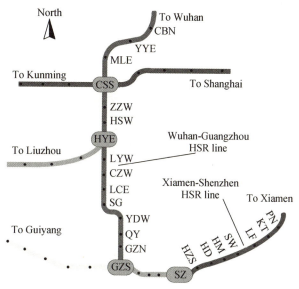

Figure 4-15   Sketch map of W-G HSR line.

The collected data of the W-G HSR include 57796 train records in the GZS-HYE segment and that of the X-S HSR line include 41186 train records. These records includetrain operation records during the period of March 24, 2015 to November 10, 2016. The scheduled/actual arrival/departure records of each train at each station, the train numbers, dates, occupied tracks, and section length are all recorded in our database and the data are recorded every minute. We conducted some pre-processing on the obtained data including: 1) filling missing data using the weighted means of the adjacent records, 2) deleting abnormal delays when the trains may be canceled due to a large delay (larger than 120 minutes), and 3) deleting abnormal delay recoveries that are larger than the scheduled buffer time in the sections. Finally, we separated the clean data into the training dataset that contained the first 75% of the delayed trains and the validating dataset that included the last 25% of the delayed trains.

4.2.4   Methodology

4.2.4.1   LSTM

The LSTM is an improved RNN for long-term dependency which has a gate mechanism to capture long-term dependencies. The LSTM can use information from a previous forward pass over the neural network to the last time step, which is capable of recognizing information conveyed by time-series data[264]. The cell architecture of the LSTM is shown in Figure 4-16. The most important part of the LSTM is its memory cell state c_t, which acts as an accumulator to store useful information obtained at each step. The cell state can be written, utilized, and cleared by its self-controlled gate mechanism. A new input enters the model for every time step, and the learned information is written in the cell state if the input gate i_t is activated. Also, the past cell state c_{t-1} can be forgotten if the forget gate f_t is on. In addition, whether the cell state c_t is mapped as output y_t is further controlled by the output gate o_t. The entire process is defined by Equations (4-16)–(4-21):

$$i_t = \sigma(W_{xi}x_t + W_{hi}h_{t-1} + W_{ci} \odot c_{t-1} + b_i) \tag{4-16}$$

$$f_t = \sigma(W_{xf}x_t + W_{hf}h_{t-1} + W_{cf} \odot c_{t-1} + b_f) \tag{4-17}$$

$$c_t = f_t \odot c_{t-1} + i_t \odot tanh(W_{xc}x_t + W_{hc}h_{t-1} + b_c) \tag{4-18}$$

$$O_t = \sigma(W_{xo}x_t + W_{ho}h_{t-1} + W_{co} \odot c_t + b_O) \tag{4-19}$$

$$h_t = o_t \odot tanh(c_t) \tag{4-20}$$

$$tanh(x) = \frac{1 - e^{-2x}}{1 + e^{-2x}}, \quad x \in (-\infty, \infty) \tag{4-21}$$

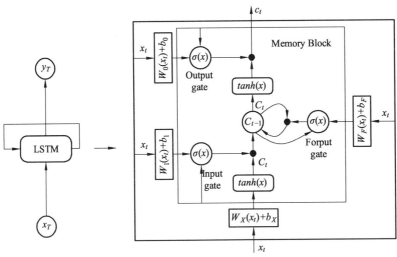

Figure 4-16　Architecture of LSTM cell.

where $\odot$ indicates the element-wise multiplication of two vectors; $tanh(x)$ is a threshold function ranging from 0 to 1 that indicates how much information is stored, utilized, and discarded; and $\sigma(x)$ is the activation function mapping the nonlinear relationship between input and output.

4.2.4.2　Architecture of LSTM-FC

Factors of time-series and non-time-series commonly influence train delays. To develop a capable architecture to handle different format data, in this section, we proposed a novel deep learning network which combines LSTM units and Fully-Connected neurons, named LSTM-FC to predict train delays. The structure of LSTM-FC is shown in Figure 4-17. The proposed LSTM-FC is composed of LSTM units and fully-connected neural layers, where the LSTM units are employed to capture the train interactions among time-series factors while the fully-connected neural layers are applied to recognize the influence of non-time-series factors. In the LSTM structure, the previous layers have a many-to-many structure to store and utilize past information, while the last layer has a many-to-one structure to map all learned information as a one-dimension vector. LSTM architecture treats every l trains as sequences, and each train represents a time-step. Assuming that we intend to predict delay of train i at s_{n+k} (train i dwells at station s_n), we use the features of train $(i-l+1)$ to i from station s_1 to s_n to predict the arrival delay of train i at s_{n+k}, and use the features of train $(i-l)$ to i-1 from station s_1 to s_n to predict the arrival delay of train i at s_{n+k}, and so forth, where i represents the ordered train number, s_n represents the station number and k represent the prediction step.

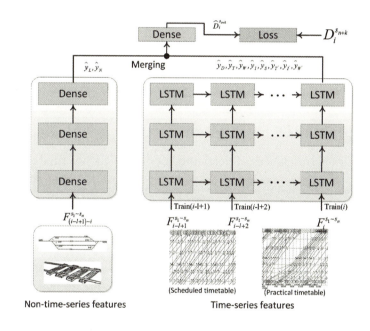

Figure 4-17　Structure of LSTM-FC.

To merge these different architectures, a fusion technique is employed to concatenate the output vectors of LSTM and fully-connected layers. In this process, the outputs of these two structures will be concatenated in horizontal axis, which means: if the output dimension of fully-connected layers is (samples, M) and LSTM is (samples, N), where M and N are determined by the number of units in the last layer, the merged vector will be (samples, M+N). Then, the merged vectors pass through a fully-connected neuron to upgrade the weights of each element. Finally, to quantify the quality of the proposed model, an objective function which compares the estimated delay $\widehat{D}_i^{S_{n+k}}$ with the observed delay $D_i^{S_{n+k}}$ to calculate the loss is chosen. In LSTM-FC, the loss function is also known as the mean squared error (MSE), shown in Equation (4-22). The loss function is gradually minimized by back-propagating the error from the output layer to input layer to update the weights and biases of each layer.

$$loss = \frac{1}{N} \sum_{i=1}^{N} (\widehat{D}_i - D_i)^2 \qquad (4\text{-}22)$$

The time-series variables are transformed into iterative sequences, as shown in Figure 4-18. For example, if there are l ($l=l_1+l_2-1$) trains in a sequence, the time-series feature set (F) of each l train is transformed into sequences that are fed into the LSTM layers. At the same time, the non-time-series variables of the l trains are fed into the FCNN architecture.

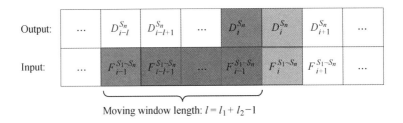

Figure 4-18   Map of time-series variables as a sequence.

4.2.4.3   Experiments for the model selection

To achieve better performances of delay prediction models, we tried different experiments on model parameters and architectures. Figure 4-19 shows the results of hidden layer and neurons selection, where bar graph represents the time cost, and scatter lines indicate the loss of the model. The left-hand graph indicates that both the training loss and validation loss decrease with the increasing of hidden layers and they reach a plateau level when the layer size is larger than 3. The right-hand graph shows the results of neuron number selection, where training and validation loss firstly decrease steadily with the growth of neurons but the validation loss will increase significantly when the neurons continue to raise. These results are intuitive: when the layers and neurons are few, the model structure is simple, and the data are under-fitted, while when the model structure is becoming complicated, the data were over-fitted. Finally, to develop a well-fitted model avoiding over-fitting, we chose the model with three LSTM hidden layers and three FCNN as our standard architecture, each LSTM layer with 70 units and each FCNN layer with 50 units.

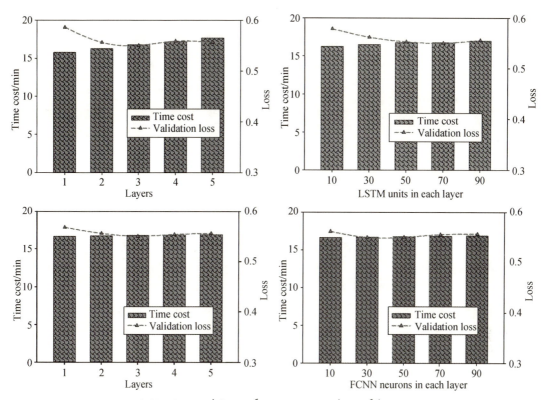

Figure 4-19　Cross-validation for sensitivity analysis of the LSTM-FC.

Because the selected model structure presented in Figure 4-19 was developed based on the prediction at HYE, the ninth station of the W-G HSR line, the input features and training and testing samples may be different when we run the model for predictions at other stations. Therefore, we further applied *ReduceLROnPlateau*techniques[275] to reduce the global learning rate to 50% when validation loss did not decline in three consecutive steps to increase the robustness of our model. Furthermore, to avoid local optima, we used the *RMSProp* optimizer[276], which updates the local learning rate according to the training process and the mini-batch technique, in which the batch-size equaled 105 (daily average trains). All selected parameters of the proposed LSTM-FC model are listed in Table 4-1.Other packages used in this research include TensorFlow[277], Scikit-learn[245], Pandas[278]1,and Numpy[279].

Table 4-1　Optional parameters used in the model optimization

Model architecture:	3 LSTM layers (70 units each)
	3 FCNN layers (50 neurons each)
Optimizer:	RMSprop
Initial learning rate:	1×10^{-3}
Techniques to avoid overfitting:	Cross-Validation
	ReduceLROnPlateau
Proportion of learning rate reduction:	50%

Training step/epochs:	50
Mini-batch-size:	105
Training/testing dataset	First 75%/last 25%

4.2.5　Model evaluation

To evaluate the performance of the proposed model, we selected three other commonly used train delay prediction models as our baseline models, namely, an ANN, an SVR, and a Markov model (MM). The brief features of each of these baseline models are:

(1) In the ANN, the neurons between the adjacent layers are fully connected and the information flow is transferred from the input layer to the output layer [259]. By comparing the fitted values with the observed values, the loss function is obtained and the errors are back-propagated from the output layer to the input layer to optimize the weights and biases of each neuron [280]. Compared with the ANN, the recurrent connection from the output layer to the input layer at each time step of the LSTM has the advantage to capture the information embedded in time-series data.

(2) The SVR, whose main principle is to map data into a high-dimensional feature space via a nonlinear relationship, is a type of SVM for regression problems [239]. Using the input X, the SVR calculates the evaluated value $\hat{Y}$ and sets a threshold ε to evaluate the difference between $\hat{Y}$ and the true value Y.

(3) An MM mainly deals with discrete-state problems based on the assumption that any state occurring at the next time checkpoint is only subject to the current state[281]. We can only use the current delay to predict the next-step delay in the case of the conditional probability of the transition between the adjacent states.

We chose three commonly used prediction error metrics, namely, the RMSE, MAE, and MAPE to evaluate our model. The definitions of the error metrics are shown in Equation (4-23), (4-24), and (4-25) where y_i is observed value; $\hat{y}_i$ is evaluated value; and N represents the sample size. The RMSE is used to evaluate the overall performance of the models, the MAE is chosen to evaluate the absolute prediction error, and the MAPE is selected to evaluate the relative prediction error.Because the main purpose of the predictive model is to analyze future states of delayed trains (i.e., states larger than 4 minutes labeled by the China Railway Corporation), all the metrics were calculated on delays. Furthermore, different lengths of delay may lead to various influences on the railway operation and in real-time dispatching, dispatchers tend to focus more on longer delays, which makes the accurate prediction of larger train delays more significant. Therefore, the proposed model was also evaluated on the largest 20% of the train delays. The distribution of the delays of all the stations is shown in Figure 4-20.

$$RMSE = \sqrt{\frac{1}{N}\sum_{i=1}^{N}(\hat{y}_i - y_i)^2} \tag{4-23}$$

$$MAE = \frac{1}{N}\sum_{i=1}^{N}\left|\hat{y}_i - y_i\right| \tag{4-24}$$

$$MAPE = \frac{100}{N}\sum_{i=1}^{N}\left|\frac{\hat{y}_i - y_i}{y_i}\right| \tag{4-25}$$

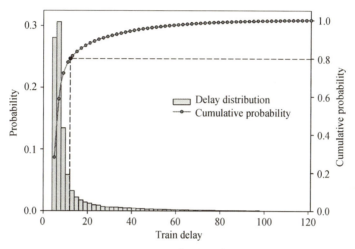

Figure 4-20　Delay distribution.

To investigate the performacne and generalizability of the proposed model, we ran it to predict train behavior at stations on the W-G HSR line and another HSR line—the X–S HSR line—that had a lower operational speed limit and a lower train density than the W–G HSR. The model performances for the W-G and X-S HSR lines are presented in Figures 4-21 and 4-22, respectively.

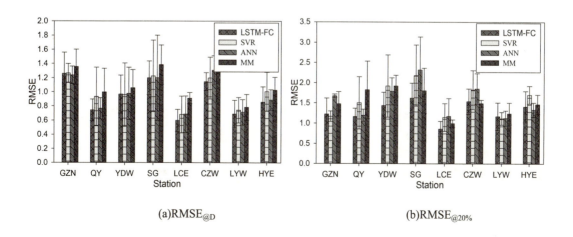

(a)RMSE$_{@D}$ (b)RMSE$_{@20\%}$

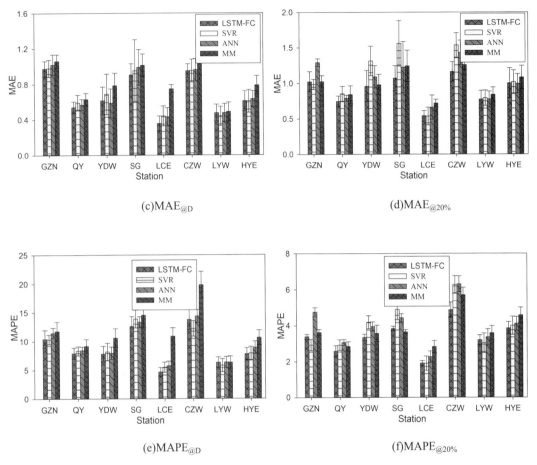

(c)MAE$_{@D}$ (d)MAE$_{@20\%}$

(e)MAPE$_{@D}$ (f)MAPE$_{@20\%}$

Figure 4-21　Model performances for W–G HSR line.

In Figures 4-21 and 4-22, the error lines in the figures represent standard deviations of the respective mini-batches. These figures indicate that the LSTM-FC model also outperforms other baseline models in terms of the RMSE, MAE, and MAPE, except for predictions at station GZN on the W–G HSR line and HD on the X–S HSR line, where some metrics of the LSTM-FC were slightly larger than those of the SVR. However, this is understandable because these two stations are the second stations in the upstream direction of their respective lines, and the inputs only included states at the previous station; in this case, the LSTM-FC, which was specially designed to capture spatiotemporal dependencies, was less suitable. In addition, as listed in Tables 4-2 and 4-3, the frequency of the delayed trains was quite low at these two stations because they were close to the original stations, resulting in fewer dependencies to be captured by the LSTM-FC. Error lines on the bars indicate that the LSTM-FC was also highly stable due to its relatively small standard deviation for mini-batch data. According to Figures 4-21 and 4-22, the prediction errors for stations differed because they were highly dependent on the scheduled running time (travel time) in previous sections, as illustrated in Figure 4-23.

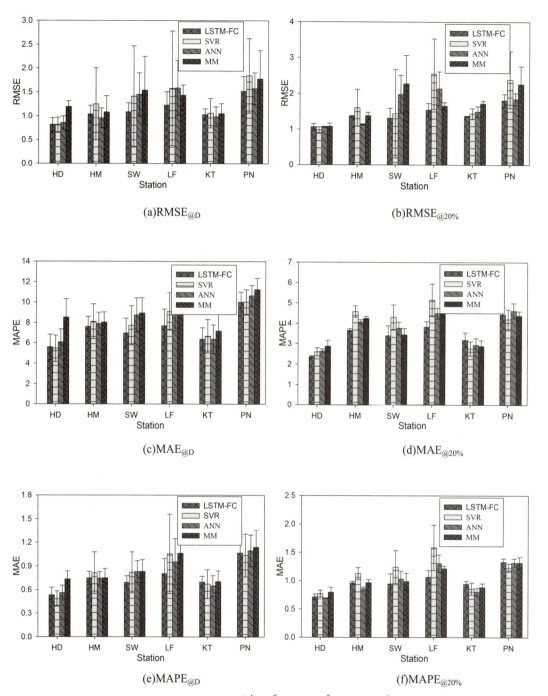

Figure 4-22　Model performances for X-S HSR line.

Table 4-2　Delay frequency for W-G HSR line

Stations	GZN	QY	YDW	SG	LCE	CZW	LYW	HYE
Training dataset	1876	7066	5469	4877	5957	8714	8869	7641
Testing dataset	894	3828	2866	3230	3863	8347	7911	6483

Table 4-3　Delay frequency for X-S HSR line

Stations	HD	HM	SW	LF	KT	PN
Training dataset	1062	1305	1538	1403	1478	1451
Testing dataset	652	871	1015	927	1032	934

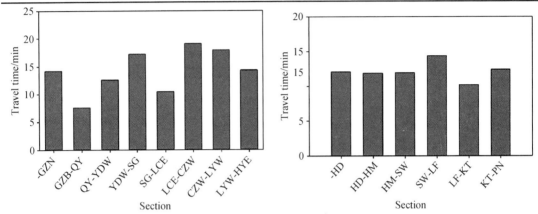

Figure 4-23　Average running time in the previous section

4.2.6　Conclusions

In this research, we developed a deep learning network to predict train delays. Viewing of that in the railway system, train interactions are very common due to the interlock of infrastructure, and we proposed a LSTM-FC model which combines LSTM and Fully-Connected (FC) neural network and takes adjacent trains as a sequence, to capture the cumulative interactions embedded in train operation data. We investigated the interactions among different trains in a group by changing input trains based on cross-validation, and carried out performance comparison with other baseline models. Then the generalization of proposed LSTM-FC model was validated on two different HSR lines. Also, the sensitivity of input features was analyzed. The following conclusions were obtained:

(1) LSTM-FC model, based on the RMSE, MAE, and MAPE error evaluation metrics, have the best performances compared with ANN, SVR, and MM.

(2) Model generalization shows that LSTM-FC model can evidently outperform other baseline models, when it has multiple past stations as inputs, or the delay frequency is relatively high, and LSTM-FC model can be well generalized to different HSR lines.

Our future work can be proceeded by considering the train heterogeneities, time and space differences in timetables, which implies that trains will be divided into different samples regarding their stops, originating time periods, and originating stations. Also, modeling train delay propagation from the view of general railway networks is also one of our interests.

Chapter 5

Confliction management of HSR

5.1 Modelling high-speed trains using triangular fuzzy number workflow nets

In this study, we propose the use of workflow nets to study the issues associated with derivation of the running states of trains. Triangular fuzzy numbers are introduced to express the train activity times and to aid in the modelling of high-speed train running processes using workflow nets. A workflow net links all the activities of train running processes in a certain sequence called a train running workflow net for high-speed trains. The main job of a triangular fuzzy number workflow net is triangular fuzzy number operation. The principles of this operation are discussed in this study. The connotations of the two modes of operation of train running workflow nets—sequential mode and alternative mode—are also analysed. In addition, methods for calculating the time duration during which a triangular fuzzy number workflow net operates, both in sequential mode and alternative mode, for high-speed trains are proposed and proved. Train activity times and running status can be forecast by executing our proposed triangular fuzzy number workflow nets.

5.1.1 Introduction

The future running states of a train are dependent on the current train running status, train operation plan, interferences, and redundancy time—the time set for relieving the delay time, improving stability, and resisting disturbance to the train diagram. A model from which the running status of a train can be derived and which can provide assistance in the making of decisions about the running of the train is needed. Understanding the real-time trajectory and deriving the train running status of high-speed rail is important as it can result in features and advantages such as high-density, high punctuality, and high security.

Due to the randomness inherent in high-speed train operations, a large number of random factors need to be considered for effective railway traffic control and so it is difficult to quantify train running processes. Studies often focus on static time modelling of train running processes in which train running times are predicted using historical track occupation data [282]. In addition, simulation methods are frequently used in these studies of train running processes [283].

The software 'RailSys' considers different railway traffic control strategies and proposes solutions when trains deviate from the plan during simulation [284]. The abovementioned studies, however, cannot state the real train running situation well. If there are disturbances in the train running process, there is usually uncertainty about the time at which the event-activities occurred in the sections and at the stations. Many optimization models and algorithms have been made for railway operations [285, 286]. A time event graph can express the train running processes in situations where timingsof the train activities are fixed; however, it does not work when these timings are variable.

The running process of trains is a series formed by the event-activities that occur both in the sections and at the stations. Event-activity is usually used to express production procedures [287]. Event-activity networks are used to model railway transportation networks[288]. Time event graphs are used to model railway systems[289] and can effectively calculate delay propagations[290]. Time event graphs are widely used for train running status derivation in the process of railway timetable rescheduling [269]. If we can describe train running processes by means of workflows, we can effectively study train running characteristics and deduce train running statuses.

The key issue associated with the expressing of a train running process is the determinationof the train running time in the sections and the station dwell time while taking into account the variety of random factors. Huisman and Boucherie [228] developed a stochastic model that captures both scheduled and unscheduled train movements in sections and from which running time distributions for each train service can be obtained. Further, Huisman [291] developed a stochastic model that can forecast delays on a section in a railway network and calculate delay distributions both for transient and stationary processes.

Train running status deduction has also been studied as a part of research into train running conflict detection and resolution. Branch-and-bound optimization algorithms such as Lagrangian relaxation, full/implicit numeration method, expert systems, and simulation methods are widely used in inter-train conflict detection and resolution [292]. The optimizing capacity utilization of the station model is established by estimating knock-on train delays[49] Mascis [293] viewed the problem of inter-train conflicts as a job-shop scheduling program with no buffer, and proposed a solution based on artificial intelligence. Cheng[294] proposed a hybrid method comprising network-based simulation and event-driven simulation to resolve resource conflicts in train traffic rescheduling. His study used a network graph model to support the calculations in the simulation to solve the problem efficiently. The stochastic models and skills mentioned above can calculate and provide a recommended value for the train running time; however, because of the uncertainty of railway operation and the inaccuracy of the model, the fuzziness characteristics of train running processes cannot be reflected effectively.

In this study, a conceptual model of train running processes is proposed in which triangular fuzzy numbers are introduced to describe the timings of the train activities. A train running workflow net with triangular fuzzy numbers is constructed by the convergence of all train activities for high-speed trains. The connotations of the two operation modes of workflow nets—sequential mode and alternative mode—are also analysed.

The remainder of this study is organised as follows. A conceptual model of a train running process is described in section 5.1.2; the basic theories underlying workflow nets, including basic Petri nets and workflow nets theory, are introduced in section 5.1.3; a workflow net for high-speed train running process modelling with triangular fuzzy numbers is constructed in section 5.1.4; and methods for calculating the time duration of a triangular fuzzy number workflow net operated both in sequential mode and alternative mode for high-speed trains are proposed and proved in section 5.1.5.

The model presented in this study takes into consideration the variable time of train running processes and can deduce the possible future running status of a train based on the train running plan and disturbances. The timings of train activities and running status can be forecast by executing the triangular fuzzy number workflow nets. It can calculate in the time domain when the trains will finish their activities. The model discussed in this study can describe the controllable stochastic of the train running process better than other models. It can be used as a very important tool for train running conflict detection and train operation adjustments.

5.1.2 Conceptual model of a train running process

Topological graph theory is a branch of graph theorythat can reflect the relationships of train activities intuitively and describe the trajectory of the running times of trains. Train activities, including arrival at stations and departure from stations, are defined as train events. Thus, the sequence of the duration of these events can be reflected by a topological graph. The arrival/departure time, the planned/actual running time, the planned/actual dwell time, the redundancy time, and the random interference time of each train can be marked in the topological graph. The running status of a train can be realized by derivation of the time along the forward direction. Figure 5-1 is an example of a conceptual model of a train running process expressed by a topological graph.

In Figure 5-1, the circles represent the arrival/departure events, $A_{i,j}$is the time at which train i arrives at station s_j, and $D_{i,j}$ is the time at which train i departs from station s_j. The one-way solid arrows reflect the relationship of train running times in the sections whereas the dashed arrows reflect the arrival-departure time relationship. The two-way solid arrow represents the constraint relations between high-speed train events.

The triple alongside each arrow indicates the train running parameters. The parameters of the triple alongside a one-way solid arrow represent,in order, the planned train running time in sections, the redundant running time, and the delayed running time. The parameters of the triple alongside a one-way dashed arrow represent, in order, the planned train dwell time in stations, the redundant dwell time, and the delayed dwell time. The parameters of the triple alongside the two-way solid arrow represent, in order, the planned intervaltime between event-activities, the redundant safety interval time (the difference between the planned safety interval time and the minimum safety interval time, which should be guaranteed), and the delayed time of the train event. In order to distinguish the delayed running time from the delayed dwell time, the delayed dwell time parameter is given in parentheses.

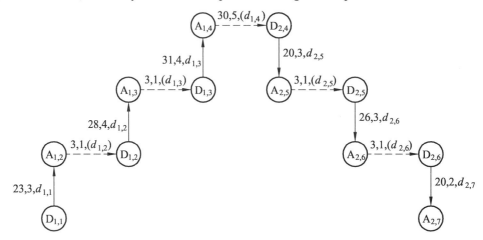

Figure 5-1　Conceptual model of a train running process expressed by topological graph.

In Figure 5-1, the triple alongside the one-way solid arrow between events $D_{1,1}$ and $A_{1,2}$ signifies that the planned time from station s_1 to station s_2 for train T_1 is 23 min, the redundant running time is 3 min, and the delayed running time may be $d_{1,1}$. The triple alongside the one-way dashed arrow between events $A_{1,2}$ and $D_{1,2}$ signifies that the planned dwell time for train T_1 in station s_2 is 3 min, the redundant dwell time is 1 min, and the delayed dwell time may be $(d_{1,2})$. The triple alongside the two-way solid arrow signifies that there is a connection event between trains T_1 and T_2. If train T_1 arrives at station s_4 and the connecting time is met, train T_2 can start from station s_4. The planned connecting time is 30 min, redundant time is 5 min, and the delayed time may be $(d_{1,4})$ due to the delayed arrival time of train T_1. The values of the delayed running time and the delayed dwell time are subject to the statistics of historical train running data or experience.

In cases where the current train running status is known, considering the planned train running time, possible delayed time, and the utilization of redundancy time, the train running status derivation can be realized by means of a topological graph. However, the train running status derivation process is not intuitive when done this way due to the complex structure of the topological graph.

5.1.3　Basic theories of workflow nets

Definition 1 (Petri net). A Petri net is a process model that can describe and reflect the evolution and development of a system. A Petri net consists of places, transitions, and arcs.

A Petri net is a five-tuple $PN = (P, T, I, O, M_0)$, where P is a finite set of states, called *places*; *T* is a finite set of *transitions*; *I* (*P* × *T*) ∪ (*T* × *P*) is a set of flow relations, called *arcs*,between *places* and *transitions* (or between *transitions* and *places*); *O* is a finite *arc* set of *T* to *P*; and M_0 is the initial mark.

Definition 2 (Workflow net).A Petri net is called a workflow net if and only if the following conditions hold:

(1) There are two special *places*, starting *placei* and ending *placeo,* in *PN*.

(2) $\forall i \in P$, st. $^{\bullet}i = \phi$;

(3) $\forall o \in P$, st. $o^{\bullet} = \phi$;

(4) $p_i,t_i \in P \bigcup T$,$p_i$and $t_i$are all on the path from *i* to *o*.

Activityis the elementary unit of a workflow net. *Transition* corresponds to the process conditions and *place* corresponds to the tasks. An activityis formed by two *transitions* and one *place* in a series connection.

Construction of workflow nets for high-speed train running processes

The high-speed train running process shown in Table 5-1 is composed of two parts: run-in-stations (including station dwell) and run-in-sections.

Table 5-1　High-speed train running process

Serial number	Train events	Remarks
1	Train departs from the starting station	(1) The stations between the starting station and the terminal station are called intermediate stations.
2	Train runs in section 1	
3	Train arrives at station 2	
4	Train stops at station 2	(2) If the train is a nonstop train at station 2, then serial numbers 3, 4, and 5 should be merged into one event called passing by station 2.
5	Train departs from station 2	
6	Train runs in section 2	
…	…	(3) In this discussion, the activities in which the trains arrive at and depart from the train depot are omitted.
i	Train runs in section *j*	
i+1	Train arrives at station *j*+1	
…	…	
n-1	Train arrives at terminal station	
n	Train stops at terminal station	

The process shown in Table 1 can be described by means of a flow chart. Thus, the process flow chart in Figure 5-2, which represents the workflow of a high-speed train running process, can be obtained.

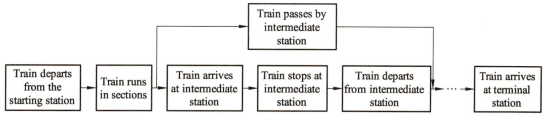

Figure 5-2　Process flow chart of a high-speed train running process.

In Figure 5-2, it can be seen that the arrival at stations and the departure from stations events are the transition points of the train running status. In Petri nets, the status of a train running in a section and stopping at a station can be expressed by *place* p_k and the arrival at the station and departure from the station events can be expressed by *transitions* t_{k1} and t_{k2}. Thus, the arrival at stations activity (running in sections) for high-speed trains can be expressed as depicted in Figure 5-3.

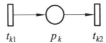

$$t_{k1} \qquad p_k \qquad t_{k2}$$

Figure 5-3 The arrival at stations activity (running in sections) for high-speed trains.

A workflow net that links all the activities of a train running process in a certain sequence is called a train running workflow net for high-speed trains (train running workflow net).

Because of the interferences from a large number of random factors in the train running process, the trains will often deviate from the operation plan. Redundant time can be utilized to absorb the delay time and make the trains recover from delay. The redundant time is a time interval in which the activity time of a train runs in a section or stops at a station. The possible time interval ranges from the minimum technically required operating time to the maximum operating time under the conditions of interferences. The planned activity time is the most common or expected time in this time interval. For example, for the activity of a train running in a section, the time interval ranges from the minimum running time t_{Rmin} in accordance with the train traction calculation, to the t_{Rmax} delayed running time; taking into consideration the interferences and the planned running time t_{Rplan} is the most common or expected time. The activity time is a fuzzy time interval due to the uncertainty of the train running process. Here, we introduce the concept of activity fuzzy time.

The activity fuzzy time of a train is the fuzzy time interval spent finishing the train activities. This activity fuzzy time comprises fuzzy time running in sections, fuzzy time stopping at stations, and fuzzy time connecting trains.

The data shown in Table 5-2 is the statistical result of the deviation time between the actual arrival (pass by) time of trains and the planned arrival (pass by) time of the five stations from South Beijing to East Dezhou. These stations are part of the High-speed Beijing–Shanghai line. The original data come from train running performances for the period June 21–24, 2012. Seventy-eight trains run in these stations every day, with a deviation time of 1560 for all the trains in four days. The maximum deviation time of early arrival at stations is 5 min and that of delayed arrival at stations is 6 min.

Table 5-2 Statistical result of deviation time from South Beijing to East Dezhou

Value of deviation time	−5	−4	−3	−2	−1	0	+1	+2	+3	+4	+5	+6
Deviation frequency	4	12	64	144	232	380	268	204	124	80	36	12

In Table 5-2, the symbol '−' represents the deviation time for early arrivals at stations and the symbol '+' represents the deviation time for delayed arrivals at stations. Deviation frequency signifies the number of times the trains deviate from the planned running time. From the results shown in Table 2, it can be seen that the deviation time of the high-speed trains satisfies a small-time large deviation principle.

We analysed the deviation time using the method of least squares linear regression and obtained regression equations. The regression equation for early arrival deviation time can be described by $y = 74.85x + 326.4$, and the regression equation for delayed arrival deviation time can be described by $y = -60.42x + 339$. The value of the significance levels are 0.918 and 0.956, respectively, and all of them are greater than 0.9. The effects of the linear regression are good. The probability of different deviation times changes linearly and satisfies the characteristics of triangular fuzzy numbers. As a result, we introduced triangular fuzzy numbers for workflow net modelling of high-speed train running processes.

Definition 3 (Triangular fuzzy number). A triangular fuzzy number is a fuzzy number in which the membership function $\mu(x)$ of the fuzzy number $\pi(\zeta) = [a,b,c]$ satisfies the following conditions:

$$\mu(x) = \begin{cases} 0 & x < a \\ \dfrac{x-a}{b-a} & x \in [a,b) \\ \dfrac{x-c}{b-c} & x \in [b,c] \\ 0 & x > c \end{cases}$$

The membership function of a triangular fuzzy number can be described as depicted in Figure 5-4.

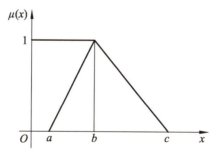

Figure 5-4   Membership function of a triangular fuzzy number.

where the membership function ranges from 0 to 1 and $0 \leqslant a \leqslant b \leqslant c \in \mathrm{R}$.

The left margin of the activity fuzzy time of the trains corresponds to point a in Figure 5-3, and the right margin of the activity fuzzy time of the trains corresponds to point c in Figure 5-3. The most common or expected time of the activity fuzzy time of the trains corresponds to point b in Figure 5-3. The relation $b-x$ ($a < x < b$) corresponds to the early arrival time deviation from the planned time, and $x-b$ ($b < x < c$) corresponds to the delayed arrival time deviation from the planned time.

*Definition 4 (Triangular fuzzy number Petri net).*A triangular fuzzy number Petri net satisfies the following conditions:

(1) It is a Petri net with a five-tuple *PN*.

(2) The triggered time of *transitions* is a set of triangular fuzzy numbers.

Thus, a triangular fuzzy number Petri net is expressed by a six-tuple $N = (P, T, I, O, M_0,$ Ж).

The meaning of the first five-tuple is the same as that of *PN*. Ж is a set of triangular fuzzy numbers that represent the triggered time of *transitions*. The time interval of the limit time for triggering a *transition* is expressed as $\pi(\zeta) = [a, b, c]$. The Ж is composed of the time interval of all the triggering times of the *transitions*. A triangular fuzzy number Petri net is depicted in Figure 5-5.

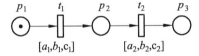

$$p_1 \quad t_1 \quad p_2 \quad t_2 \quad p_3$$

$$[a_1,b_1,c_1] \qquad [a_2,b_2,c_2]$$

Figure 5-5　Triangular fuzzy number Petri net.

*Definition 5 (Triangular fuzzy number workflow net).*A triangular fuzzy number workflow net is a workflow net that is modelled by a triangular fuzzy number Petri net.

The triangular fuzzy number workflow net and the triangular fuzzy number Petri net are similar in form. Their difference is that Ж represents the time duration of the activityin the workflow net, and the triggering time of the *transitions* is zero.

$\pi(\zeta)$ is labelled along with the *places* of the triangular fuzzy number workflow net. The first element of $\pi(\zeta)$ is the minimum train running time in sections or the minimum train stopping time at stations. The second element of $\pi(\zeta)$ is the planned train running time in sections or the planned train stopping time at stations. The third element of $\pi(\zeta)$ is the maximum train running time in sections or the planned train stopping time at stations with the condition of disturbances.

The main job of the triangular fuzzy number workflow net operation is the triangular fuzzy number operation. Its principles of operation are as follows:

(1) Generalizedplus of triangular fuzzy number ($\oplus$)

We have $\pi(\zeta_1) = [a_1, b_1, c_1]$ and $\pi(\zeta_2) = [a_2, b_2, c_2]$, then $\pi(\zeta_1)$ and $\pi(\zeta_2)$ makes $\pi_1(\zeta)$

$$\pi_1(\zeta) = \pi(\zeta_1) \; \oplus \pi(\zeta_2) = [a_1 + a_2, b_1 + b_2, c_1 + c_2] \tag{5-1}$$

(2) Generalized minusof triangular fuzzy number ($\ominus$)

$\pi(\zeta_1)$ minus$\pi(\zeta_2)$ makes $\pi_2(\zeta)$

$$\pi_2(\zeta) = \pi(\zeta_1) \; \ominus \; \pi(\zeta_2) = [a_1 - a_2, b_1 - b_2, c_1 - c_2] \tag{5-2}$$

Take the construction of a workflow net for train T_1in Figure 1 as an example. Train T_1stops at station s_j ($j = 2, 3, 4$) and the motor train unit needs to run with another train number T_2immediately. That is to say, there is a connection activity between trains$T_1$and T_2. There are six activitiesin the whole process of train T_1. These are shown in Table 5-3.

Table 5-3   Activities of train T_1

Activitynumber	Content of activity	Fuzzy time of activity
1	Train T_1runs in the section between stations $s_1$and s_2.	$[20, 23, 23 + d_{1,1}]$
2	Train T_1stops at station s_2.	$[2, 3, 3 +(d_{1,2})]$
3	Train T_1runs in the section between stations $s_2$and s_3.	$[24, 28, 28 + d_{1,2}]$
4	Train T_1stops at station s_3.	$[2, 3, 3 +(d_{1,3})]$
5	Train T_1runs in the section between stations $s_3$and s_4.	$[27, 31, 31 + d_{1,3}]$
6	Connection at station s_4.	$[25, 30, 30 +(d_{1,4})]$

In order to facilitate the discussion in the following section, parameter $d_{i,j}$is given the following delayed time values: $d_{1,1}= 3$, $(d_{1,2}) = 2$, $d_{1,2}= 4$, $(d_{1,3}) = 0.5$, $d_{1,3}= 4$, $(d_{1,4}) = 3$.

Figure 5-6 is the triangular fuzzy number workflow net for train T_1, where $p_s$is the *place* representing the start of the process and p_e is the *place* representing the end of the process. The triangular fuzzy time for p_s and $p_e$is $[0, 0, 0]$ and the dark spot in $p_s$is the train token.

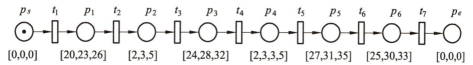

Figure 5-6   Triangular fuzzy number workflow net for train T1.

5.1.4   Operating modes of workflow nets for high-speed trains

A workflow net usually has three basic operating modes: sequential mode, alternative mode, and parallel mode. Parallel mode means that several follow-up activities can be triggered simultaneously and conducted in parallel after one activity is finished. In a high-speed rail system, there may be several activities taking place at the same time in a station. For example, the activitiesin of train inspections and passenger boarding and alighting can take place simultaneously after the trains stop at the stations. This study, however, focuses on the macro-status issue of the train running processes. The activities of train inspections and passenger boarding and alighting are included in the train stopping at stations activity. In workflow nets for high-speed trains, the macro-status of trains stopping at a station, trains running in a section, and trains connecting do not take place simultaneously. Hence, the parallel mode of workflow nets is not discussed in this study.

Sequential mode of workflow nets for high-speed trains

The sequential mode is the operating mode in which the follow-up activity can start only after the current activity has ended. All the activities take place in accordance with a planned sequence in turn. If we project the timings of the train activities for a single train to the timeline in chronological order, the running of a single train can be considered as a workflow net running in sequential mode.

Proposition 1. The time duration $\sum_{\pi(\xi)}(O)$ of a triangular fuzzy number workflow net operating in sequential mode and composed of n activities, p_1, p_2, ..., p_i, ..., p_n, can be formulated as

$$\sum_{\pi(\xi)}(O)=\left[\sum_{i=1}^{n}a_i,\sum_{i=1}^{n}b_i,\sum_{i=1}^{n}c_i\right] \tag{5-3}$$

Proof.(By Mathematical Induction)

Basis Step. According to the definition of triangular fuzzy number workflow nets, there exists $\sum_{\pi(\xi)}{}^1(O)=[a_1,b_1,c_1]$ when $n=1$ and equation (3) holds apparently.

Inductive Step. Assume that equation (3) holds too when $n=k$, then

$$\sum_{\pi(\xi)}{}^k(O)=[\sum_{i=1}^{k}a_i,\sum_{i=1}^{k}b_i,\sum_{i=1}^{k}c_i]$$

When $n=k+1$, according to the principle of generalizedplus of triangular fuzzy numbers,

$$\sum_{\pi(\xi)}{}^{k+1}(O)=\sum_{\pi(\xi)}{}^k\oplus\pi(\xi_{k+1})$$

$$=[\sum_{i=1}^{k}a_i+a_{k+1},\sum_{i=1}^{k}b_i+b_{k+1},\sum_{i=1}^{k}c_i+c_{k+1}]$$

$$=[\sum_{i=1}^{k+1}a_i,\sum_{i=1}^{k+1}b_i,\sum_{i=1}^{k+1}c_i]$$

So equation (3) holds as well when $n=k+1$.

Since both the basis and the inductive steps have been proven, it has now been proved by mathematical induction that $\sum_{\pi(\xi)}(O)=[\sum_{i=1}^{n}a_i,\sum_{i=1}^{n}b_i,\sum_{i=1}^{n}c_i]$ holds for all natural$n$.

In the case where the time at which the current activity of a train finishes is given and the fuzzy time of the train activities sequentially being executed are determined, the time derivation of the train can be realized by calculating the duration of a triangular fuzzy number workflow net operated in sequential mode for high-speed trains. It can be used to detect train running conflicts by comparing the finish time of the workflow nets with the operating activities time of the other train, including conflicts between train running and maintenance times, connecting trains time conflicts, cross-line time conflicts, conflicts between train operation, and passenger transfer times.

5.1.4.1 Alternative mode

If the trains run according to the plan, the workflow net of each train will run in sequential mode independently. There are always disturbances transmitted in the vertical, which lead to deviations in the timings of the activities of the train running workflow nets. The disturbances transmitted in the horizontal may lead to competition for transportation resources and concurrency conflicts between train running workflow nets $w_1$and w_2 when they occupy the same transportation resources at the same time. The dispatchers need to make decisions and determine the order of execution for w_1 and w_2. One of the train running workflow nets will run prior and the other later. The operating mode of the workflow nets mentioned above is called the alternative mode. w_1 and w_2 are called sub-nets. For example, two train running workflow nets execute to the activity of 'stopping at the arrival/departure line I' at time t on account that train 2 deviates from the planned running time. If sub-net w_1 executes first, train 1 will occupy arrival/departure line I first. Figure 5-7 is an example of the alternative operating mode of the workflow nets for high-speed trains. This figure can be used to illustrate the situation of competition to use the resources of arrival/departure lines, sections, and stations.

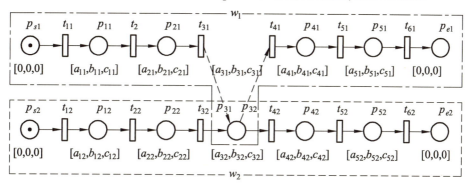

Figure 5-7   The alternative operating mode of the workflow nets for high-speed trains.

The upper half of Figure 5-7 is sub-net w_1 and the lower half is sub-net w_2. The dark spots in p_{s1} and p_{s2} are the train tokens. Activity p_{31} of w_1 competes with p_{32} of w_2. Only w_1/w_2 can be executed first, and w_2/w_1 can subsequently be executed.

Proposition 2. With a train running workflow net operating in alternative mode, if we assume that w_2/w_1 is executed first when there is trigger time competition p_i, and the queuing times of w_1/w_2 are τ; then, the time duration $\sum_{\pi(\xi)}(S_{w_1})$ of w_1 and the time duration $\sum_{\pi(\xi)}(S_{w_2})$ of w_2 are as follows:

$$\sum_{\pi(\xi)}(S_{w_1}) = \left[\sum_{i=1}^{n} a_{i1} + \beta\tau, \sum_{i=1}^{n} b_{i1} + \beta\tau, \sum_{i=1}^{n} c_{i1} + \beta\tau\right] \tag{5-4}$$

$$\sum_{\pi(\xi)}(S_{w_2}) = \left[\sum_{i=1}^{n} a_{i2} + (1-\beta)\tau, \sum_{i=1}^{n} b_{i2} + (1-\beta)\tau, \sum_{i=1}^{n} c_{i2} + (1-\beta)\tau\right] \tag{5-5}$$

Where, β is a 0-1 variable, and $\beta = 1$ when w_2 is executed first and $\beta = 0$ when w_1 is executed first.

Proof of equation (4). Because of the fact that w_2 is executed first when there is trigger time competition p_i, and w_1 runs in sequential mode, the time duration from p_s to p_{i-1} is $\sum_{\pi(\xi)}(O_{i-1}) = \left[\sum_{i=1}^{i-1} a_{i1}, \sum_{i=1}^{i-1} b_{i1}, \sum_{i=1}^{i-1} c_{i1}\right]$. The queuing times of w_1 is $\beta\tau$, $\beta = 1$. The time $\beta\tau$ can be expressed as the triangular fuzzy number $[\beta\tau, \beta\tau, \beta\tau]$. The equation will hold when $\beta\tau$ is added to the time duration from p_i to p_e.

$$\sum\nolimits_{\pi(\xi)}(O_n)=[\beta\tau,\beta\tau,\beta\tau]\oplus[\sum_i^n a_{i1},\sum_i^n b_{i1},\sum_i^n c_{i1}]=[\sum_i^n a_{i1}+\beta\tau,\sum_i^n b_{i1}+\beta\tau,\sum_i^n c_{i1}+\beta\tau],$$

due to $\sum\nolimits_{\pi(\xi)}(S_{w_1})=\sum\nolimits_{\pi(\xi)}(O_{i-1})\oplus\sum\nolimits_{\pi(\xi)}(O_n)$,

so, $\sum\nolimits_{\pi(\xi)}(S_{w_1})=[\sum_{i=1}^n a_{i1}+\beta\tau,\sum_{i=1}^n b_{i1}+\beta\tau,\sum_{i=1}^n c_{i1}+\beta\tau]$.

Thus, equation (5-4) holds. Equation (5-5) can be proved in the same way.

The time derivation of the train can be realized by calculating the time duration of a triangular fuzzy number workflow net operated in alternative mode for high-speed trains in the case where the time at which the current activity of a train finishes is given and the fuzzy time of the train activities are determined. It can be used to detect section occupation conflicts, station interval conflicts, utilization of arrival and departure track conflicts, and so on. It can also be used to determine the occupation time and the order of the transportation resources.

5.1.5 Conclusions

In summary, the timings of train activities and running status can be forecast using the characteristics of the sequential mode and the alternative mode of triangular fuzzy number workflow nets for high-speed trains. Using this model, the possible time at which the train's activities will finish can be calculated and any train running conflicts can be determined by comparing the given deadline time of the activities and the possible time at which the activities will finish. Our next step is to study methods and principles of detecting train running conflicts by calculating the time duration of triangular fuzzy number workflow nets operated both in sequential mode and alternative mode for high-speed trains. In addition, we plan to calculate the probability of conflicts and propose train running conflict prediction methods in our next study. Based on these studies, we will discuss methods for forecasting train running conflicts. This will provide a theoretical foundation for train operation adjustment and railway optimization.

5.2 Predicting high-speed train operation conflicts using workflow nets and triangular fuzzy numbers

The dispatching system of a high-speed railway is the basis and guarantee of trains that run with high speed, high density, high security and good punctuality. The prediction of train operation conflicts is the main issue of train operation adjustment. In this study, we propose the use of workflow nets and triangular fuzzy numbers to study the issues associated with predicting train operation conflicts. The linked lists for conflict prediction are built and used as tools to derive the train running states corresponding to the two operating modes of train workflow nets: the sequential mode and the alternative mode. According to the current train running status and the triangular fuzzy numbers of times for future activities in train operation, the probabilities of all kinds of train operation conflicts that may occur can be obtained by comparing the possible end times of the workflow nets with the fixed deadlines. Hence, the prediction of train operation conflicts is realized.

5.2.1 Introduction

Train operation conflict refers to the mutual restraint and the opposition effect that occur when two trains will need to use the same technical equipment or train path when a train deviates from operational plan. There are many uncertainties in the train operation process due to disturbances from equipment factors, human factors and external environmental factors. Uncertainties such as the uncertain running time in a section and the uncertain stopping time at the station make uncertain the time that technical equipment and other resources will be kept occupied by trains.

Train operation conflicts in the train diagram can be shown by figure 5-8. In figure 5-8, i and j are the train paths,while a,b and c are stations, $\bigcirc$ denotes the conflict point.

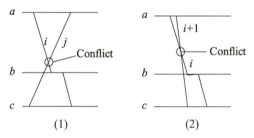

(1)   (2)

Figure 5-8　Train operation conflicts in the train diagram

There are seven types of train operation conflicts:

Station interval conflict-When the arrival or departure time does not satisfy the time standard of necessary technical working, the conflicts will occur. In the case of two adjacent trains in figure 5-9, there is $\left|D_{i,j}-D_{k,j}\right|<I$ or $\left|A_{i,j+1}-A_{k,j+1}\right|<I$, a Station interval conflictoccurs.where $A_{i,\,j+1}$, $A_{k,\,j+1}$are arrival time at station$j+1$ of train i and train k,$D_{i,\,j}$, $D_{k,\,j}$are departure time from station j of train i and train k, and $I$is station interval spaced by automatic block signals.

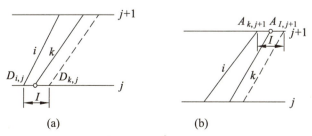

(a)   (b)

Figure 5-9　Station interval conflict between trains spaced by automatic block signals

Section occupation conflicts - When two trains run at the same block section at the same time, the section occupation conflicts will happen. In figure 5-10, if $(A_{i,j+1} - D_{k,j+1})(D_{i,j} - A_{k,j}) < 0$, a section occupation conflictoccurs.

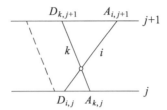

Figure 5-10　Section occupation conflicts

Utilization conflicts of arrival and departure tracks - If the total number of arrival trains in a station is exceed thearrival and departure tracks, the train operation order will be disturbed and the conflict will occur.

Conflicts between train operation and maintenance work-Cross-line trains should depart from the station before the beginning of maintenance work or they should also arrive at the station before the ending of maintenance work. That is to say, if $D_{i,j} \in [T_B, T_E] \cup A_{i,j} \in [T_B, T_E]$ in figure 5-11, there will be a conflict. Where $T_B$is beginning time of maintenance and $T_E$is ending time of maintenance.

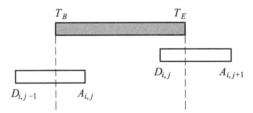

Figure 5-11　Conflict between train operation and maintenance work

Conflicts between train operation and passenger transfers- At station j, in order to meet the need of passengers' transferring between trains, the arrival time of train i should not late than the departure time of train k, which will receive a large number passengers transferred from train i. If $A_{i,j} + T_z \geqslant D_{k,j}$ in figure 5-12, there will be a conflict. Where T_z is redundancy time of transferring for passengers.

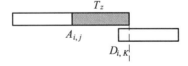

Figure 5-12　Conflicts between train operation and passenger transfers

Time conflicts for connecting electric multiple units (EMUs)-The connecting time between the arrival EMU and its departure that undertakes another transport mission again need to be sufficient. At station j, if an EMU undertakes both the transport mission of train i andtrain k, the arrival time of train i should not late than the departure time of train k.

If $A_{i,j} + T_c \geq D_{k,j}$, there will be a conflict. Where T_c is time period between an EMU arrives at the station and departs from the station again undertakes another transport mission.

Time conflicts due to cross-line trains entering high-speed line- In order to avoid the interference to the operation of high-speed trains, the time of cross-line trains entering high-speed line should be controlled strictly. The entering time of cross-line trains should be included in the time-domain of $[T_{J1}, T_{J2}]$ that was set in advance in the railway timetable. If $D_{i,g} \notin [T_{J1}, T_{J2}]$, there will be a conflict. Where $D_{i,g}$ is time of cross-line train i entering high-speed lines at station g.

Resolving the conflicts caused by unpredictable factors is the most complex and most important job of dispatchers. The main tasks of railway dispatching are determining the kind and level of each train operation conflict, analysing the conflicts according to certain optimization objectives, and determining a reasonable sequence of trains. Exposing the developmental and evolutionary rules for operation conflicts of high-speed trains through a specific model and then forecasting the conflicts that may arise during train operation is of great significance for enhancing the level of traffic organization for high-speed rail.

The operation conflicts of high-speed trains can be predicted by calculating the probability of a future time conflict of trains on the basis of train running status and future operation plans. In the final analysis, this is the process of deriving the time trajectories of train activities and discovering the time conflicts.

Due to the randomness inherent in high-speed train operations, a large number of random factors need to be considered; thus, it is difficult to quantify the running processes of a train. Simulation methods are frequently used in the study of train running processes. [295, 296] The networked rail transit simulation software Opentrack can deduce the running states of trains in both normal and disturbed situations[297]. The software RailSys considers different railway traffic control strategies and can provide solutions for trains deviating from the operational plan. [298]

Mazzarello and Ottaviani[148] studied the relationship between the running density and train operation delays, concluding that a higher running density leads to higher probabilities of train operation delays and train operation conflicts. Moreover, a graph of the relation between running density and train operation delay was given.

Tsang and Ho[299] pointed out that an inter-train conflict will occur when two trains arrive at a railway convergence point at the same time, and the conflict will then cause train running delays, reduce the punctuality rate of trains and lower the quality of railway service. Cheng[294, 300] studied the issue of resource conflicts in train operation processes by using a hybrid simulation method that was event driven and road-net based. With the network diagram model, Cheng put forward three dispatching strategies: train arrivals first, local optimization and the critical path method. Mascis et al.[293] viewed the problem of inter-train conflicts as a job-shop scheduling program with no buffer, and they proposed a solution based on an artificial intelligence approach.

During a study on the problem of train operation diagram optimization, D'Ariano et al.[138]researched the issues of speed matching and conflict resolution. Using the method of decision trees, they achieved the goal of detecting potential train route conflicts in real time, which can assist in the establishment and optimization of a train operation adjustment plan. Fay[144]emphasized that forecasting train operation conflicts is the cornerstone of train dispatching work. Stolk[301] introduced conflict detection and advanced decision support systems in the control of route setting operations. Hallowell and Harker[302] adopted the method of computer simulation to forecast delays in train operation. They obtained a series of simulation data and thereby analysed the reasons for train delays. Huisman[291] developed a stochastic model that can forecast delays on a track section in a railway network and calculate delay distributions for both transient and stationary processes. Yuan and Hansen[49] established an optimal capacity utilization model for a station by estimating knock-on train delays. Wen[303]proposed a conflict prediction method and implemented the process by deriving train operation states and judging conflicts circularly. However, in that paper, the time of a train event is not a random parameter and is only an estimated time range.

The existing studies are inadequate in the area of train operation affected by the combination of train disturbances and diagram buffer time and in the area of train operation conflict forecasting methods based on the derivation of train running states. Wen et al.[109] introduced triangular fuzzy numbers not only to express train activity times but also to aid in using workflow nets for modelling the running processes of high-speed trains.

This work isa development of literature 17, in this study, we analyse the running status of a train by considering disturbances and diagram buffer time, westudy the possible future running status of a train by using workflow nets, and we explore the probabilities of various kinds of conflicts by verifying the time consistency of the workflow net of train operation. When constructing the workflow net of high-speed rail, two modes (the sequential mode and the alternative mode) were selected as the time projection modes of each train operation process.

5.2.2 Time consistency verification for workflow net of high-speed train operation

The running conflicts of high-speed trains can be predicted by dynamically monitoring the timing of the workflow net of train operation; that is, by examining the time consistency of the workflow net dynamically in real time.

A workflow net that links all the activities of a train running process in a certain sequence is called a train running workflow net for high-speed trains (train running workflow net). How to modellhigh-speed trains using triangular fuzzy number workflow nets can reference literature 17.

In a triangular fuzzy number[a, b, c], the left margin "a"corresponds to the minimumactivity time of a train, the right margin"c"corresponds to the maximumactivity time of a train, and "b"corresponds to the most common or expected activity time of a train.

Definition 1(Train activities deadline). Let $\forall\, p_i \in P$ represent one activity in the workflow net of train operation. The latest start time or end time of p_i is defined as a fixed value $E(p_i)$, which is called the deadline of train activities and is a definite time in the form year/month/day/hour/minute/second.

Definition 2 (Time verification for workflow net of train operation). Time verification for a workflow net of train operation is the contrast between the end time and the latest allowable time $E_{max}(P)$ to finish related works stipulated by the train operation diagram, with $E(P)$ calculated through the workflow net. If $E(P) \leqslant E_{max}(P)$, the result of the time verification is consistency, which means there are no conflicts.

The prognosis for conflicts in high-speed train operation includes two aspects of the workflow. One aspect is for a time conflict between the end of train activities and the deadline of the workflow net, which is also the time verification process of the sequential mode of the workflow net. The other aspect is for a time conflict in the workflow net of two high-speed trains using the same transport resources, which is also the time verification process of the alternative mode of the workflow net.

In the case where the time at which the current activity of a train finishes is given and the fuzzy time of the train activities sequentially being executed are determined, the time derivation of the train can be realized by calculating the duration of a triangular fuzzy number workflow net operated in sequential mode for high-speed trains. It can be used to detect train running conflicts by comparing the finish time of the workflow nets with the operating activities time of the other train, including conflicts between train operation and maintenance work, Conflicts between train operation and passenger transfers, Time conflicts for connecting electric multiple units (EMUs), Time conflicts due to cross-line trains entering high-speed line. The time derivation of the train can be realized by calculating the time duration of a triangular fuzzy number workflow net operated in alternative mode for high-speed trains in the case where the time at which the current activity of a train finishes is given and the fuzzy time of the train activities are determined. It can be used to detect station time interval conflicts, section occupation conflicts, and arrival and departure track utilization conflicts, and so on. It can also be used to determine the occupation time and the order of the transportation resources.

Time verification of the sequential mode of a workflow net for high-speed train operation can be realized by the following method. Let p_i, $p_j \in P$ be two activities. Let $E(p_i)$ and $E(p_j)$ be the end times for executing those activities, with activity p_i executed first. Once activity p_i has finished, if the predicted $E(p_j)$ is less than the allowable finish time $E_{max}(P)$, the result of the test is consistency. Verification is shown in Figure 5-13.

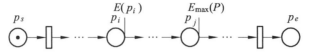

Figure 5-13　Dynamic verification of train activity deadlines

The task consists of the following steps:

(1) Due to the actual finish time of activity p_i in the workflow netis fixed time, the earliest finish time and the latest finishtimeof trainsactivities are equate to the planned finish time. That is to say, there is a=b=c, then, the actual finish time of activity p_i in the workflow netis expressed in the form of triangular fuzzy numbers $[E(p_i), E(p_i), E(p_i)]$.

(2) The execution time of train activities from p_i to p_j in Figure 6 is calculated as

$$\sum_{\pi(\xi)}(O_j)=[\sum_i^j a_i, \sum_i^j b_i, \sum_i^j c_i].$$

Where $\sum_i^j a_i$ isthe sum of the minim execute time of each trainactivity from p_i to p_j,

$\sum_i^j b_i$ isthe sum of the planned execute time of each trainactivity from p_i to p_j, and $\sum_i^j c_i$ is the sum of the maximum execute time of each trainactivity from p_i to p_j.

(3) The finish time of activity p_j is predicted as

$$E(p_j) =[\sum_i^j a_i+E(p_i), \sum_i^j b_i+E(p_i), \sum_i^j c_i+E(p_i)].$$

(4) If $\sum_i^j c_i+E(p_i) \leq E_{max}(P)$, then the result of the time verification of train activity p_j in the workflow net is consistency, which means that no conflict arises; otherwise, a conflict arises.

Time verification of the alternative mode of a workflow net for high-speed train operation can be realized by the following method.

The disturbances transmitted in the horizontal may lead to competition for transportation resources and concurrency conflicts between train running workflow nets w_1 and w_2 when they occupy the same transportation resources at the same time. One of the train running workflow nets will run prior and the other later. w_1 and w_2 are called sub-nets in the alternative mode of train running workflow nets. If the finish times of activity p_j in two workflow nets w_1 and w_2 have intersections, the result of time verification for these is inconsistency, which means that a conflict will arise between them when activity p_j is executed. The task consists of the following steps:

(1) Calculate the start times of activity p_i in the workflow nets w_1 and w_2 as

$$\sum_{\pi(\xi)}(O^{w_1}) =[\sum a_{j1}, \sum b_{j1}, \sum c_{j1}] \text{ and } \sum_{\pi(\xi)}(O^{w_2}) =[\sum a_{j2}, \sum b_{j2}, \sum c_{j2}] .$$

The calculation must obey the operational rule of triangular fuzzy numbers.

(2) Compare $\sum_{\pi(\xi)}(O^{w_1})$ with $\sum_{\pi(\xi)}(O^{w_2})$ to determine whether these have an intersection. If so, there may be a time conflict.

5.2.3 Probability computation for conflicts in high-speed train operation

On the basis of the current train running status, the probability of conflicts between trains under two modes of operation (the sequential and alternative modes) can be calculated using the time consistency verification method for workflow nets of high-speed train operations. The goal is to predict train running conflicts.

Probability computation for various types of train running conflicts in sequential mode

Definition 3. Let $\pi(\zeta) = [a,b,c]$ be the estimated start time or finish time of the workflow net of high-speed train operation, and let $E_{\max}(P_i)$ be the corresponding deadline as shown in Figure 5-14. Then, the probability of a conflict between the workflow net and the deadline is

$$P_1(C) = \begin{cases} 1 - \dfrac{\displaystyle\int_a^{E_{\max}(P_i)} \mu(x)dx}{\displaystyle\int_a^c \mu(x)dx} & E_{\max}(P_i) \in [a,b) \\[4mm] \dfrac{\displaystyle\int_{E_{\max}(P_i)}^c \mu(x)dx}{\displaystyle\int_a^c \mu(x)dx} & E_{\max}(P_i) \in [b,c] \\[4mm] 1 & E_{\max}(P_i) < a \\[2mm] 0 & E_{\max}(P_i) > c \end{cases} \tag{5-6}$$

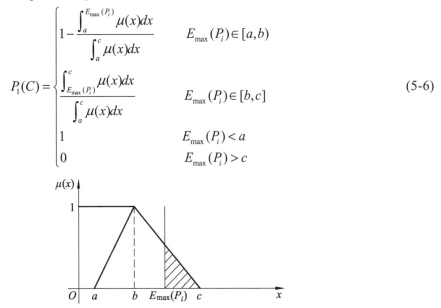

Figure 5-14   Contrast between the running time and the deadline of a train workflow net.

Obviously, the geometrical meaning of $P_1(C)$ is the ratio of the areas of the shaded triangle and larger triangle in Figure 5-14. Moreover, $[E_{\max}(P_i),c]$ is the conflict period.

Proposition 1. If $E_{\max}(P_i) \geqslant c$, then $P_1(C) = 0$ and there will not be any conflict between the estimated finish time and the deadline $E_{\max}(P_i)$ of train activity p_i. If $E_{\max}(P_i) \leqslant a$, then $P_1(C) = 1$ and there will inevitably be a conflict.

Proof. If $E_{\max}(P_i) \geqslant c$, then $\displaystyle\int_{E_{\max}(P_i)}^c \mu(x)dx = 0 \Rightarrow P_1(C) = 0$.

If $E_{\max}(P_i) \leqslant a$, then $\dfrac{\displaystyle\int_a^{E_{\max}(P_i)} \mu(x)dx}{\displaystyle\int_a^c \mu(x)dx} = 0 \Rightarrow P_1(C) = 1$.

Since $P_1(C)$ is monotonically decreasing in the domain of definition, $0 \leqslant P_1(C) \leqslant 1$ is valid.

Since equation (5-6) involves too many integration steps, converting it into the form implied by its geometrical meaning will greatly reduce its computational complexity:

$$P_{11}(C) = \begin{cases} 1 - \dfrac{[E_{\max}(P_i) - a]^2}{(b-a)(c-a)} & E_{\max}(P_i) \in [a,b] \\[3mm] \dfrac{[c - E_{\max}(P_i)]^2}{(c-b)(c-a)} & E_{\max}(P_i) \in [b,c] \\[3mm] 1 & E_{\max}(P_i) < a \\[2mm] 0 & E_{\max}(P_i) > c \end{cases} \tag{5-7}$$

For example, suppose that the estimated finish time of activity p_i in a workflow net is $\pi(\zeta)$ = [60, 65, 72] and the standard connecting time for an EMU is 15 min. Combining this with the expected end time of p_i, we obtain the revised finish time $\pi(\zeta)$ = [75, 80, 87]. If the deadline of p_i is 78, the conflict probability is 0.85. If the deadline is 82, the conflict probability is 0.3.

When the deadline in equation (5-7) changes to the latest allowable time for transferring a large number of passengers to other trains, the start time of comprehensive skylight maintenance, or the permissible time for a cross-line train to enter high-speed lines, as described above, we can forecast the probability of a conflict between train operations and passenger transfers, a conflict between traffic operations and maintenance work, or a conflict due to cross-line trains entering high-speed lines. The probability computation method for a conflict between train operations and passenger transfers is the same as that for a conflict due to EMU connecting time. However, a conflict due to comprehensive skylight maintenance or a cross-line train is another case. Because the execution time is then an interval $[A_s, A_e]$, not a point, we have to transform the interval $[A_s, A_e]$ into a rectangle composed of four points: (A_s, 0), (A_s, 1), (A_e, 1) and (A_e, 0). The conflict probability is equal to the ratio of the areas of the shaded triangle and larger triangle in Figure 5-15. The shaded area is the intersection between the triangle and the rectangle.

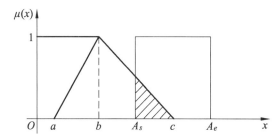

Figure 5-15　Conflict probability as intersection between triangular fuzzy numbers and the time interval.

If the time interval for comprehensive skylight maintenance is $[A_{s1}, A_{e1}]$, the calculation of the probability of a time conflict between high-speed train operation and comprehensive skylight maintenance in sequential mode is described by equation (5-8). If the crossing time interval of a cross-line train is $[A_{s2}, A_{e2}]$, the calculation of the probability of a time conflict for cross-line trains entering high-speed lines is described by equation (5-9).

$$P_{12}(C) = \begin{cases} 1 & A_s \leqslant a \wedge c \leqslant A_e \\[2mm] \dfrac{[A_{e1}-a]^2 -[A_{s1}-a]^2}{(b-a)(c-a)} & a < A_s \wedge b > A_e \\[4mm] \dfrac{[A_{e1}-a]^2}{(b-a)(c-a)} & A_s < a < A_e \leqslant b \\[4mm] 1-\dfrac{[c-A_{e1}]^2}{(c-b)(c-a)} & A_s < a < b < A_e < c \\[4mm] \dfrac{[c-A_{s1}]^2 -[c-A_{e1}]^2}{(c-b)(c-a)} & b < A_s \wedge c > A_e \\[4mm] \dfrac{[c-A_{s1}]^2}{(c-b)(c-a)} & b < A_s < c \leqslant A_e \\[4mm] 1-\dfrac{[A_{e1}-a]^2}{(b-a)(c-a)} -\dfrac{[c-A_{s1}]^2}{(c-b)(c-a)} & a < A_s < b \wedge b < A_e < c \\[4mm] 0 & A_s > c \vee A_e < a \end{cases} \qquad (5\text{-}8)$$

$$P_{13}(C) = \begin{cases} 0 & A_s \leqslant a \wedge c \leqslant A_e \\[2mm] 1-\dfrac{[A_{e2}-a]^2 -[A_{s2}-a]^2}{(b-a)(c-a)} & a < A_s \wedge b > A_e \\[4mm] 1-\dfrac{[A_{e2}-a]^2}{(b-a)(c-a)} & A_s < a < A_e \leqslant b \\[4mm] \dfrac{[c-A_{e2}]^2}{(c-b)(c-a)} & A_s < a \wedge b < A_e < c \\[4mm] 1-\dfrac{[c-A_{s2}]^2 -[c-A_{e2}]^2}{(c-b)(c-a)} & b < A_s \wedge c > A_e \\[4mm] 1-\dfrac{[c-A_{s2}]^2}{(c-b)(c-a)} & b < A_s < c \leqslant A_e \\[4mm] \dfrac{[A_{e2}-a]^2}{(b-a)(c-a)} +\dfrac{[c-A_{s2}]^2}{(c-b)(c-a)} & a < A_s < b \wedge b < A_e < c \\[4mm] 1 & A_s > c \vee A_e < a \end{cases} \qquad (5\text{-}9)$$

In equation (5-8), the value of the conflict probability refers the ratio of the areas of the shaded triangle and the rectangle. For example, when $A_s < a < b < A_e < c$, it means the shaded triangle is the whole triangular, therefore, the conflict probability is 1. When $b < A_s < c \leqslant A_e$, the shaded triangle is showed in Figure 5-15, and the conflict probability is $\dfrac{[c-A_{s1}]^2}{(c-b)(c-a)}$. In the same way, each conflict probability in equation (5-8) and equation (5-9) can be calculated due to different relationship between the estimated finish time of activity p_i in a workflow net and the time interval for comprehensive skylight maintenance or the crossing time interval of a cross-line train.

Definition 4 (Conflict time). Assume that the predicted finish time of workflow net w_i of a high-speed train is expressed in the form of triangular fuzzy numbers as $[A_i, B_i, C_i]$ and the deadline of the workflow net is $[A_s, A_e]$. If $P_{1i}(C) \neq 0$, the conflict time of the workflow net is $T_{Ci}=[A_i, C_i] \cap [A_s, A_e]$.

For a conflict due to EMU connecting time, a conflict between train operations and passenger transfers, a conflict between train operations and maintenance work, or a conflict due to cross-line trains entering high-speed lines, the forecast is obtained by time verification of the sequential mode of the workflow net for high-speed train operation. Hence, for prediction of train conflicts under the sequential operation mode, a linked list is used to assist the analysis process, just as Table 5-4 shows.

Table 5-4　Linked list for prediction of train conflicts under sequential operation mode

Train activity	Fuzzy time of activity	Earliest end time constraints	Actual finish time of activity	Expected end time of workflow net	Deadline	Conflict probability $P_1(C_{Pi})$ (%)	Conflict time
p_1							
p_2							
...							
p_i							

The first column of Table 5-4 represents the sequence of train activities. The second column represents the fuzzy time of each train activity, which is described by a relative time that indicates the possible consumption of time for completing the corresponding job. The third column represents the expected earliest end time of each train activity, which is an absolute time and generally refers to the earliest departure time of the train at the station. As the train operation activities must strictly obey the basic running principle (the earliest departure time of the train at the station is not earlier than the planned outset time), the earliest start time of the next activity (the train leaves the station) should not be earlier than the planned time, even if a method shortening the section time is adopted and the train reaches the station and completes the corresponding activities before the planned time. That is, when computing the specific time of a train running in the workflow net, if the time of the train leaving station s_i is

$$\pi(\zeta) = \left[\sum_1^i a_i, \sum_1^i b_i, \sum_1^i c_i \right]$$ and the planned departure time is $t_E(s_i)$, then $$\pi(\zeta) = \left[\max(\sum_1^i a_i, t_E(S_i), \right.$$

$$\left. \sum_1^i b_i, \sum_1^i c_i \right].$$ The fourth column represents the actual finish time of train activity, which is an absolute time determined. The fifth column represents the expected end time of the workflow net, which is an absolute time based on the known train running state from the fourth column and obtained from the operational rule of triangular fuzzy numbers once the current train activity has been executed. The sixth column represents the deadline of the workflow net, which is an absolute time or time interval determined by the EMU connecting time, skylight arrangement time, passenger transfer time and cross-line time. The seventh column represents a conflict possibility sequence, which is the result of time consistency verification of the workflow net and conflict probability computation for train operation after the completion of

each train activity. The eighth column represents the possible occurrence period of each conflict.

Take, for instance, the specific operational data of train No. G6002 from South Guangzhou Station to South Changsha Station (data collected on 1 July 2011 with an unadjusted operation diagram). The following describes the specific method of conflict prediction for a high-speed train running in the sequential mode. Table 5-5 is the linked list for conflict prediction of the EMU connecting times of train No. G6002. For convenience of calculation, all times in the table are expressed in minutes. The absolute time starts with 0:00, and the planned departure time of train No. G6002 from South Guangzhou Station is 6:55, so its absolute departure time is 415. Similarly, the planned arrival time of the train at South Changsha Station is 559. In the second column, the first element within the brackets is chosen according to the train pulling data and the minimum stopping time standard of the Wuhan-Guangzhou High-speed Railway, the second element is the scheduled time in a train diagram, and the third element is the statistical mean value of the section running time or stopping time under interference conditions. The deadline in the sixth column is the latest allowable time for train No. G6002 to arrive at South Changsha Station, otherwise the train turn-back operation that is required to turn around immediately at South Changsha Station will be delayed. The time listed is 590, so the deadline of the workflow net of train No. G6002 is 590. The standard connecting time for an EMU is 20 min, so the data in the seventh column are the results of adding the standard EMU connecting time to the data in the fifth column and checking the post-addition values for consistency with the datum in the sixth column.

Table 5-5　Linked list for prediction of connecting time conflicts for train No. G6002

Train activity	Fuzzy time of activity	Earliest end time constraints	Actual finish time of activity	Expected end time of workflow net	Deadline	Conflict probability $P_1(C_{Pi})$ (%)	Conflict time
p_1	[65,70,74]		489	[556,563,573]	590	12.86	[590,593]
p_2	[1,1,2]	486	492	[557,565,574]		25.40	[590,594]
p_3	[18,20,22]		510	[557,563,570]		0	—
p_4	[1,1,2]	507	511	[557,563,569]		0	—
p_5	[22,25,27]		540	[564,567,571]		3.6	[590,591]
p_6	[1,1,2]	533	541	[564,567,570]		0	—
p_7	[23,26,29]		564	—		0	—

With the execution of train activities in the workflow net, the future activities of the train will become completed activities one by one. The estimated end time of a workflow net for high-speed train operation varies with the actual completion time of train activities, and the possibility of conflict changes accordingly. Due to the influence of interference, train activity p_1 is delayed by 4 min (415 + 70 + 4 = 489), so the planned finish time of the workflow net after the execution of activity p_1 conflicts with the deadline and the probability of the conflict is 12.86%. Then, train activity p_2 is delayed by 2 min, which increases the probability of the conflict between the planned finish time of the workflow netand the deadline to 25.40% after the execution of activity p_2. Activities p_3 and p_4 are undisturbed, and the train takes full advantage of the redundant time in the diagram. The train implements activities p_3 and p_4 in accordance with the minimum standards, which reduces to zero the probability of a conflict between the planned finish time of those activitiesand the deadline. Analogously, train activity p_5 suffers interference that increases the conflict probability, but the undisturbed activities p_6 and p_7 use the buffer time in the diagram to decrease the conflict probability to zero.

Probability computation for various types of train running conflicts in alternative mode

Since the high-speed rail transport system is a queuing system and track sections, receiving-departure track, and other technical equipment are all scarce resources, trains must always compete for the same transport resources. This is also the reason for station time interval conflicts, section occupation conflicts, and utilization conflicts for arrival and departure track.

Proposition 2. Assume that sub-nets $w_1$and w_2 form an alternative mode workflow net and that a conflict will occur when activity p_j is executed. The finish time of p_j in workflow net w_1 is $\sum_{\pi(\xi)}(O^{w_1})$ and the finish time of p_j in workflow net w_2 is $\sum_{\pi(\xi)}(O^{w_2})$. Therefore,

$$\sum_{\pi(\xi)}(O^{w_1})=[\sum a_{j1},\sum b_{j1},\sum c_{j1}]$$

$$\sum_{\pi(\xi)}(O^{w_2})=[\sum a_{j2},\sum b_{j2},\sum c_{j2}]$$

If the inequality $\sum_{\pi(\xi)}(O^{w_1})\cap\sum_{\pi(\xi)}(O^{w_2})\neq\phi$ is satisfied, net $w_1$will conflict with net w_2 and the conflict time will be [max($\sum a_{j1}$, $\sum a_{j2}$),δ, min($\sum c_{j1}$, $\sum c_{j2}$)]. Note that δ represents the value between max($\sum a_{j1}$, $\sum a_{j2}$) and min($\sum c_{j1}$, $\sum c_{j2}$) that is the most likely value of the conflict time and is where the membership functions attain their peak values.

The above proposition can easily be proved by the graphic method. Figure 5-16 shows two triangular fuzzy numbers $\pi(\zeta_1) = [a_1,b_1,c_1]$ and $\pi(\zeta_2) = [a_2,b_2,c_2]$. The shaded area is their intersection $\pi(\zeta_1)\cap\pi(\zeta_2) = [\ a_2,\ \delta,\ c_1]$, where $\delta=\dfrac{b_2c_1-a_2b_1}{c_1+b_2-a_2-b_1}$ and $\mu(\delta)=\dfrac{c_1-a_2}{c_1+b_2-a_2-b_1}$.

Replacing $\pi(\zeta_1)$ and $\pi(\zeta_2)$ with $\sum_{\pi(\xi)}(O^{w_1})$ and $\sum_{\pi(\xi)}(O^{w_2})$, respectively, Proposition 1 is obtained. For example, if $\pi(\zeta_1) = [1,3,6]$ and $\pi(\zeta_2) = [4,5,7]$, then $\delta = 4.5$ and $\mu(\delta) = 0.5$. In particular, if $\pi(\zeta_1) = \pi(\zeta_2)$, then $\delta= b_1=b_2$ and $\mu(\delta)=1$.

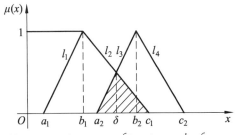

Figure 5-16　Intersection map of two triangular fuzzy numbers.

As shown in Figure 5-16, let $y = \mu(x)$, and let the equations of four segments l_1, l_2, l_3 and l_4 be $y = k_1 x + d_1$ ($x \in [a_1,b_1]$), $y = k_2 x + d_2$ ($x \in [b_1,c_1]$), $y = k_3 x + d_3$ ($x \in [a_2,b_2]$) and $y = k_4 x + d_4$ ($x \in [b_2,c_2]$). Let $h_1 = \dfrac{y - d_1}{k_1}$, $h_2 = \dfrac{y - d_2}{k_2}$, $h_3 = \dfrac{y - d_3}{k_3}$ and $h_4 = \dfrac{y - d_4}{k_4}$.

Definition 5. Assume that two trains compete for the same resource M and that the fuzzy times corresponding to finished activities are $\pi(\zeta_1) = [a_1,b_1,c_1]$ and $\pi(\zeta_2) = [a_2,b_2,c_2]$. If $\pi(\zeta_1) \cap \pi(\zeta_2) = [\max(a_1, a_2),\ \delta,\ \min(c_1, c_2)]$ and the membership function of δ is $\mu(\delta)$, then the probability of a time conflict between the two workflow nets in the alternative mode is given by equation (5-10).

$$P_2(C) = \frac{\int_0^{\mu(\delta)} (h_2 - h_3)\,dy}{\int_0^1 (h_2 - h_1 + h_4 - h_3)\,dy - \int_0^{\mu(\delta)} (h_2 - h_3)\,dy} \tag{5-10}$$

As can be seen in Figure 9, the probability of a time conflict between two trains is associated with the conflict time, the ratio of the fuzzy time spans of two train activities, and the ratio between the membership degree of the conflict time and that of the fuzzy time of two train activities. Obviously, the numerator of equation (5) is the area of the intersection between the two triangles shown in Figure 5-11, while the denominator is the area of the union of the triangles. Hence, the probability of a time conflict is equal to the ratio of the intersection to the union in terms of the triangular fuzzy times of two train activities.

Proposition 3. If $c_1 \leqslant a_2$, then $P_2(C) = 0$, which means no conflict exists between two trains. If $\pi(\zeta_1) = \pi(\zeta_2)$, then $P_2(C) = 1$, which means the trains are bound to conflict. The range of $P_2(C)$ is $[0,1]$.

Proof. If $c_1 \leqslant a_2$, then $\mu(\delta) = 0 \Rightarrow \int_0^{\mu(\delta)} (h_2 - h_3)\,dy = 0 \Rightarrow P_2(C) = 0$.

If $\pi(\zeta_1) = \pi(\zeta_2)$, then $a_1 = a_2$, $b_1 = b_2$, $c_1 - c_2 \Rightarrow \mu(\delta) = 1$

$\Rightarrow \int_0^1 (h_2 - h_1 + h_4 - h_3)\,dy - \int_0^{\mu(\delta)} (h_2 - h_3)\,dy = \int_0^{\mu(\delta)} (h_2 - h_3)\,dy \Rightarrow P_2(C) = 1$

Further, $\int_0^{\mu(\delta)} (h_2 - h_3)\,dy \leqslant \int_0^1 (h_2 - h_1 + h_4 - h_3)\,dy - \int_0^{\mu(\delta)} (h_2 - h_3)\,dy$

$\Rightarrow 0 \leqslant P_2(C) \leqslant 1$.

Similarly, equation (5-10) can be expressed in terms of the elements of triangular fuzzy numbers:

$$P_2(C) = \begin{cases} \dfrac{[\min(c_1 - a_2, c_2 - a_1)]^2}{(c_1 + c_2 - a_1 - a_2)(b_1 + c_2 - a_1 - b_2) - [\min(c_1 - a_2, c_2 - a_1)]^2} & \pi(\zeta_1) \cap \pi(\zeta_2) \neq \phi \\ 0 & otherwise \end{cases} \tag{5-11}$$

If $c_1 < c_2$, the values of a_1, b_1, and c_1 must be added to the safety time interval of two trains when using equation (5-11) to compute the probability of a train operation conflict. If $c_1 \geqslant c_2$, the values of a_2, b_2, and c_2 must be added to the safety time interval of two trains when using (5-11).

For example, two trains use the same transport resources M, the fuzzy times of finished train activities are $\pi(\zeta_1) = [87, 92, 98]$ and $\pi(\zeta_2) = [81, 86, 93]$, and the safety time interval of the trains is 3min. When calculating the conflict probability, each element of $\pi(\zeta_2)$ must be added to the safety time interval 3 to use equation (6). The calculated conflict probability is 0.48 and the conflict time interval is [87, 96].

Prediction for station time interval conflicts, section occupation conflicts, and arrival and departure track utilization conflicts is realized by time verification of the workflow net for high-speed train operation in the alternative mode As with the verification of the sequential mode, a linked list is used to assist the analysis process for prediction of train conflicts under the alternative operation mode, as Table 5-6 shows. The conflicts between sub-nets are calculated when the trains competed for transport resources $m_1, m_2, \ldots$, and m_k successively. The first column in the table is the name of the transport resource competed for by two trains on their running paths. The second and third columns are the actual completion times of their previous activities, and these are absolute times that can be calculated with equations (5-9) and (5-10), respectively. The fourth and fifth columns are the fuzzy times of two corresponding train activities finished while occupying the current transportation resource, and each is expressed by a relative time that represents the likely consumption of time for completing the corresponding activity. The sixth column is the conflict possibility sequence, which represent the probability of a time conflict between the triangular fuzzy numbers of two train workflow nets after the completion of the current activity. The seventh column is the possible occurrence period of each conflict.

Table 5-6   Linked list for prediction of train conflicts under alternative operation mode

Transport resource	Completion time of previous activity of workflow net w_1	Completion time of previous activity of workflow net w_2	Fuzzy time of train activity in workflow net w_1	Fuzzy time of train activity in workflow net w_2	Conflict probability $P_2(C_{Pi})$ (%)	Conflict time interval
m_1						
m_2						
...						
m_k						

Take, for instance, the specific operational data of train No. G1022 and train No. G6002 from South Guangzhou Station to South Changsha Station. The following describes the specific method of conflict prediction for a high-speed train running in the alternative mode. The results are listed in Table 5-7. The planned departure time of train No. G1022 from South Guangzhou Station is 6:50, and its transformed absolute time is 410, which is 5 min earlier than that of train No. G6002. The above trains have the same running route and the stops are South Guangzhou Station, North Guangzhou Station, Qingyuan Station, Shaoguan Station, West Chenzhou Station, West Leiyang Station, East Hengyang Station, West Hengshan Station, West Zhuzhou Station and South Changsha Station. All of the 10 stations and nine sections are locations where trains may compete for transport resources and train operation conflicts are likely to occur.

Table 5-7 Linked list for prediction of tracking interval conflicts between trains No. G1022 and No. G6002

Transport resource	Completion time of previous activity of workflow net w_1	Completion time of previous activity of workflow net w_2	Train activity fuzzy time of workflow net w_1	Train activity fuzzy time of workflow net w_2	Conflict probability $P_2(C_{Pi})$ (%)	Conflict time interval
m_1	410	415	[65,69,74]	[66,71,76]	26.67	[481,487]
m_2	479	484	[24,26,29]	[26,29,31]	2.56	[510,511]
m_3	508	511	[26,28,30]	[27,30,32]	33.33	[538,541]
m_4	536	546	[12,14,16]	[13,14,15]	0	—

Because the traffic density of the Wuhan-Guangzhou High-speed Railway at the present stage is not great and there are no cross-line trains, receiving-departure track conflicts generally do not appear, except in the situation of a line failure or unfavourable weather conditions, which cause the appearance of conflicts due to shortages of arrival and departure tracks. Influenced by the snow of 19 to 20 January 2011, trains on the Wuhan-Guangzhou High-speed Railway had to run with reduced speed, which finally led to arrival-departure line conflicts at all stations along the way. The station time interval conflict is the most common form of conflict in daily running. Table 4 is the linked list for prediction of tracking interval conflicts between train No. G1022 and train No. G6002, where the branch network w_1 acts on behalf of the workflow net of train No. G1022 and w_2 acts on behalf of that of train No. G6002. After the running process in section q_{i-1} is finished, if the arrival time interval of trains at station s_i does not meet the time standards, a tracking interval conflict between the trains will be produced. Taking into account the small influence that the stopping time at the station has on the whole running process of a train, we only select train operation activities of the main interval as examination subjects to reduce the amount of calculation. Moreover, the time consumption of station parking activity has been included in the range of section activity. The transport resources in the first column of Table 4 are the sections from South Guangzhou to West Chenzhou, from West Chenzhou to East Hengyang, from East Hengyang to West Zhuzhou and from West Zhuzhou to South Changsha. These are represented by m_1 to m_4, respectively. Column 2 is the time for train No. G1022 to enter the corresponding section, and column 3 is the time for train No. G6002 to enter. Column 4 is the triangle fuzzy number of the running section of train No. G1022, and column 5 is that of train No. G6002. Column 6 is the probability of conflict between the triangle fuzzy numbers in columns 4 and 5. When computing the conflict probability of two trains, the completion time of the preceding train activities should be added to a constant minimum tracking interval between two trains before the consistency verification with the end times of the train activities performed.

During train running process, the dispatchers always make decisions to reduce the conflict probability after conflict prediction. In table 4, since the actual running timeof train No. G6002 in section m_2 is greater than that of train No. G1022, the time conflict probability of the trains expected to arrive at east Hengyang station is small. However, the running of train No. G1022 in section m_2 is disturbed by 3 min, and train No. G6002 runs in this section at the same time with a compressed time standard, which reduces the actual arrival time gap of the trains to 3 min at East Hengyang Station and increases the possibility of a train tracking interval conflict at West Zhuzhou Station to 33.33%, according to the fuzzy time operation of train activities in section m_3. During the actual running in section m_3, the dispatcher will let train No. G1022 run as planned and train No. G6002 run with compressed time standard in order to reduce the probability of the tracking interval conflict between the trains, so the forecast conflict probability of the trains after the execution of the activity in section m_4 will then be reduced to zero.

Suppose that the running performance of train No. G1022 declines in section m_1 such that the speed is reduced (but the operation safety is not affected) and the actual completion time is 500 min. Due to the influence of train No. G1022, train No. G6002 has to run with the minimal tracking interval, for safety apparently, and the actual running time in section m_1 is 503 min for train No. G6002. If the original running order is not changed, train No. G6002 will always be influenced by the speed of the preceding train No. G1022 and will not make full use of the redundant time in its follow-up trip to counteract the interference suffered in section m_1. The completion time of activities in workflow net w_2 is bound to be greater than 570 min, which will conflict with the deadline and affect the normal continuation of EMUs. In order to ensure the normal continuation of train No. G6002, the strategy of train running order adjustment can be adopted to regulate the sequence in which the trains occupy transport resources. In this instance, train No. G6002 can depart West Chenzhou Station at 503 min to be the preceding train and run with the minimum times in its subsequent sections. The finish time of the activities in workflow net w_2 is then 569 min (< 570 min), which eliminates the connecting time conflict of train No. G6002. In addition, due to the reduction in speed, the running time of train No. G1022 must be extended in all sections. The competition for transportation resources between the above trains will no longer appear in the subsequent trip, and so other kinds of conflicts arise in the alternative mode.

The circumstances of competition between multiple trains for the same transport resources can be divided by selecting the resource occupation order for trains in a pairwise manner. The calculation method is the same as that described above. The only differences are the repetition of the calculation and the increase in computation time.

As can be seen from the above analysis, in the alternative mode of the workflow net of a high-speed train, the selection and determination of the running order of branch nets should avoid increases of conflict probability under the sequential and alternative operation modes to achieve the goal of overall optimization of the workflow net.

5.2.4 Conclusions

This study mainly focuses on conflict prediction for the running of high-speed trains. A detailed analysis has been presented. The main results include the following:

(1) A workflow net for high-speed train operation has two modes: the sequential mode and the alternative mode. The sequential mode of a workflow net for high-speed train operation describes conflicts between traffic operations and maintenance jobs, conflicts due to EMU connecting time, conflicts between train operation and passenger transfers time, and time conflicts of cross-line trains going across the line. Conversely, station time interval conflicts, section conflicts, and usage conflicts of receiving-departure lines are described in the alternative mode.

(2) The prediction of running conflicts for high-speed trains is achieved by time consistency verification of workflow net activities. According to the current train running status and the triangular fuzzy numbers of times for future activities in train operation, the probabilities of all kinds of train operation conflicts that may occur can be obtained by comparing the possible end times of the workflow nets with the fixed deadlines. Hence, the prediction of train operation conflicts is realized.

However, the conflicts can be predicted using workflow nets and triangular fuzzy numbers, but the method depends on the fuzzy time of train activities, the variation mechanism of fuzzy time after the dispatcher intervened in the process of train operation should studied in-depth, and how the conflict prediction method used in train operation conflict resolution and train operation adjustment scheme reschedule are the main work that we are striving for.

Chapter 6

Delay recovery and Supplement time allocation

6.1   Forecasting Primary Delay Recovery of High-Speed Railway Using Data-driven Methods

Accurate prediction of recoverable train delay can support the train dispatchers' decision-making with timetable rescheduling and improving service reliability. In this chapter, we present the results of an effort aimed to develop primary delay recovery (PDR) predictor model using train operation records from Wuhan-Guangzhou (W-G) High-speed Railway (HSR). To this end, we identified the main variables that contribute to delay, including dwell buffer time (DBT), running buffer time(RBT), magnitude of primary delay (PDT), and individual sections' influence. Different models are applied and calibrated to predict the PDR. The validation results on test datasets indicate that the Random Forest Regression (RFR) model outperforms other three alternative models, namely, Multiple Linear Regression (MLR), Support Vector Machine (SVM), and Artificial Neural Networks (ANN) regarding prediction accuracy measure. Specifically, the evaluation results show that when the prediction tolerance is less than 1 minute, the RFR model can achieve up to 80.4% of prediction accuracy, while the accuracy level is 44.4%, 78.5% and 78.5% for MLR, SVM,and ANN models, respectively.

6.1.1   Introduction

Despite the availability of advanced communication and control technologies, HSR lines could still be subject to significant delay in their daily operations due to various unexpected disruptions such as bad weather events, power issues, and facilities failure [25]. For example, according to the statistics of the China Railway Corporation, the average departure punctuality for China's 22,000 km HSR network is as high as 98.8%. However, due to various disturbances during their operations, the average punctuality at the final destination stations is less than 90% [188].

When a train is disturbed (delayed) due to an unexpected event, the resulting delay is called primary delay. This delay could propagate to the downstream stops; however, the propagated delay at the downstream stops are often lower due to the fact that the train could catch up by running faster or taking lower dwell time at the stations. Train delays, if not managed properly, may lead to poor performances of the railway service, longer travel time, and missing transfers. Any of these can impose higher costs both on the users and operators of the railway, and affect their expectations about service quality and desired punctuality. Generally, the dispatchers use delay recovery and rescheduling models along with train waiting rules in train running decisions to update timetables and avoid further delays. A general goal is to recover the delayed train to the normal situation as soon as possible. For these reasons, the ability to predict delay recovery plays an important role in estimating running and dwell times that are essential parts of managing any railway transport services[99].

Significant efforts have been devoted to the understanding of delay and predicting delay recovery. Over the past decades, both analytical and simulation models have been developed for proactive and retroactive disturbance management in train operations. However, due to lack of detailed operational data, these models are mostly limited in incorporating real-world statistics and prediction power. Recent advances in train positioning and communication technologies have enabled building models of higher accuracy. This research was motivated by this opportunity to contribute data-driven delay recovery prediction models to the train delay management. Using ten months of train operation records from the W-G HSR line in China, with the established models, the delay recovery potential can be predicted according to the values of the observatory variables. Our comprehensive comparison results on the real-world test datasets indicate that data-driven both models have good performance, yet the random forest model outperforms the other models regarding accuracy and robustness measures. The benefits of the proposed prediction model are manifold as follows. For train operators, by predicting primary delay recovery (PDR), and reducing the delay propagation, and improving overall train operation services. For passengers, by improving train operation and helping them to experience a higher quality of service regarding punctuality and reliability. For further studies and research by contributing new data-driven models of PDR, derived from a wealth of station-level and section-level observations on train operations.

The remainder of this studyis organized as follows. Section 6.1.2 briefly reviews disturbances management literature. Section 6.1.3 provides a formal description of the primary delay recovery problem as well as the operational data collected from the W-G HSR line. In section 6.1.4 we discuss the details of the presented models and the calibration of RFR model. Next, in Section 6.1.5, the validation and comparison results between the proposed model and other potential models are presented. Finally, conclusions and future study directions are discussed in Section 6.1.6.

6.1.2 Literature Review

Punctuality is considered as one of the most important performance measures in any transit mode including HSR [249, 304]. A train service, once delayed at a station or in a section, could continue arriving and departing late at the downstream stations, which is commonly referred as to delay propagation. A delayed train can cause delays to several other trains over a large operating area and time period. Even worse, the delay of just one train may cause a whole cascade of delays to other trains over the entire railway network [35] and further delays and conflicts at train interactions and transferring points [36]. How fast a train service can recover from its delay in the subsequent stations, called delay recovery, and is an important performance measure that shows the reliability and robustness of the service being provided.

Disturbances management issue has raised considerable interests in the literature [33, 305]. A few of researchers focused on the topic of primary delay management particularly. The analysis of the primary and the secondary delays, and their characteristics are studied by [189]. The intensity of primary delay recognized as one of the factors in evaluating the effectiveness of different conflict resolution strategies [306]. Timetable performance evaluation and mathematical methods combined with sophisticated models, algorithms, and simulations for executing timetable are used during rescheduling timetable after delay assessing [194]. It is pointed out that data about stochastic disturbances and the causes of the delays are hard to be collected and measured. There are just a few papers dedicated to incorporating the stochastic disturbances in simulation tools for the automatic calibration of disturbance parameters for the purpose of disturbances management [88].

Estimating and updating running times is a common practice in preventing delay propagation and delay recovery operations. The running time estimation depends on the disturbances and the buffer times that the trains have during their entire operation. Kecman and Goverde focused on the running time prediction and estimation as a reflection of the delay [99]. An exact lower bound rule is applied to estimate the least train delay for resolving the remaining crossing conflicts in a partial schedule and dominance rule is used to reduce search space by eliminating less promising nodes [307]. When there is historical data on train delays, data-driven models are thought more reliable to estimate train delay as they tend to have better fitness. Generally, the most classical data-driven models are regression model and Artificial Neural Networks. [80, 227, 274] all regard the dependence of train delay as a linear relationship, while in Machine Learning (ML) field, ANNs are one of the most popular models for delay prediction [116, 117, 272, 308, 309]. Then, [118] prove that Support Vector Machine model outperforms ANN on train delay prediction while applying SVM model on train delay prediction in Serbian railway system. Other applications based on data-driven models such as a fuzzy Petri net (FPN) model for estimating train delays is proposed to calculate train delays [310]. Van der Meer et al. mined peak hours, rolling stock, weather data as the primary contributors to running time, and developed predictive model involving the mining of track occupation data for the estimation delays [86]. A model that estimates station dwelling time is proposed in [311], which works based on the input parameters of vehicle type, infrastructure and demand for transport. Workflow nets and fuzzy triangular numbers are applied by [38] to study the issues associated with predicting train operation conflicts. However, the most common limitation of these work is that there are limited in incorporating real data on train operations to illustrate and validate the presented models practically.

There are two types of delay recovery models, one is based on simulation and theoretical hypotheses, and the other is based on historical data. In the former type, the issue of delay recovery was usually handled in the timetable rescheduling. A review of methods for real-time scheduling and recovery problems was carried out by [121]. They reviewed three classes of real-time schedule recovery: vehicle rescheduling for road-based services, train-based rescheduling, and airline schedule recovery problems. Another overview of recovery models and algorithms for real-time railway disturbance and disruption management was presented in [8] that mainly summarized the methods on real-time timetable rescheduling of the rolling stock and crew duties. The size of primary delays (and possibly primary delays) and the ability of a timetable to absorb primary delays are characterized as two important ingredients for timetable robustness and performances measurement [218]. For the latter type, [306] presented a delay propagation model in which train path conflicts and dispatching decisions are taken into account, and parameters are estimated by offline statistical analysis of historical train detection data. However, this work does not address the delay probabilities at each station and in each section. [22] uses a data-mining approach for analyzing rail transport delay chains, with data from passenger train traffic on the Finnish rail network. However, the data of train operations was limited only to one month record. The empirical data from Dutch [306], Spanish [124], Finnish [22], Britain [23], and China [29, 30, 145] were used for modeling. Among this data, only the data of China came from the HSR. Simulation models were also applied to investigate the problem of timetable rescheduling and delay recovery [190]. The concept of resilience has been introduced as a criterion to measure the system ability in absorbing perturbations, and its ability to recover rapidly from perturbations [312]. Khadilkar studied the delay probability distributions and found the mean recovery rate of 0.13 minute/km based on historical data from the Indian Railways network, which is used in modeling delay recovery[25]. However, this approach can affect the prediction accuracy of the model, since assigning a fixed recovery ratio can barely reflect the real recovery potential of train operations on different stations and sections.

Recently some mathematical models and algorithms have been developed to support the dispatchers in their decision-making process. Most of the papers look at the railway system at a microscopic level rather than at a macroscopic level, and the corresponding papers explicitly focus on minimizing the delays of passenger or freight trains. Reviewing the literature, the optimizing of timetable and rolling stock schedules using Operation Research methods were found as the most popular approaches in delay recovery modeling. The application of mathematical recovery models for solving real-time train rescheduling is thought to be a more effective way of dealing with disturbances and disruptions. Minimizing maximum delay [313], minimizing the total train delay [103], and minimizing delay cost [314] were all taken as the optimization objectives. Mixed-integer linear programming is widely used for modeling [315]. However, these approaches cannot handle large-scale real-world railway networks that require fast and efficient solutions to cope with unexpected disturbances during trains' operation.

Moreover, due to lack of detailed operational data, the presented models in the existing literature are mostly limited to incorporating real train operation records.

6.1.3　Problem Definition and Data Description

6.1.3.1　Problem Definition

Train operations on a HSR line is a dynamic process, affected by many factors including train schedules, operating constraints, and various perturbations. When a train is held back on a track or at a station due to some external disturbances, the resulting delay is called *primary delay* or initial delay. A late train could affect the operations of other trains at the downstream stations and sections. The delay caused to other trains is commonly referred as *knock-on delay* or *secondary delay*. This study is concerned with the primary type of delays. When a delay occurs to a HSR train, various mitigation actions could be taken, mostly initiated by dispatchers, such as adjusting running speeds and dwell times to absorb the incurred delay. The ability to predict delay recovery, especially at the terminal stations, plays an important role in adjusting running and dwell times to manage delay and reduce further delay in the downstream stations. The underlying process of delay propagation and recovery estimation is depicted in Figure 6-1, and formulated in Equations (6-1) and (6-2). Stations, indexed by k, are numbered sequentially from 1 to n. Consider a particular train servicing the line, starting from the first station (1) and running sequentially toward the terminal station (n). Assume the train have experienced a primary delay of PDT_0 at a station (note that this delay could equivalently be initiated at the section preceding the station), which is the difference between the actual departure and the scheduled departure time at the station. This delay will propagate downstream but could also be reduced through operational adjustments such as increasing train speed and reducing dwell time. The amount of delay recovered by a specific downstream station (k), denoted by RT_k, is defined as the difference between the amount of the primary delay the train suffered (PDT_0), and its arrival delay at the station k, as shown in Equation (6-1).

$$RT_k = PDT_0 - (AAT_k - SAT_k) \qquad (6-1)$$

where SAT_k, and AAT_k, respectively, are the scheduled arrival time and actual arrival time of the train at station k. In this research, we are particularly concerned with predicting the delay recovery time at the destination station, i.e., RT_n.

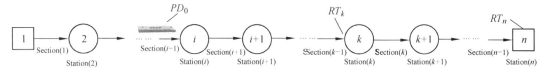

Fig.6-1　Sketch of train operation and delay propagation in a HSR line

The buffer time that scheduled in the sections and at the stations can be used for delay recovering after the train is delayed by (PDT_0) in section (i-1), and there are Equations (6-2)

and (6-3).

$$DBT = \sum_i dbt_i \qquad\qquad (6\text{-}2)$$

$$RBT = \sum_{i+1} rbt_{i+1} \qquad\qquad (6\text{-}3)$$

whereDBT, and $RBT$are the total dwell buffer time and the total running buffer time respectively in the rest of the train journey once delayed. While dbt_i is the dwell buffer time at station i of the train, and there is $dbt_i=0$ if station is a non-stop station of the train. And rbt_{i+1} is the running buffer time in section i +1, and there is rbt_{i+1} if there is no buffer time scheduled in section$i$ +1.

6.1.3.2   Wuhan-Guangzhou HSR

A case study is conducted in this research using train operation records from the W-G HSR in Guangzhou Railway Corporation. As shown in Figure 6-2, W-G HSR connects Wuhan (Hubei province) to Guangzhou (Guangdong province) with a total of 1096 km of double-tracks and 18 stations. In this research, only the operation data for trains connecting GuangzhouNorth and ChibiNorth were available (including 14 stations). The train operation data were obtained for the period from February 24, 2015 to November 30, 2015, including a total of 29,662 records.

Fig.6-2   Map of Wuhan-Guangzhou HSR

All HSR train operations in China are fully controlled by the Centralized Traffic Control (CTC) system that records all operational events and data on a second by second intervals. The trains are continuously monitored by a remote control system via the signal block system. When a train passes a station signal, this event is recorded by a remote control system and simultaneously transmitted to the CTC system. The CTC records and displays the data with its exact time, to the second. The data gathered from CTC include the arrival and departure times at individual stations, which describe the overall running process of the trains. Table 6-1 shows a sample of train operation records. We use these data to determine the arrival delays, departure delays, and dwell times at each station. Table 6-2 provides some information and descriptive statistics regarding each station. Since a train could be delayed at multiple locations along the tracks in sections or at stations, in this research, we assume that trains only experience a single delay. More explicitly, once a train is delayed, it does not suffer further disturbances in the downstream sections and stations. Figure 6-3 shows an instance of a delayed train and the corresponding propagation of arrival delay at the downstream stations. In this example, the train initially was delayed for 20 minutes at GZN. It recovered one minute after the section QY-YDW, one minute after the YDW–SG, five minutes during running at the section CZW-LYW, and four minutes during running at the section ZZW-CSS. Overall, a total of 11 minutes of buffer time were used to recover the initial delay of 20 minutes. In the next section, we focus on developing models to predict trains delay recovery, using historical data from the W-G HSR line from GZN station to the CBN station.

Table 6-1   Train running records in a database

Train NO.	Date	Station	Scheduled Arrival	Scheduled Departure	Actual Arrival	Actual Departure
G634	2015-2-24	GZN	17:26:00	17:26:00	17:28:00	17:28:00
G6152	2015-2-24	QY	17:16:00	17:18:00	17:18:00	17:20:00
G9694	2015-2-24	YDW	19:00:00	19:02:00	19:00:00	19:03:00
G548	2015-2-24	SG	17:26:00	17:29:00	17:25:00	17:29:00

Table 6-2   Stations' delay data and descriptive statistics

	Station		Arrival Delay (min)		Departure Delay (min)	
NO.	Code	Name	Mean	Sd.	Mean	Sd.
1	GZN	GuangzhouNorth	1.26	5.70	1.28	5.73
2	QY	Qingyuan	1.92	6.41	1.90	6.47
3	YDW	YingdeWest	1.71	6.83	1.73	6.95
4	SG	Shaoguan	1.59	7.10	1.55	7.19
5	LCE	LechangEast	1.81	7.34	1.82	7.38
6	CZW	ChenzhouWest	2.18	7.66	2.14	7.77
7	LYW	LeiyangWest	2.25	7.90	2.24	7.96
8	HYE	HengyangEast	1.95	7.74	2.01	8.03
9	HSW	HengshanWest	2.47	8.32	2.45	8.40
10	ZZW	ZhuzhouWest	2.43	8.70	2.42	8.78
11	CSS	ChangshaSouth	1.42	8.46	1.38	8.47
12	MLE	MiluoEast	1.64	8.62	1.61	8.60
13	YYE	YueyangEast	1.59	8.68	1.50	8.69
14	CBN	ChibiNorth	1.37	8.89	1.36	8.88

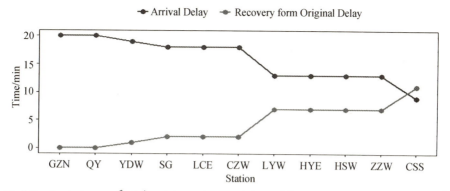

Fig.6-3 An instance of a delayed train at GZN station, delay recovery and propagation of delay from GZN to CSS (colored online)

6.1.4 Modeling Framework for Delay Recovery

6.1.4.1 Delay Recovery Analysis

The *PDT* is the main factor causing trains' late arrivals at, or departures from stations. To keep a timetable flexible and to recover trains from primary delays, a certain amount of buffer time is usually included in the timetable. The supplementary times are allocated in the form of additional dwell times at individual stations, andadditional running times over individual sections. Buffer time is the difference between the scheduled running time (dwell time) in the timetable and the minimum required running time (dwell time). To understand the potentials of delay recovery, we analyzed the arrival and departure events of the delayed trains during their dwelling at the stations or running over the sections case-by-case. Figure 6-4 shows a scatter chart of the pair-wise relationship between the departure delays and the arrival delays at individual stops. As can be seen, some arrival delays were completely absorbed at the stations, while others (those that are between the diagonal line and the red dashed line) were partially recovered. However, there were also instances when delays were further increased after trains' stop at the stations, as shown by these points above the diagonal line, which could be attributed to the demand surging or other incidents at the stations. Table 6-3 shows the average delay recovery ratio – the ratio of the number of trains recovered from primary delay divided by the total number of trains being delayed – for each station (section), respectively. We see that the recovery ratios of the stations are much higher than those in the sections, except for the ZZW station and the ZZW-CSS section. In the same way, Figure 6-5 compares the weighted average recovery time at the stations and their adjacent proceeding sections from the historical train operation data. The weighted average recovery time at a station is defined as the weighted buffer time used by the late arrived trains. The weighted average recovery time in a section is defined as the weighted buffer time used by the late departed trains from a station while running over the adjacent section. Figure 6-4、6-5 and Table 6-3 clearly show that the buffer times allocated at stations and in sections play very significant roles when recovering the delays.

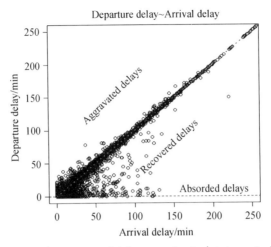

Fig.6-4　Departure delays vs. arrival delays at individual stations (colored online)

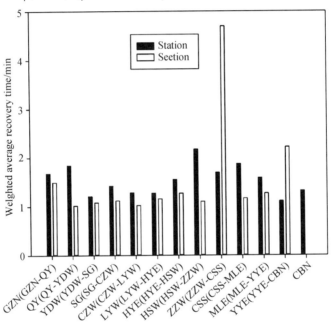

Fig.6-5　Average recovery time at individual stations and sections

Table 6-3　Delay recovery ratio of each individual station (section)

Station (Section)	Recovery ratio%	Station (Section)	Recovery ratio%
GZN(GZN-QY)	41.46 (0.12)	HSW (HSW-ZZW)	49.35 (21.54)
QY(QY-YDW)	51.53 (28.07)	ZZW (ZZW-CSS)	29.86 (45.65)
YDW (YDW-SG)	43.50 (32.81)	CSS (CSS-MLE)	62.49 (0.91)
SG(SG-CZW)	45.15 (11.10)	MLE (MLE-YYE)	69.44 (34.52)
CZW (CZW-LYW)	39.84 (21.13)	YYE (YYE-CBN)	76.05 (42.86)
LYW (LYW-HYE)	43.93 (31.86)	CBN (NA)	14.76 (NA)
HYE (HYE-HSW)	27.89 (1.55)	—	—

Figure (6-5) shows that the weighted average recovery time of the stations are slightly higher than those in the sections, except for ZZW station and its adjacent section (ZZW-CSS). Especially, we see that the delayed trains have significant recovery potential, more than 4 minutes, when they pass through the ZZW-CSS section. This shows that the ZZW-CSS section plays a significant role in recovering delayed trains. We use this finding to distinguish trains which are passing through this section (ZZW-CSS). Moreover, our findings support that the dwell times at the stations and buffer times in the sections can help reduce the propagation of delays in the network. As a result, we use *DBT* and *RBT* to include their effects in the recovering from the delay.

So far, we have identified the main factors that may contribute to the delay recovery of trains (*RT*), namely, *PDT, DBT, RBT*. *PDT* represents the severity (duration) of the delayed event. *DBT* is the total scheduled dwell time for all stations between the points at which the train has experienced a primary delay and the terminal station. *RBT* is the total (scheduled) buffer times in all of the downstream sections up to the terminal station. Moreover, as it was revealed, among all the stations and sections, the ZZW-CSS section has a significant effect on reducing the propagation of the passing trains' delay. To incorporate this factor, we introduce a binary variable *ZC* in our models to distinguish those delayed trains that pass through this section. Finally, the recovery time *RT* is the dependent variable in our models, representing the total delay recovered during the rest of the trip, once a train is delayed.

Table 6-4 shows five instances of delay recovery that are derived from the train operation records to help explain the inputs of our models. In this table, the first column indicates the train number who suffered a primary delay, and the second column shows the delay occurrence date. The column "Station.1" denotes the station where the delay occurred; or the first adjacent station the train just passed, in case the delay happened in a section. "Station.2" denotes the station at which the train recovered from the delay, or the destination station. For instance, the Train G554, on 24 February 2015, departed 15 minutes late from CZW, *PDT* = 15 minutes. For this train, we set the CBN station to be the final station as its destination station is out of the domain that the data covers. During its journey from CZW to CBN, the total dwell time for the train is *DBT* = 10 minutes, and the total running buffer time is *RBT* = 47 minutes. Since this train passes through ZZW-CSS section, we set *ZC* = 1. From the last column, we see that this train totally recovered its delay when it arrives at CBN, *RT* = 15 minutes.

Table 6-4　Instances of delay recovery

Train No.	Date	Station.1	Station.2	PD*	TD*	RB*	ZC	RT*
G554	2015-02-24	CZW	CBN	15	10	47	1	15
G1130	2015-03-06	GZS	CBN	8	4	16	0	8
G76	2015-05-13	GZN	CZW	5	2	9	0	5
G1404	2015-05-19	HYE	CSS	37	6	14	1	9
G1134	2015-07-04	QY	YYE	9	12	42	1	9

6.1.4.2 Relation investigation of variables

According to most European railway companies, trains arriving less than 5 minutes late are not considered to be delayed[189]. We followed the same convention by excluding these observations with a delay less than 5 minutes or above 60 minutes. Furthermore, the data that represent secondary delay records were also excluded. The filtered data set includes a total of 917 observations or events with primary delays. The summary statistics of the model variables are shown in Table 6-5, and the histogram of the samples given each variable is shown in Figure 6-6, and the scatter matrix graphs of every continuous variable are shown in Figure 6-7. Particularly, Figure 6-6 indicates that extracted variables do not follow the Gauss distribution hypothesis of the traditional statistical model, and from Figure 6-7, we see that the correlation between each pair of factors are relatively weak, allowing us to use them together as independent variables without the concern of multicollinearity. Therefore, the distribution and relationship of variables motivated us to use a computational intelligence approach to model *RT* and its influential factors.

We divided our data into training and test datasets. To achieve a reliable model regarding stability measures, we attempted different sizes of random samples from our training data to compare the stability of the models. As a criterion, we used the mean of squared residuals of 100 experiments under each proportion. Figure 6-8 shows the Mean Squared Error (MSE) distribution under different proportion of training data, where each model was run 100 times. The figure indicates that a higher training sample size results in a better stability level of the model, with a more concentrated residuals distribution. In addition, when more than 70% of the samples are selected for training data, the models can acquire good performances. As a result, to obtain adequate testing dataset, we finally randomly took 70% of the sample for modeling, and used the rest of 30% of the observations for validation.

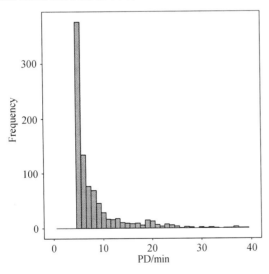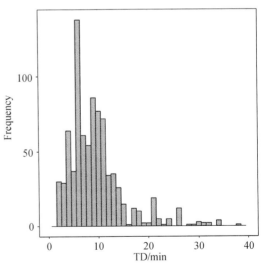

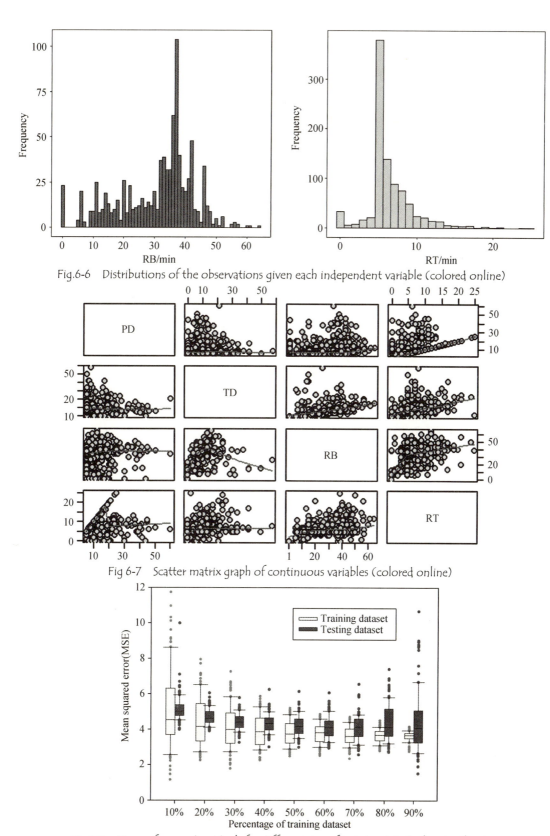

Fig.6-6 Distributions of the observations given each independent variable (colored online)

Fig 6-7 Scatter matrix graph of continuous variables (colored online)

Fig.6-8 Mean of squared residuals for different size of training data (colored online)

Table 6-5 Summary of the descriptive statistics of the identified factors

Variable	N	Min*	Max*	Mean	SD*	Correlation			
						PD	TD	RB	RT
PD	917	5.00	64.00	8.98	7.24	1	0.14	0.11	0.59
TD	917	0.00	58.00	8.90	6.53	0.14	1	0.45	0.34
RB	917	0.00	64.00	30.66	12.33	0.11	0.45	1	0.28
RT	917	0.00	25.00	6.38	3.10	0.59	0.34	0.28	1

6.1.4.3 Random Forest Regression Model

Random Forest is a machine learning method for classification and regression. This modeling approach uses an ensemble of decision trees $\{h(X, \beta_k), k = 1, ...\}$ for mapping a relationship between a vector of predictor and dependent variables. Each tree is a decision tree without pruning and it is established according to CART algorithm. For each tree, X is the input vector, β_k is an independent stochastic variable which decides the growth of every tree. The output of the model is the modes of the classes (classification) or mean prediction (regression) of the individual trees (Breiman, 2001) and [257]. In our RFR modeling there are four predictor variables, as a result of constructing each node of a decision tree, we considered four different scenarios each with a different number of variables, and all the scenarios are processed with Mean Squared Error (MSE) being the loss function of our model, shown in Equation (6-4). Figure 6-9 depicts the number of variables at each split and the nodes (tree size) of the trees. Figure 6-9(a) shows the mean of the squared residuals (errors) under a different number of selected variables. As it can be seen, when two variables are selected, the smallest mean of squared residuals can be obtained. Figure 9(b) shows the complexity of a tree, and that the forest is quite complex when 74 to 132 nodes are included in each tree.

$$MSE = \frac{1}{N} \sum_{k=1}^{N} (\widehat{RT_k} - RT_k)^2 \tag{6-4}$$

To find a reasonable forest scale (number of trees) and get a balance between the accuracy and computational speed, we examined prediction errors under different tree sizes. More explicitly, using RFR models with 1 to 500 decision trees, we examined prediction errors from the respective forest size, see Figure 6-10.

The result shows that errors do not change significantly when the number of trees is higher than 200, suggesting that a forest with about 200 trees should be efficient for modeling PDR. Consequently, we built a forest with 231 decision trees where each tree has two variables on each node, and the corresponding root mean squared residuals (RMSE) is 4.89 (see Figure 6-8(a)). There is no certain formulation for a RFR model. However, we can derive the main coefficients of the variables of the model, as provided in Table 6-6. The coefficients show that *PDT* plays the most important role, then *DBT*, and *RBT* comes next, and the variable *CZ* has the least importance.

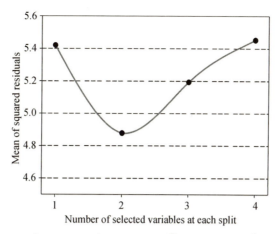

Fig.6-9   Errors, and tree's complexity under different number of variables (nodes)

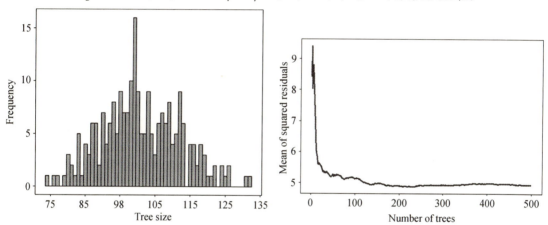

Fig.6-10   Prediction errors of models given different number of decision trees

Table 6-6   Coefficients of the identified factors in RF model

Variable	PD	TD	RB	ZC
Coefficient	49.33	14.51	11.85	6.67

6.1.5   Validation and Performance Comparison

To examine the effectiveness of the presented models, we compared the distribution of MAE for predictions, shown in Equation (6-5), with other three classical models in train delay/recovery prediction against the testing dataset. The testing dataset includes 275 (30%) cases of delay recovery. The standard models that were compared with RFR include:Support Vector Machine (SVM): The main principle of SVM is to map data into a high-dimensional feature space via a nonlinear relationship and then perform a linear regression within this space. In SVM, for the input X, SVM calculates the evaluated value $\hat{Y}$ and a threshold ε is set, only when the difference between evaluated value $\hat{Y}$ and the true value Y is larger than the threshold ε, the cost is calculated, otherwise, it is regarded as the correct prediction.

Artificial Neural Networks (ANN): it is one of the most commonly used models in

Machine Learning. In ANN, neurons between adjacent layers are fully connectedand the information is transferred from the input layer to output layer to calculate the predicted values. By comparing the predicted values with true value, errors are obtained and back-propagated from the output layer to input layer to update the weights and biases of each neuron

Multiple Linear Regression (MLR): Generally, regression models are used to construct a relationship between two or more explanatory variables (independent) and a response (dependent) variable by fitting a linear equation to the data. MLR must meet many assumptions, such as normality of error distribution, homogeneity of variance and independence of errors.

The comparison results are depicted in Figure (6-11). It shows that a great proportion of the residuals are around zero in RFR, SVM and ANN models, meaning that the accuracy of these three models is higher. Then, Table 6-7 quantitatively shows the MAE and accuracy of every model in different allowance error, which means that RFR model has smaller MAE and higher accuracy. Therefore, RFR model is the best model to predict the train delay recovery.

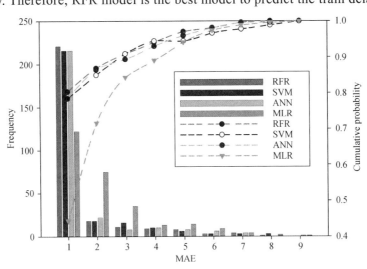

Fig.6-11   Accuracy comparison of RFR, SVM, ANN and MLR models (colored online)

Table 6-7   Accuracy of predicting models

Allowance Error	1 min	2 min	3 min	4 min	5 min	6 min	7 min	8 min	9 min	Mean error
RFR	0.804	0.869	0.909	0.942	0.971	0.982	0.996	1	1	0.762
SVM	0.785	0.850	0.909	0.945	0.945	0.967	0.978	0.989	1	0.866
ANN	0.785	0.865	0.894	0.931	0.960	0.981	0.996	0.996	1	0.858
MLR	0.444	0.716	0.844	0.891	0.942	0.974	0.989	0.996	1	1.726

Moreover, to evaluate the robustness of the presented models, we look at the prediction obtained from models and compared the prediction residuals at different observed *PDT*, and *RT* levels, see Figure 6-12. In these figures, we cannot see any systematic pattern in the range of residuals at the observed *PDT*, and *RT* levels. For example, the range of residuals does not increase or jump when the values of *PDT*, and *RT* are increasing.

The comprehensive evaluation showed that the RFR model is more reliable than other three models in predicting delay recovery. To further test the effectiveness of the RFR model, we compared its performance with two other prediction approaches. Namely, we applied the Extreme Learning Machine (ELM) and Stochastic Gradient Descent (SGD) methods [128] and [129] under the same explanatory variables and the same dataset. It was found that the RFR still led to the highest prediction accuracy. Indeed, the comparison of the residual variances of RFR and ELM under a *t*-test reported a *p*-value less than 0.00, and statistically, the variance of residuals in RFR was found significantly lower than ELM. Additionally, when the variance of the residuals of RFR was compared with SGD's, a *p*-value less than 0.00 was reported that confirms the superiority of RFR model. These comparisons motivate us to emphasize on proposing the RFR as a delay recovery prediction model.

$$MAE = \frac{1}{N} \sum_{k=1}^{N} \left| \widehat{RT_k} - RT_k \right| \qquad (6\text{-}5)$$

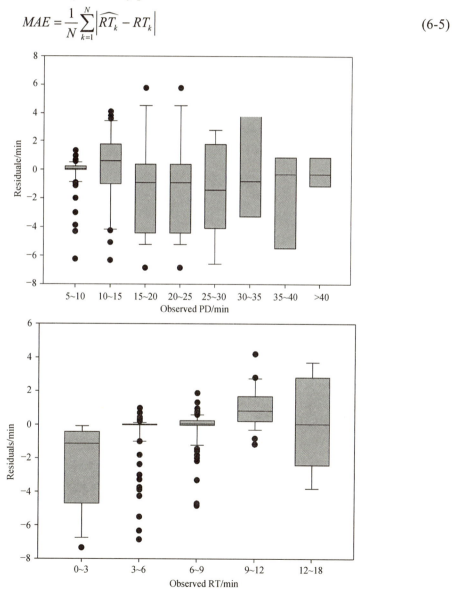

Fig.6-12　Comparison of robustness at different observed RTs and PDTs level (RFR model)

6.1.6 Conclusions and Future Research

In this study, a RFR model was proposed for predicting delay recovery of HSR trains that suffer from a primary delay. Results from different performance examinations indicate that RFR model can achievea better performance level than other classical delay prediction models. Though the model was established using data from W-G HSR, it can be extended to other HSR networks with similar characteristics. Furthermore, our model can be beneficial to both practitioners and researchers in the field of disturbances management.

The research presented in this study represents the first step toward the development of a comprehensive service management system for a HSR network. Our ongoing work focuses on developing a general framework and model construct that can be applied to any HSR line. This will involve investigating different HSR lines using real operation records with a greater spatial and temporal coverage. We will also examine the individual distributions of arrival and departure delays at the station- and section-levels. Additionally, we will consider the delay recovery distributions of each station and section. The last but not the least, we will combine the primary and knock-on delays into an integrated delay recovery model for optimizing service operations and timetabling of HSR.

6.2 A data-driven time supplements allocation model for train operations on high-speed railways

This study presents a time supplements allocation (TSA) method that incorporates historical train operation data to optimize buffer-time distribution in the sections and stations of a published timetable. First, delay recovery behavior is investigated and key influential factors are identified using real-world train movement records from the Wuhan–Guangzhou High-speed Railway (W-G HSR) in China. Then, a ridge regression model is proposed that explains delay recovery time (RT) regarding buffer times at station (BTA), buffer times in section (BTE), and the severity of the primary delay (PD). Next, a TSA model is presented that takes the quantitative effects of identified factors as input to optimize time supplements locally. This model adjusts the scheduled BTA and BTE in the timetable based on delay occurrence probabilities in each section and station. The presented model is applied to a case study comparing the existing and optimized timetables of 24 trains operating during peak morning hours. Results indicate an average 12.9% improvement in delay recovery measures of these trains.

6.2.1 Introduction

In railway networks, despite advanced communication, monitoring, and control facilities, train operations are still subject to uncertainties that can disrupt train services and cause unexpected delays. Train punctuality is a key service measure in passengers' perceptions of the quality of offered services that motivates travelers to choose to travel via rail. It is also one of the main criteria used by train operating companies to evaluate train operation performance and the effectiveness of delay management decisions. Once train service is disrupted (or otherwise delayed) due to an unexpected event, the resulting delay is called a primary delay (*PD*). This delay can propagate to downstream stops or other trains, called secondary (knock-on) delays. Any delay, if not managed well, may reduce the performance of railway services, lengthen travel time, cause travelers to miss transfers, and reduce service quality.

When a train is delayed, dispatchers apply counteractive recovery policies to resolve the delay as swiftly as possible or reduce its effect on passengers and subsequent train operations. In this regard, time supplements are one of the few resources used to recover from delays and increase the stability and robustness of train operations in the case of unexpected disturbances [316]. Time supplements, also called *buffer times*, are either added to minimum operating times or between successive operations. They allow a train to experience disruptions while adhering to scheduled operations as much as possible. In practice, a fixed amount of buffer time is generally added between successive train operations; however, this can reduce operational capacity in a heavily utilized network by contributing to longer travel times. Also, due to the non-storability of buffer times, the unused buffer times in sections or at stations cannot be used by the trains at downstream sections or stations. To retain service punctuality at the desired level and absorb delays while avoiding capacity loss, time supplements must be allocated effectively [42].

In this study, we address time supplement allocation in high-speed railway (HSR) train operations and attempt to determine how and to what extent buffer times affect delay recovery. We also address characteristics of train operations in sections and stations to identify how available buffer times should be distributed among different sections or stations to recover effectively from delays. We present a time supplements allocation (TSA) model that incorporates delay recovery factors along with train operation characteristics obtained from train operation records on China's Wuhan–Guangzhou High-speed Railway (W-G HSR). First, a ridge regression model (RRM) of delay recovery is generated to explain delay severity and buffer-time effects in reducing or recovering from primary delays. Next, using results from the regression model, an integer linear programming (ILP) model is presented that allocates time supplements to train operations at each station or section while considering the delay priorities of sections/stations and restrictions on the total travel time for each train. Case study results suggest that the proposed model can achieve better buffer-time allocation and thus improve delay recovery measures.

The remainder of this study is organized as follows. Section 6.2.2 briefly reviews the literature on delay recovery, timetable optimization, and time supplements allocation. The issues of PD and TSA, and modeling data from W-G HSR, are reported in Section 6.2.3. The influence factors of recovery time (RT) from delay are investigated, and functional relationships between RT and these influence factors are established and validated in Section 6.2.4. In Section 6.2.5, an ILP model is presented for redistributing buffer times, aiming to obtain a better timetable regarding stability and robustness. Finally, conclusions and future study directions are discussed in Section 6.2.6.

6.2.2 Literature review

The concepts and characteristics of primary (source) and secondary (knock-on) delays, which are precursors to delay propagation and recovery studies, were studied in [189]. Large travel disruptions due to primary delays can propagate to other trains in the network, hence requiring short-term adjustments in the timetable to limit delay propagation [219]. The severity of primary delays and the ability of a timetable to absorb them are defined as two main components of timetable robustness and stability measurement [218]. The concept of resilience was introduced in [312] to measure the capacity of a system to absorb and recover from perturbations.

To increase the robustness of a timetable against delay propagation, the scheduled running time in sections and the dwell time at stations are often larger than the minimum required running and dwell times [157]. However, allocation of excessive time supplements can lead to longer travel times for trains along with infrastructure capacity loss [1]. Designing an operative timetable has thus garnered attention from researchers and practitioners, giving rise to terms in the literature such as minimal headway, time supplements, frequency, regularity, flexibility, punctuality, robustness, resilience, recovery, and layover times. Time supplements such as running and dwell buffer times are added to the minimum required times between successive train operations in track sections. Their main function is to ensure safe operations and maximize operational adherence to scheduled times by preventing delay propagation and recovering from time lost due to disturbances in train operations [317]. Therefore, the TSA should be addressed during timetable scheduling and rescheduling by considering delay occurrence and recovery factors. After analyzing historical data and distributing buffer times in a complex and busy junction with minimum delay propagation, Yuan and Hansen concluded that as buffer times between trains decreased, knock-on delays increased exponentially [49, 151]. This finding confirms that the quality of BTA is necessary to reduce behavioral responses and resource waste. To investigate the quality of TSA and to assess whether the supplement in existing timetables fits actual needs and is used properly, Fabrizio et al. presented a statistical approach to analyze historical data of train timekeeping in Denmark [318].

To measure the effectiveness of buffer times, the weighted average distance (WAD) and buffer index were proposed. Vormans defined the WAD as the weighted average distance of supplements from the starting point of the train line, calculated based on historical trips of trains [152]. The WAD of an entire line is calculated as the mean of all WADs of trains on the line, intended to indicate the degree to which a supplement or buffer is biased towards the start of the line, the end, or evenly distributed throughout. Similarly, WADs have been incorporated into an approach combining linear programming with stochastic programming and robust optimization techniques to improve timetable robustness [153]. Andersson et al. developed the strategy of placing margins at critical points [154]. Kroon et al. introduced a stochastic optimization model that can be used to modify a given cyclic timetable, in which WAD was used as a measure [155]. The authors observed that with different amounts of total slack allocated optimally, the distribution favored early buffer supplement (low WAD) when less total buffer supplement was available. The buffer index, used to identify which part of the timetable should be amended and the extent to which arrival/departure times should be changed, is calculated based on a delay and buffer time for each train and station, representing a delay characteristic with respect to causing knock-on delays [62]. Subsequently, buffer indices have been used as criteria in an algorithm based on a Monte Carlo simulation to modify a given timetable and make it more robust, helping to identify which part of a timetable must be modified and how best to modify it.

As described in [25], the mean recovery rate provided by time supplements between two stations was calculated from more than 38,000 train arrival/departure records from the Indian Railway Network. However, the obtained mean recovery rate of 0.13 min/km hardly reflected recovery effects of corrective operations at stations or sections, as limited data from 175 sections over 15 days cannot fully represent actual operations. Şahin obtained transition probability matrices of section runs and conflict resolution based on historical data, in which the running time supplement was, on average, 13% of the minimum journey time [26]. According to the UIC CODE 451-1 OR published by the International Union of Railways, regular running time supplements are added to every train path in the timetable in three different ways: based on distance driven (min/km), travel time (%), and fixed supplements per station or junction (min) [158]. Supplements vary in different countries due to local circumstances. For instance, running time supplements were approximately 7% for all trains in the Netherlands and for passenger trains in Switzerland compared to 11% for freight trains in Switzerland.

Dispatching decisions are partly focused on allocating sufficient time supplements to trains' operations on the network [159] to compensate trains' stochastic arrival and departure delays [160].Goverde and Hansen emphasized that the time allowance (buffer times) is a significant indicator of timetable stability in terms of the effectiveness of avoiding or reducing delay propagation to another train [157]. They presented the recommended BTA principles in German railways and in railways in the Netherland based on their operation experiences. The running time allowance and dwell time allowance (supplements) in the United Kingdom were not explicitly defined but were optimized according to past performance obtained from historical operation data in a particular railway section from [161]. Vansteenwegen and Oudheusden first investigated desired buffer times in a timetable and established a linear problem that penalizes positive and negative deviation from desired values [162]. These ideal buffer times were calculated to safeguard connections when the arriving train is late. Buffer times were based on delay distributions of arriving trains and on weighing different types of waiting times obtained from train operation data in Belgium.

Overall, Although there were some studies aiming to improve the utilization of buffer time[319, 320], and some data-drive methods have been proposed to study the delay issues[235, 321], few models have incorporated real-world timetable performance indices such as the buffer time utilization ratio and delay probability derived from historical records. Because delay propagation and recovery problems depend heavily on the operational factors and conditions of train operations, in practice, TSA should be carried out by considering the characteristics of implemented timetables. This study aims to bridge this gap by presenting a TSA model based on the historical performance of influence factors related to timetable robustness. This model was developed out of a motivation to enhance timetable robustness and diminish capacity loss.

6.2.3 Problem description and dataset

6.2.3.1 Problem statement

Consider a typical HSR train run, as depicted in Figure 6-13, in which a train departs from the origin station (1) to arrive at the destination station (S), where A_i and D_i are the arrival and departure times at station i, respectively. The train may encounter unexpected disturbances, with approximately predictable probabilities, which results in a delay. The disturbances usually caused by unpredictable events, such as bad weather conditions, failure of facilities and operations, or can be caused by other trains. Whether the delay is passed on from other trains or caused by an exogenous factor, it is called a primary delay at the first point that it disturbs an operation. However, dispatchers can use pre-scheduled buffer times at the stations and in the sections to recover or partially absorb the delayed operation. In this case, the recovered time (RT) for a train with an arrival delay of T_f at the destination station n, which incurred a primary delay T_0 at any previous station or section, is defined:

$$RT = T_0 - T_f \qquad (6\text{-}6)$$

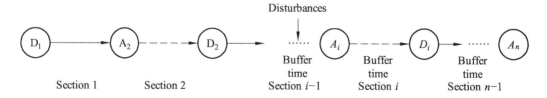

Figure 6-13 Sketch of delay occurrence and delay recovery in a HSR train operation.

In Figure 6-13, a train is delayed by T_0 in section $i-1$ ($i \geqslant 2$), then, the dispatcher will use or adjust the pre-scheduled buffer times in the following sections and stations, if possible. The RT depends on the total buffer times allocated to its following journey after incurring a delay. Given the example above, the RT can also be theoretically defined as:

$$
RT = \sum_{q=i-1}^{n-1} r_q + \sum_{s=i}^{n-1} r_s
$$
$$
0 \leqslant r_s \leqslant R_s, s = 1, 2, \cdots, n \tag{6-7}
$$
$$
0 \leqslant r_q \leqslant R_q, q = 1, 2, \cdots, n-1
$$

where r_q and r_s are the utilized buffer times allocated to the operations on the following sections (q) and stations (s), respectively. Similarly, R_q and R_s are the maximum buffer times that are pre-scheduled in section (q) and at the station (s). If the delayed train is fully recovered before its arrival at the station (s), there will be no buffer time used after station (s). However, when the value of R_q and R_s are too small, there will be insufficient resources to recover from the delay. On the contrary, if the value of R_q and R_s are too high, there will be a capacity lost, since excessive buffer times make operations take a longer time to complete. Due to the differences in operational circumstances in (at) different sections (stations), it is hard to figure out the optimumvalues of R_q and R_s in the timetable design step to achieve best delay recovery and travel time plans. However, having historical observations from HSR train operations, one can explore the behavior of delay occurrence and recoveries from real data, in (at) the section-(stations-) level. Moreover, it is possible to understand the delay recovery potentials of allocated historical buffer times. Motivated by these analyses, we build a data-driven model for allocating or adjusting buffer times that account for delay recovery and occurrence potentials. Therefore, we focus on investigating how train delays can be recovered if no further disturbances happen; and given historical data, how to allocate time supplements to better recover from delays.

6.2.3.2　Data description and analysis

The data used in this study comes from the W-G HSR line, which is shown in Fig. 6-2. According to Chinese Railway Corporation, late arrival over 4 minutes is recorded as a delay; when trains are delayed too much, the dispatching decision usually changes to cancel large-scale delayed trains. Therefore, we delete trains delayed over 60 minutes and use the clean data to calculate the actual and planned travel times, delay occurrence and recovery patterns and time supplements for each train service. Figure 6-14 shows three delay recovery samples extracted from the data. For instance, we can see that train G6014 has recovered part of its primary delay in GZN, 11 out of 20 minutes, at its arrival time to CSS.

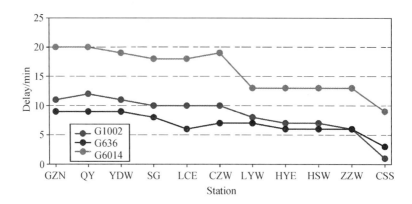

Figure 6-14　Three instances of delayed trains with delay recovery.

6.2.4　Delay recovery analyses

6.2.4.1　Identification of influence factors

Buffer times, which are allocated in each section and station, are considered the source of delay recovery. Figure 6-15 displays the delay recovery obtained from historical data, which denotes the difference between the average scheduled running (dwell) time and average practical running (dwell) time in each section or at each station. Comparisons of bar pairs indicate that the practical running and dwelling times are smaller than the scheduled running and dwelling time, implying that buffer times were somewhat effective in decreasing delays in sections and at stations. To understand the utilization rate of buffer time, we also calculated the recovery ratio (φ) of every section/station, shown in Equation (6-8). As depicted in Figure 6-16, the average recovery ratios of sections were found to be much higher than those of stations. Based on analysis of Figure 6-15 and Figure 6-16, the historical performance of the current timetable of W-H HSR appears to demonstrate a higher recovery ratio in sections than at stations, whereas scheduled buffer times in sections are smaller than at stations.

$$\varphi = \frac{RT_i}{R_i} \tag{6-8}$$

where　φ　is the recovery ratio in each section or station;　RT_i　is the observed recovery time in each section or station; and　R_i　is the total buffer time pre-scheduled in each section or station.

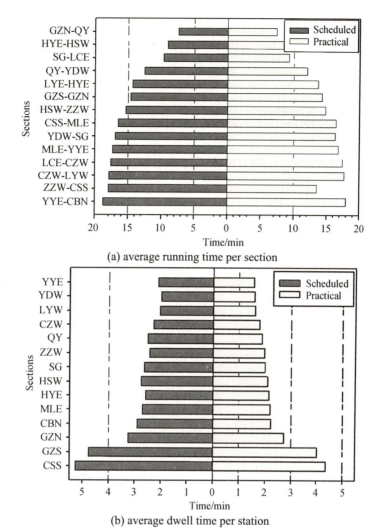

(a) average running time per section

(b) average dwell time per station

Figure 6-15　Comparison between scheduled and observed

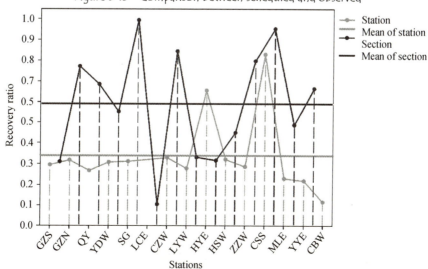

Figure 6-16　Absorptivity of sections and stations.

Given statistics derived from historical data and domain knowledge, we identified that for each train m, the buffer time in a section (BTE) and buffer time at a station (BTA)are influential factors on RT; see Equations (6-9) and (6-10):

$$BTE_m = \sum_{q=i}^{n-1} R_q^m \qquad (6\text{-}9)$$

$$BTA_m = \sum_{s=i}^{n} R_s^m \qquad (6\text{-}10)$$

where m represents the train number. For a railway line with n stations and $n\text{-}1$ sections, if train m isdelayed by T_0in section $i\text{-}1$ or station i, then R_q^m and R_s^m are the pre-scheduled buffer times in section (q), $i \leqslant q \leqslant n-1$, and at station (s), $i \leqslant s \leqslant n$.

In addition, RT can be related to a primary delay, which confines the maximum recovery for each delayed train. Therefore, the severity of the primary delay (PD) is also a key factor affecting recovery time (RT).Finally,the influential factors on RT considered in this study include:

- ➢ BTA: the total buffer time at stations
- ➢ BTE: the total buffer time in sections
- ➢ PD: the primary delay

where BTA and BTEare the time supplement factors that measure buffer time utilization, and PDdenotes the severity of a primary delay.

After data pre-processing, 3074 cases were extracted from historical train operation records of the W-G HSR line. Table 6-8 lists the findings from five cases.

Table 6-8   RT and its influential factors.

Trains	Date	Delay station	End station	BTA	BTE	PD	RT
G1134	04/08/15	CSS	CBN	5	2	14	6
G66	05/24/15	CSS	CBN	2	2	5	5
G1104	01/06/16	CSS	CBN	4	3	67	3
G1110	05/05/15	CZW	YYE	4	13	4	4
G1304	05/09/15	CZW	CSS	8	9	11	7

6.2.4.2   Variable correlation analyses

To obtain a more reliable model to explain the relationship between RT and its influential factors, we first investigated the distribution and correlation of the extracted variables. Figure 6 shows the distribution of extracted variables, and Table 6-9 shows their correlation coefficients. As presented in Figure 6-17 and Table 6-9, the distributions of variables violate the normal-distribution hypothesis, and the partialcorrelation coefficients indicate strong multicollinearitiesamong independent variables. These evidences allowed us to model RT and its influence factors using more advanced approaches compared to a traditional statistical regression model.

Table 6-9   Partial correlation coefficient.

	BTA	BTE	PD	RT
BTA	1.000	0.144	0.201	0.095
BTE	0.144	1.000	−0.005	0.277
PD	0.201	−0.005	1.000	0.080
RT	0.095	0.277	0.080	1.000

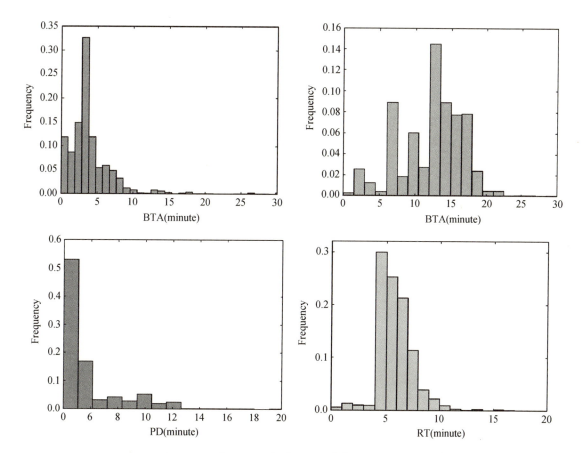

Figure 6-17   Distribution and relations of all continuous variables.

6.2.4.3   Ridge regression

A RRM is a machine learning model used to address the multicollinearity problem among independent variables [322]. In a traditional multiple linear regression model, the estimation of coefficients β based on the least squares method (LSM) is $\beta = (X'X)^{-1}X'Y$. The existence of multicollinearity among independent variables will lead to $|X'X| \approx 0$, which results in inaccurate coefficient estimation. To address this problem, we proposed an RRM to estimate the coefficients ofRT and its influential factors. The principle of RRM is to add a penalty to the loss function of the traditional model to restrict the ranges of coefficients. The loss function of ridge regression is:

$$J(\beta) = \min \left\{ \sum_{i=1}^{N} \left(y_i - \beta_0 - \sum_{j=1}^{p} x_{ij}\beta_j \right)^2 + \alpha \sum_{j=1}^{p} \beta_j^2 \right\} \tag{6-11}$$

where $\sum_{i=1}^{N} \left(y_i - \beta_0 - \sum_{j=1}^{p} x_{ij}\beta_j \right)^2$ is the loss function of LSM; $\sum_{j=1}^{p} \beta_j^2$ is the penalty function;

and α is the weight of the penalty function.

To establish ridge regression, one of the most important factors is choosing a reasonable weight for the penalty function because different correlations among independent variables call for different penalties. Therefore, to select a reasonable value for α, we trained our model based on cross-validation using the stochastic gradient descent (SGD) optimizer and investigated the final fitting error of different α, as shown in Figure 6-18. Finally, the weight of penalty function $\alpha=2.7 \times 10^3$ was chosen.The coefficients of every influential factor estimated by the proposed RRM are shown in Table 6-10.

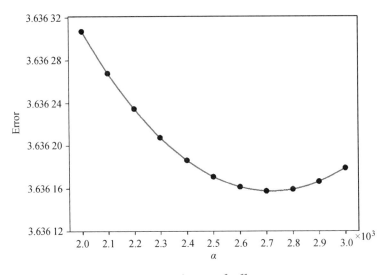

Figure 6-18   Final error of different α.

Table 6-10   Coefficients of explanatory variables.

Variables	BTA	BTE	PD
Coefficients	0.082	0.288	0.257

The coefficients of RRM suggest that an average of 0.082 minutes can be used for delay recovery to account for 1 minute of pre-scheduled dwell buffer time at a station, whereas an average of 0.288 minutes can be used for a delay recovery of 1 minute of pre-scheduled running supplement time in a section. These conclusions align with the results presented in Figure 6-17, wherein the recovery ratios of the running buffer time are larger than those of the dwelling buffer time.

6.2.5 Time supplements allocation

In this section, we first report the proposed TSA model based on RRM to optimize the allocation of buffer times according to historical recovery observations from train operation data. When establishing the TSA model, we only examined timetable-related factors (i.e., BTA and BTE). Then, to consider PD factors, we distributed the total dwelling and running buffer time according to the delay occurrence at every station and section, respectively. Finally, we took 24 trains operating during peak morning hours as examples to compare delay recovery improvements after buffer time reallocation.

6.2.5.1 TSA optimization model

To build the optimization model, we made the following simplifying assumptions:
- the minimum pre-scheduled dwell time of trains at stations can meet passengers' boarding and alighting demands; and
- all delayed trains can reach their maximum speed in sections.

To construct the TSA model, we defined the following sets, parameters, and decision variables.

R: ordered set of trains, $m \in \{1, 2, \dots, |R|\}$; a lower-numbered train precedes a higher-numbered one.

S: ordered set of stations, $i, j \in \{1, 2, \dots, |S|\}1$; S_{ij} is the segment from station i to station j.

t_{start}: additional time for accelerating when a train departs from a station.

t_{stop}: additional time for deaccelerating when a train arrives at a station.

T^m: total travel time from the origin station to the destination station of the mth train (last station the railway bureau controls).

t_{min}^k: minimum dwell time at station k for all trains.

t_{max}^k: maximum dwell time at station k for all trains.

$t_{min}^{k,k+1}$: minimum running time in section $[k, k+1]$ for all trains.

$t_{max}^{k,k+1}$: maximum running time in section $[k, k+1]$ for all trains.

$x^{m,k}$ a binary variable: if train m stops at station k, $x^{m,k}=1$; otherwise, $x^{m,k}=0$.

$t_A^{m,k}$: arrival time of train m at station k.

$t_D^{m,k}$: departure time of train m at station k.

I_1: minimum running interval.

I_2: minimum arrival/departure interval.

BTE^m : total buffer time of train m to be scheduled in a section (decision variable).

BTA^m : total buffer time of train m to be scheduled at a station (decision variable).

The TSA aims to obtain a better delay recovery plan, for each train $m \in R$, to improve the robustness of the timetable. More explicitly, the objective of our model is to maximize train delay recovery time. For each train m, the objective function of the ILP model can be expressed as follows:

$$\max(RT^m) = \max(0.082 \cdot BTA^m + 0.288 \cdot BTE^m) \tag{6-12}$$

All running trains considered in the model should satisfy the following constraints during their trips from station i to station j. The total dwell time of each train should satisfy the minimum required and maximum allowable dwell time restrictions:

$$BTA^m + \sum_{i \leqslant k \leqslant j} t_{min}^k \geqslant \sum_{i \leqslant k \leqslant j} t_{min}^k \tag{6-13}$$

$$BTA^m + \sum_{i \leqslant k \leqslant j} t_{min}^k \leqslant \sum_{i \leqslant k \leqslant j} t_{max}^k \tag{6-14}$$

When a train is delayed, the dispatcher can accelerate the train to recover the delay as much as possible. However, the train is not allowed to exceed the highest speed, nor is it allowed to move below the minimum speed; otherwise, it will affect the regular operation of subsequent trains:

$$BTE^m + \sum_{i \leqslant k \leqslant j-1} t_{min}^{k,k+1} \geqslant \sum_{i \leqslant k \leqslant j-1} t_{min}^{k,k+1} \tag{6-15}$$

$$BTE^m + \sum_{i \leqslant k \leqslant j-1} t_{min}^{k,k+1} \leqslant \sum_{i \leqslant k \leqslant j-1} t_{max}^{k,k+1} \tag{6-16}$$

The total travel time of each train as defined in the published timetable should remain unchanged when buffer times are reallocated:

$$BTA^m + \sum_{i \leqslant k \leqslant j} t_{min}^k + BTE^m + \sum_{i \leqslant k \leqslant j-1} t_{min}^{k,k+1} + (t_{start} + t_{stop}) \cdot \sum_{i+1 \leqslant k \leqslant j-1} x_k^m + t_{start} \cdot x_i^m + t_{stop} \cdot x_j^m = T^m \tag{6-17}$$

Through the above constraints and objective, only reasonable BTE and BTA values of individual trains were obtained. The minimum intervals of adjacent trains should also be satisfied to optimize a whole timetable. Therefore, when optimizing an entire timetable, we also considered restrictions in that the headways between successive trains should not be less than the minimum intervals, defined as follows in sections/stations:

$$t_A^{m,k} - t_A^{m-1,k} \geqslant I_1, k \in S, m \in R \tag{6-18}$$

$$(t_D^{m,k} - t_D^{m-1,k}) \cdot x^{m,k} \cdot x^{m-1,k} \geqslant I_2 \cdot x^{m,k} \cdot x^{m-1,k}, k \in S, m \in R \tag{6-19}$$

Because the proposed model locally optimizes buffer times in the published timetable, the order of operations in the optimized timetable will be the same as the original. The proposed

TSA model can optimize buffer time distribution in sections/stations based on their historical performance. One of the contributions of the proposed TSA model is that after optimization, the buffer time allocation can be more reasonable without capacity loss; this is of great significance for HSR lines due to the small intervals between trains.

6.2.5.2 Parameter setting and solution approach

The values of input parameters were obtained from documents and timetables provided by the Guangzhou Railway Bureau. For example, the value of T^m was obtained from the scheduled timetable, and the respective values of t_{min}^k, t_{max}^k, $t_{min}^{k,k+1}$, $t_{max}^{k,k+1}$, and $x^{m,k}$ were obtained from the practical timetable. For trains using electric multiple units (EMU) CRH3 locomotives, the values of t_{start}^m and t_{start}^m were recorded as 2 and 3 minutes, respectively. According to technical requirements, the values of I_1 and I_2 were defined as 3 and 5 minutes in HSR, respectively. We obtained the values of dwell and running time parameters from historical data as shown in Tables 6-11 and 6-12.

Table 6-11   Maximum and minimum dwell times at stations.

Station	GZS	GZN	QY	YDW	SG	CZW	LYW	HYE	HSW	ZZW	CSS
Max dwell	14	8	8	2	15	13	8	21	9	7	14
Min dwell	2	1	1	1	1	1	1	1	1	1	2

Table 6-12   Maximum and minimum running times in sections (t_{start} and t_{stop} are not included).

Section	GZS-GZN	GZN-QY	QY-YDW	YDW-SG	SG-LCE	LCE-CZW	CZW-LYW	LYE-HYE	HYE-HSW	HSW-ZZW	ZZW-CSS
Max running	14	9	13	17	11	20	18	14	9	16	36
Min running	9	7	11	14	9	16	15	10	8	13	8

In this model, the buffer times for each train were locally optimized in three stages based on the current timetable. In the first stage, to identify overtaking stations, the railway line was divided into $N+1$ segments once there were N overtaking stations between two trains, and then the total buffer times were calculated. Next, the parameters of each train were concatenated as an |R| length vector to input the ILP model to reallocate the defined running and dwell buffer times between sections and stations. The third stage was carried out in three steps: a) the running buffer time of each section, not exceeding the maximum running buffer time of each section, was allocated according to the occurrence probability of a departure delay at former station; b) the remaining running buffer time after step a was allocated to sections whose buffer times did not exceed the maximum limit; and c) if any buffer time remained after Step b, it could be allocated to operations at the stations according to the occurrence probabilities of arrival delays in former section.

6.2.5.3 Case study

The timetable of the GZS-CSS segment of the W-G HSR line, with 12 stations and an average of 112 daily trains, was taken as an example. Trains operating in this segment are all EMU CRH3 high-speed series. For this section, TSA is solved to optimize the buffer times of 24 trains operating during peak morning hours. Information on these trains, extracted from the scheduled timetable, is presented in Table 6-13.

Table 6-13   Trains operating information.

Train	From	To	Departure	Arrival	Travel time (min)	Stops	Dwelling time (min)
G1102	GZS	CSS	7:00	9:42	162	4	9
G6102	GZS	CSS	7:06	9:48	162	3	6
G832	GZS	CSS	7:11	9:53	162	4	9
G6132	GZS	CSS	7:23	9:59	156	3	8
G1002	GZS	CSS	7:33	10:09	156	4	11
G94	GZS	CSS	7:40	10:15	155	3	10
G1104	GZS	CSS	7:46	10:26	160	3	13
G6012	GZS	CSS	7:53	10:35	162	3	13
G86	GZS	CSS	8:01	10:21	140	1	3
G682	GZS	CSS	8:05	10:41	156	3	8
G280	GZS	CSS	8:11	10:59	168	5	20
G72	GZS	CSS	8:28	11:09	161	5	17
G1106	GZS	CSS	8:34	11:22	168	4	20
G6014	GZS	CSS	8:42	11:28	166	4	13
G96	GZS	CSS	8:55	11:17	142	1	3
G6142	GZS	CSS	9:01	11:38	157	4	26
G1004	GZS	CSS	9:07	11:43	156	4	14
G636	GZS	CSS	9:17	11:55	158	5	14
G1108	GZS	CSS	9:22	12:00	158	5	16
G6104	GZS	CSS	9:27	12:05	158	4	11
G74	GZS	CSS	9:32	12:10	158	5	13
G552	GZS	CSS	9:35	12:28	173	6	18
G542	GZS	CSS	9:46	12:34	168	4	16
G6106	GZS	CSS	9:53	12:41	168	3	11

The ILP model was solved using the "Rglpk" packages of *R-programming,* and total BTE and BTA distribution were obtained. Then, to include PD factors, the buffer times were distributed based on the delay occurrence probabilities in the former section or station. For instance, the buffer time allocated to station i was proportional to arrival delays at station i, and the buffer time allocated to section $S_{i,i+1}$ was proportional to departure delays at station i. Statistics on disturbance probabilities along GZS-CSS are displayed in Figure 6-19.

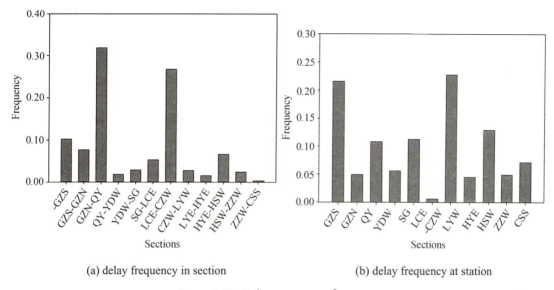

(a) delay frequency in section (b) delay frequency at station

Figure 6-19　Delay occurrence frequency

Figure 6-20 presents part of the scheduled train operations (red lines) and optimized operations (blue lines). Observed delay recoveries, and those calculated by RRM after optimization, are shown in Figure 6-21. Results indicate that the delay recovery measures of these 24 trains were improved by 12.9% on average after TSA optimization.

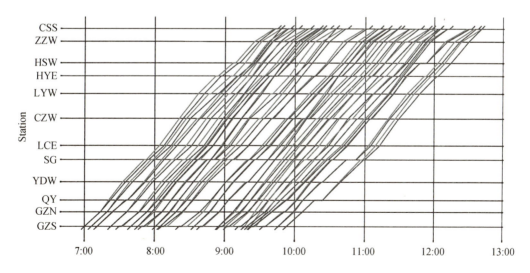

Figure 6-20　Operating and optimized timetables.

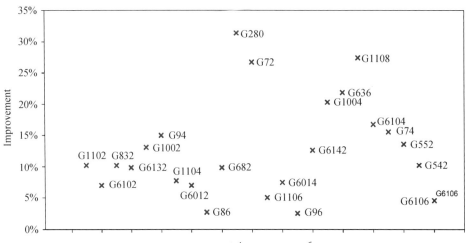

Figure 6-21 Improvements in delay recovery after optimization.

6.2.6 Conclusions

This study presents a data-driven TSA problem using results from an RRM delay recovery prediction model developed based on 20 months of HSR train operation data from Guangzhou railway in China. The established RRM model combines three independent explanatory variables that explain trains' delay recovery behavior in case of a primary delay. Next, an ILP model is presented thattakes the quantitative effects of delay recovery variables to optimize TSA locally, given delay occurrence probabilities. The results of a case study indicate that the optimized timetable performs better than the published one in recovering train operations from a delay. The presented model can thus be used as an effective tool to support TSA decisions in settings where a global model is infeasible. Even though this model was designed for the specified line, it can be applied to others with some modifications.

Moreover, the RRM model established in this study reveals the quantitative relationships between delay recovery time and its influence factors. The ILP model provides a buffer time optimization solution for the scheduled timetable. Both models can hence be used as a foundation for delay recovery simulations and other theoretical studies to consider delay propagation or recovery potential. Also, our data-driven TSA model can significantly improve timetable robustness without capacity loss.

This work is part of our research on analyzing and managing delays based on real-world HSR train operations in China. Some limitations should be addressed in future work. For instance, the minimum dwell time at each station, as well as passengers' alighting and boarding flow effects, should be considered as determining factors. Adding the possibility of changing the order of trains or operations would extend the proposed model. Future research can also include a delay recovery model that combines primary and knock-on delay effects in the allocation of time supplements concerning delay distributions.

References

[1] Mattsson L-G. Railway capacity and train delay relationships. Critical Infrastructure: Springer; 2007. p. 129-150.

[2] Peppard L, Gourishankar V. Optimal control of a string of moving vehicles. IEEE Transactions on Automatic Control. 1970;15 (3):386-387.

[3] Quaglietta E, Pellegrini P, Goverde RM, Albrecht T, Jaekel B, Marlière G, Rodriguez J, Dollevoet T, Ambrogio B, Carcasole D. The ON-TIME real-time railway traffic management framework: A proof-of-concept using a scalable standardised data communication architecture. Transportation Research Part C: Emerging Technologies. 2016;63:23-50.

[4] Kong CUoH. Safety, Reliability, and Disruption Management of High Speed Rail and Metro Systems. http://wwwcityeduhk/csie/TBRS/about/introduction/ [Internet]. 2016.

[5] Velasquez M, Hester PT. An analysis of multi-criteria decision making methods. International Journal of Operations Research. 2013;10 (2):56-66.

[6] Lamorgese L, Mannino C, Pacciarelli D, Krasemann JT. Train Dispatching. Handbook of Optimization in the Railway Industry: Springer; 2018. p. 265-283.

[7] Cacchiani V, Huisman D, Kidd M, Kroon L, Toth P, Veelenturf L, Wagenaar J. An overview of recovery models and algorithms for real-time railway rescheduling. Transportation Research Part B: Methodological. 2014;63:15-37. 10.1016/j.trb.2014. 01.009.

[8] Corman F, Meng L. A review of online dynamic models and algorithms for railway traffic management. IEEE Transactions on Intelligent Transportation Systems. 2015;16 (3): 1274-1284.

[9] Thaduri A, Galar D, Kumar U. Railway assets: a potential domain for big data analytics. Procedia Computer Science. 2015;53:457-467.

[10] Ghofrani F, He Q, Goverde RM, Liu X. Recent applications of big data analytics in railway transportation systems: A survey. Transportation Research Part C: Emerging Technologies. 2018;90:226-246.

[11] Briola D, Caccia R, Bozzano M, Locoro A. Ontologica: Exploiting ontologies and natural language for railway management. Design, implementation and usage examples. International Journal of Knowledge-based and Intelligent Engineering Systems. 2013;17 (1):3-15.

[12] Thorleuchter D, Van den Poel D. Web mining based extraction of problem solution ideas. Expert Systems with Applications. 2013;40 (10):3961-3969.

[13] Cambria E, Schuller B, Xia Y, Havasi C. New avenues in opinion mining and sentiment

analysis. IEEE Intelligent Systems. 2013;28 (2):15-21.

[14] Tutcher J, Ontology-driven data integration for railway asset monitoring applications; IEEE; 2014.

[15] Ochiai Y, Nishimura J, Tomii N. Punctuality analysis by the microscopic simulation and visualization of web-based train information system data. WIT Transactions on The Built Environment. 2014;135:537-549. doi:10.2495/cr140441.

[16] Goverde R, Hansen I. TNV-Prepare: analysis of Dutch railway operations based on train detection data. Computers in Railways. 2000;7:779-788. doi:10.2495/CR000751.

[17] Graffagnino T. Ensuring timetable stability with train traffic data. Computers in Railways XIII: Computer System Design and Operation in the Railway and Other Transit Systems. 2013:427-438. doi:10.2495/cr120361.

[18] De Fabris S, Longo G, Medeossi G. Automated analysis of train event recorder data to improve micro-simulation models. Timetable Planning and Information Quality. 2010: 125-134.

[19] Nash A, Ullius M. Optimizing railway timetables with OpenTimeTable. WIT Transactions on The Built Environment. 2004;74.

[20] Oneto L, Fumeo E, Clerico G, Canepa R, Papa F, Dambra C, Mazzino N, Anguita D. Train delay prediction systems: A big data analytics perspective. Big Data Research. 2017.

[21] Cerreto F, Nielsen OA, Harrod S, Nielsen BF, Causal Analysis of Railway Running Delays. Milan, Italy; World Congress on Railway Research; 2016 29 May to 2 June

[22] Wallander J, Makitalo M. Data mining in rail transport delay chain analysis. Int J Ship Trans Log. 2012;4 (3):269-285.

[23] Jaroszweski D, Hooper E, Baker C, Chapman L, Quinn A. The impacts of the 28 June 2012 storms on UK road and rail transport. Meteorol Appl. 2015;22 (3):470-476. 10.1002/met.1477.

[24] Komori M, Tomii N. Visualization of train traffic records to realize more robust timetable. The 1st Asian Conference on Railway Infrastructure and Transportation; 2016 October 19-20, 2016.

[25] Khadilkar H. Data-enabled stochastic modeling for evaluating schedule robustness of railway networks. Transportation Science. 2016;51 (4):1161-1176.

[26] Şahin İ. Markov chain model for delay distribution in train schedules: Assessing the effectiveness of time allowances. Journal of Rail Transport Planning & Management. 2017;7 (3):101-113. 10.1016/j.jrtpm.2017.08.006.

[27] Gorman MF. Statistical estimation of railroad congestion delay. Transportation Research Part E: Logistics and Transportation Review. 2009;45 (3):446-456.

[28] Milinković S, Marković M, Vesković S, Ivić M, Pavlović N. A fuzzy Petri net model to estimate train delays. Simulation Modelling Practice and Theory. 2013;33:144-157.

[29] Wen C, Li Z, Lessan J, Fu L, Huang P, Jiang C. Statistical investigation on train primary

delay based on real records: evidence from Wuhan–Guangzhou HSR. International Journal of Rail Transportation. 2017;5 (3):170-189. doi:10.1080/23248378.2017. 1307144.

[30] Jong JC, Lin TH, Lee CK, Hu HL. The analysis of train reliability for the Taiwan High Speed Rail. 2010;1:169-180. 10.2495/cr100171.

[31] Şahin İ. Markov chain model for delay distribution in train schedules: Assessing the effectiveness of time allowances. Journal of Rail Transport Planning & Management. 2017.

[32] D'Ariano A, Pranzo M. An Advanced Real-Time Train Dispatching System for Minimizing the Propagation of Delays in a Dispatching Area Under Severe Disturbances. Netw Spat Econ. 2009;9 (1):63-84. 10.1007/s11067-008-9088-1.

[33] Corman F, D'Ariano A. Assessment of Advanced Dispatching Measures for Recovering Disrupted Railway Traffic Situations. Transp Res Record. 2012(2289):1-9.

[34] Fang W, Yang S, Yao X. A survey on problem models and solution approaches to rescheduling in railway networks. IEEE Transactions on Intelligent Transportation Systems. 2015;16 (6):2997-3016.

[35] Vromans MJCM, Dekker R, Kroon LG. Reliability and heterogeneity of railway services. European Journal of Operational Research. 2006;172 (2):647-665.

[36] Delorme X, Gandibleux X, Rodriguez J. Stability evaluation of a railway timetable at station level. European Journal of Operational Research. 2009;195 (3):780-790. 10.1016/j.ejor.2007.06.062.

[37] Goverde RM, Meng L. Advanced monitoring and management information of railway operations. Journal of Rail Transport Planning & Management. 2011;1 (2):69-79.

[38] Wen C, Li JG, Peng QY, Li BY, Ren JJ. Predicting high-speed train operation conflicts using workflow nets and triangular fuzzy numbers. P I Mech Eng F-J Rai. 2015;229 (3):268-279. doi:10.1177/0954409713509978.

[39] Giuliari M, Pellegrini F, Savio S. Moving block and traffic management in railway applications: The EU project COMBINE. WIT Transactions on The Built Environment. 2000;50.

[40] Kecman P, Goverde RM. Process mining of train describer event data and automatic conflict identification. Computers in railways XIII, WIT transactions on the built environment. 2013;127:227-238.

[41] Şahin İ. Railway traffic control and train scheduling based oninter-train conflict management. Transportation Research Part B: Methodological. 1999;33 (7):511-534.

[42] Jovanović P, Kecman P, Bojović N, Mandić D. Optimal allocation of buffer times to increase train schedule robustness. European Journal of Operational Research. 2017;256 (1):44-54.

[43] Solomatine D, See LM, Abrahart R. Data-driven modelling: concepts, approaches and experiences. Practical hydroinformatics: Springer; 2009. p. 17-30.

[44] Zhang J, Wang F-Y, Wang K, Lin W-H, Xu X, Chen C. Data-driven intelligent transportation systems: A survey. IEEE Transactions on Intelligent Transportation Systems. 2011;12 (4):1624-1639.

[45] Roberts C, Easton JM, Kumar AVS, Kohli S. Innovative Applications of Big Data in the Railway Industry: IGI Global; 2017.

[46] Nash A, Huerlimann D. Railroad simulation using OpenTrack. WIT Transactions on The Built Environment. 2004;74.

[47] Bendfeldt J, Mohr U, Muller L. RailSys, a system to plan future railway needs. WIT Transactions on The Built Environment. 2000;50.

[48] Hansen IA, Goverde RM, van der Meer DJ, Online train delay recognition and running time prediction; IEEE; 2010.

[49] Yuan J, Hansen IA. Optimizing capacity utilization of stations by estimating knock-on train delays. Transportation Research Part B: Methodological. 2007;41 (2):202-217. 10.1016/j.trb.2006.02.004.

[50] Flier H, Gelashvili R, Graffagnino T, Nunkesser M. Mining Railway Delay Dependencies in Large-Scale Real-World Delay Data. Robust and online large-scale optimization. 2009;5868:354-368.

[51] Richter T. Systematic analyses of train run deviations from the timetable. WIT Transactions on The Built Environment. 2010(114):651-662.

[52] Jiang C, Huang P, Lessan J, Fu L, Wen C. Forecasting Primary Delay Recovery of High-Speed Railway Using Multiple Linear Regression, Supporting Vector Machine, Artificial Neural Network and Random Forest Regression. Canadian Journal of Civil Engineering. 2018(ja).

[53] Turner C, Tiwari A, Starr A, Blacktop K. A review of key planning and scheduling in the rail industry in Europe and UK. Proceedings of the Institution of Mechanical Engineers, Part F: Journal of Rail and Rapid Transit. 2016;230 (3):984-998.

[54] Conte C. Identifying dependencies among delays [Ph.D]: Georg-August University of Göttingen; 2008.

[55] Olsson NOE, Haugland H. Influencing factors on train punctuality—results from some Norwegian studies. Transport Policy. 2004;11 (4):387-397. 10.1016/j.tranpol.2004.07. 001.

[56] Palmqvist C-W, Olsson N, Hiselius L, Some Influencing Factors For Passenger Train Punctuality In Sweden; 2017.

[57] Brazil W, White A, Nogal M, Caulfield B, O'Connor A, Morton C. Weather and rail delays: Analysis of metropolitan rail in Dublin. Journal of Transport Geography. 2017;59:69-76.

[58] Veiseth M, Olsson N, Saetermo I. Infrastructure's influence on rail punctuality. WIT Transactions on the Built Environment. 2007;96.

[59] Gibson S, Cooper G, Ball B. Developments in transport policy: The evolution of capacity

charges on the UK rail network. Journal of Transport Economics and Policy (JTEP). 2002;36 (2):341-354.

[60] Hasan N. Direct Fixation Fastener (Dff) Spacing And Stiffness Design. Proceedings Of the Asme/Asce/Ieee Joint Rail Conference. 2012:11-17.

[61] Xu P, Corman F, Peng Q. Analyzing railway disruptions and their impact on delayed traffic in Chinese high-speed railway. IFAC-PapersOnLine. 2016;49 (3):84-89. doi:10. 1016/j.ifacol.2016.07.015.

[62] Ushida K, Makino S, Tomii N, Increasing robustness of dense timetables by visualization of train traffic record data and Monte Carlo simulation. Lille, France; 2011 May 22-26.

[63] Porter K, Ramer K. Estimating earthquake-induced failure probability and downtime of critical facilities. Journal of business continuity & emergency planning. 2012;5 (4):352-364.

[64] Liu P, Yang L, Gao Z, Li S, Gao Y. Fault tree analysis combined with quantitative analysis for high-speed railway accidents. Safety science. 2015;79:344-357.

[65] Ma J, Bai Y, Shen J, Zhou F. Examining the impact of adverse weather on urban rail transit facilities on the basis of fault tree analysis and fuzzy synthetic evaluation. Journal of transportation engineering. 2013;140 (3):04013011.

[66] Li H, Parikh D, He Q, Qian B, Li Z, Fang D, Hampapur A. Improving rail network velocity: A machine learning approach to predictive maintenance. Transportation Research Part C: Emerging Technologies. 2014;45:17-26.

[67] Oneto L, Fumeo E, Clerico G, Canepa R, Papa F, Dambra C, Mazzino N, Anguita D, Advanced Analytics for Train Delay Prediction Systems by Including Exogenous Weather Data; IEEE; 2016.

[68] Lee W-H, Yen L-H, Chou C-M. A delay root cause discovery and timetable adjustment model for enhancing the punctuality of railway services. Transportation Research Part C: Emerging Technologies. 2016;73:49-64.

[69] Yamamura A, Koresawa M, Adachi S, Tomii N. Taking effective delay reduction measures and using delay elements as indices for Tokyo's metropolitan railways. 2014;1:3-15. doi:10.2495/cr140011.

[70] Cerreto F, Nielsen BF, Nielsen OA, Harrod SS. Application of data clustering to railway delay pattern recognition. Journal of Advanced Transportation. 2018;2018.

[71] Adenso-Dıaz B, González MO, González-Torre P. On-line timetable re-scheduling in regional train services. Transportation Research Part B: Methodological. 1999;33 (6): 387-398.

[72] Oneto L, Fumeo E, Clerico G, Canepa R, Papa F, Dambra C, Mazzino N, Anguita D. Dynamic Delay Predictions for Large-Scale Railway Networks: Deep and Shallow Extreme Learning Machines Tuned via Thresholdout. IEEE Transactions on Systems, Man, and Cybernetics: Systems. 2017.

[73] Richter T. Systematic analyses of train run deviations from the timetable. 2010;1:651-662.

10.2495/cr100601.

[74] Richter T. Data aggregation for detailed analysis of train delays. Computers in Railways XIII: Computer System Design and Operation in the Railway and Other Transit Systems. 2013;127:239.

[75] Carey M, Kwieciński A. Stochastic approximation to the effects of headways on knock-on delays of trains. Transportation Research Part B: Methodological. 1994;28 (4):251-267.

[76] Goverde RM, Hansen I, Hooghiemstra G, Lopuhaa H, Delay distributions in railway stations; WCTRS; 2001.

[77] Yuan J, Statistical analyses of train delays at The Hague HS. Delft, The Netherlands; TRAIL, Delft, The Netherlands; 2001.

[78] Huisman T, Boucherie RJ, van Dijk NM. A solvable queueing network model for railway networks and its validation and applications for the Netherlands. European Journal of Operational Research. 2002;142 (1):30-51.

[79] Briggs K, Beck C. Modelling train delays with q-exponential functions. Physica A: Statistical Mechanics and its Applications. 2007;378 (2):498-504. doi:10.1016/j.physa. 2006.11.084.

[80] Yuan J, Goverde R, Hansen I. Propagation of train delays in stations. WIT Transactions on The Built Environment. 2002;61. doi:10.2495/CR020961.

[81] Yuan J. Stochastic modelling of train delays and delay propagation in stations 2006.

[82] Büker T, Seybold B. Stochastic modelling of delay propagation in large networks. Journal of Rail Transport Planning & Management. 2012;2 (1):34-50.

[83] Wen C, Li Z, Lessan J, Fu L, Huang P, Jiang C, Muresan MI. Analysis of Causes and Effects of Primary Delays in a High-Speed Rail System. 2018.

[84] Lessan J, Fu L, Wen C, Huang P, Jiang C. Stochastic Model of Train Running Time and Arrival Delay: A Case Study of Wuhan–Guangzhou High-Speed Rail. Journal of the Transportation Research Board. 2018;2672 (10):215-223.

[85] Harrod S, Pournaras G, Nielsen BF, Distribution Fitting for Very Large Railway Delay Data Sets with Discrete Values; 2018.

[86] Van der Meer DJ, Goverde RM, Hansen IA. Prediction of train running times using historical track occupation data. Delft University of Technology, 2009.

[87] Zilko A, Hanea A, Kurowicka D, Goverde R, Non-Parametric Bayesian Network to Forecast Railway Disruption Lengths. Ajaccio, France; 2014 April 8-11, 2014.

[88] Cui Y, Martin U, Zhao W. Calibration of disturbance parameters in railway operational simulation based on reinforcement learning. Journal of Rail Transport Planning & Management. 2016;6 (1):1-12. doi:10.1016/j.jrtpm.2016.03.001.

[89] Meng-Cheng N, Kwok-Leung T, Yang Z. A Data Driven Method for Delay Duration Estimation of High Speed Train. 97th Transportation Research Board Annual Meeting; 2018 January 7-11.

[90] Tang Y, Wen C, Huang P, Li J, Yang Y. Support Vector Regression Models for Influenced Time Prediction in High-Speed Rail System. 97th Transportation Research Board Annual Meeting; 2018 January 7-11.

[91] Code U. 450-2 (2009). International Union of Railways, Assessment of the performance of the network related to rail traffic operation for the purpose of quality analyses-delay coding and delay cause attribution process2009.

[92] Chang C, Thia B. Online rescheduling of mass rapid transit systems: fuzzy expert system approach. Iee P-Elect Pow Appl. 1996;143 (4):307-316.

[93] Meester LE, Muns S. Stochastic delay propagation in railway networks and phase-type distributions. Transportation Research Part B: Methodological. 2007;41 (2):218-230.

[94] Wiggenraad P. Alighting and boarding times of passengers at Dutch railway stations. TRAIL Research School, Delft. 2001.

[95] Buchmueller S, Weidmann U, Nash A. Development of a dwell time calculation model for timetable planning. WIT Transactions on The Built Environment. 2008;103:525-534.

[96] Murali P, Dessouky M, Ordóñez F, Palmer K. A delay estimation technique for single and double-track railroads. Transportation Research Part E: Logistics and Transportation Review. 2010;46 (4):483-495.

[97] Guo J, Meng L, Kecman P, Corman F, Modeling delay relations based on mining historical train monitoring data: a Chinese railway case. In:Proceedings of 6th International Conference on Railway Operations Modelling and Analysis – RailTokyo 2015. Tokyo; International Association of Railway Operations Research; March 23 - 26 2015.

[98] Flier H, Graffagnino T, Nunkesser M. Finding Robust Train Paths in Dense Corridors. IAROR RailZurich 2009. 2009.

[99] Kecman P, Goverde RM. Predictive modelling of running and dwell times in railway traffic. Public Transport. 2015;7 (3):295-319.

[100] Li D, Daamen W, Goverde RMP. Estimation of train dwell time at short stops based on track occupation event data: A study at a Dutch railway station. Journal of Advanced Transportation. 2016;50 (5):877-896. 10.1002/atr.1380.

[101] Fukami K, Yamamoto H, Hatanaka T, Terada T. A new delay forecasting system for the Passenger Information Control system (PIC) of the Tokaido-Sanyo Shinkansen. 2006;1:199-203. 10.2495/cr060201.

[102] Kecman P, Goverde RMP. Online Data-Driven Adaptive Prediction of Train Event Times. IEEE Transactions on Intelligent Transportation Systems. 2015;16 (1):465-474. 10.1109/tits.2014.2347136.

[103] D'ariano A, Pacciarelli D, Pranzo M. A branch and bound algorithm for scheduling trains in a railway network. European Journal of Operational Research. 2007;183 (2):643-657. doi:A branch and bound algorithm for scheduling trains in a railway network.

[104] D'Ariano A, Albrecht T. Running time re-optimization during real-time timetable perturbations. WIT Transactions on the Built Environment. 2006;88.

[105] Barta J, Rizzoli AE, Salani M, Gambardella LM. Statistical Modelling Of Delays In a Rail Freight Transportation Network. Wint Simul C Proc. 2012.

[106] Kecman P, Corman F, Meng L, Train delay evolution as a stochastic process; 2015.

[107] Wang SL, Ma JH. Variable-Carriage Vehicle Scheduling Based on Segment Point. 2013 International Conference on Computer Science And Artificial Intelligence (Iccsai 2013). 2013:16-20.

[108] Cheng Y-H, Yang L-A. A Fuzzy Petri Nets approach for railway traffic control in case of abnormality: Evidence from Taiwan railway system. Expert Systems with Applications. 2009;36 (4):8040-8048.

[109] Wen C, Peng Q, Chen Y, Ren J. Modelling the running states of high-speed trains using triangular fuzzy number workflow nets. Proceedings of the Institution of Mechanical Engineers, Part F: Journal of Rail and Rapid Transit. 2014;228 (4):422-430. doi:10. 1177/0954409713480488.

[110] Zilko AA, Kurowicka D, Goverde RM. Modeling railway disruption lengths with Copula Bayesian Networks. Transportation Research Part C: Emerging Technologies. 2016; 68: 350-368.

[111] Lessan J, Fu L, Wen C. A Hybrid Bayesian Network Model for Predicting Delays in Train Operations. Comput Ind Eng. 2018; 127: 1214-1222.

[112] Martin LJ, Predictive reasoning and machine learning for the enhancement of reliability in railway systems; Springer; 2016.

[113] Martin LJ, Romanovsky A, A Formal Approach to Designing Reliable Advisory Systems; Springer; 2016.

[114] Lulli A, Oneto L, Canepa R, Petralli S, Anguita D, Large-scale railway networks train movements: a dynamic, interpretable, and robust hybrid data analytics system; IEEE; 2018.

[115] Pongnumkul S, Pechprasarn T, Kunaseth N, Chaipah K, Improving arrival time prediction of Thailand's passenger trains using historical travel times; IEEE; 2014.

[116] Peters J, Emig B, Jung M, Schmidt S, Prediction of delays in public transportation using neural networks; IEEE; 2005.

[117] Yaghini M, Khoshraftar MM, Seyedabadi M. Railway passenger train delay prediction via neural network model. Journal of advanced transportation. 2013; 47 (3): 355-368.

[118] Marković N, Milinković S, Tikhonov KS, Schonfeld P. Analyzing passenger train arrival delays with support vector regression. Transportation Research Part C: Emerging Technologies. 2015; 56: 251-262.

[119] Barbour W, Mori JCM, Kuppa S, Work DB. Prediction of arrival times of freight traffic on US railroads using support vector regression. Transportation Research Part C: Emerging Technologies. 2018; 93: 211-227.

[120] Chen D, Wang L, Li L. Position computation models for high-speed train based on support vector machine approach. Applied Soft Computing. 2015;30:758-766. 10.1016/j.asoc.2015.01.017.

[121] Visentini MS, Borenstein D, Li J-Q, Mirchandani PB. Review of real-time vehicle schedule recovery methods in transportation services. Journal of Scheduling. 2014;17 (6):541-567.

[122] Naohiko H, Osamu N, Shigeru M, Hitoshi I, Norio T. Recovery measure of disruption in train operation in Tokyo Metropolitan Area. Transportation Research Procedia. 2017;25:4374-4384.

[123] Liebchen C, Lübbecke M, Möhring R, Stiller S. The concept of recoverable robustness, linear programming recovery, and railway applications. Robust and online large-scale optimization: Springer; 2009. p. 1-27.

[124] Cadarso L, Marín Á, Maróti G. Recovery of disruptions in rapid transit networks. Transportation Research Part E: Logistics and Transportation Review. 2013;53:15-33. 10.1016/j.tre.2013.01.013.

[125] Cadarso L, Marín Á. Recovery of disruptions in rapid Transit networks with origin-destination demand. Procedia-Social and Behavioral Sciences. 2014;111:528-537.

[126] Khadilkar H. Data-Enabled Stochastic Modeling for Evaluating Schedule Robustness of Railway Networks. Transportation Science. 2016.

[127] Wen C, Lessan J, Fu L, Huang P, Jiang C, Data-driven models for predicting delay recovery in high-speed rail; IEEE; 2017.

[128] Bottou L. Large-scale machine learning with stochastic gradient descent. Proceedings of COMPSTAT'2010: Springer; 2010. p. 177-186.

[129] Huang G-B, Zhu Q-Y, Siew C-K, Extreme learning machine: a new learning scheme of feedforward neural networks; IEEE; 2004.

[130] Chao W. Train operation conflict management research status of high-speed railways. Journal of Transportation Security. 2011;4 (3):231-246.

[131] Chen B, Harker PT. Two moments estimation of the delay on single-track rail lines with scheduled traffic. Transportation Science. 1990;24 (4):261-275.

[132] Higgins A, Kozan E, Ferreira L. Modelling delay risks associated with train schedules. Transportation Planning and Technology. 1995;19 (2):89-108.

[133] Ferreira L, Higgins A. Modeling reliability of train arrival times. Journal of transportation engineering. 1996;122 (6):414-420.

[134] Medeossi G, Longo G, de Fabris S. A method for using stochastic blocking times to improve timetable planning. Journal of Rail Transport Planning & Management. 2011;1 (1):1-13.

[135] D'Addio G, Mazzucchelli M, Savio S. Automatic conflict detection and resolution in metrorail systems: evaluation approach for MARCO EU project. WIT Transactions on The Built Environment. 1998;36.

[136] Hooghiemstra JS, Kroon LG, Odijk MA, Salomon M, Zwaneveld PJ. Decision support systems support the search for win-win solutions in railway network design. Interfaces. 1999;29 (2):15-32.

[137] Giannettoni M, Savio S. The European project COMBINE 2 to improve knowledge on future rail traffic management systems. WIT Transactions on The Built Environment. 2004;74.

[138] D'Ariano A, Pranzo M, Hansen IA. Conflict resolution and train speed coordination for solving real-time timetable perturbations. Ieee Transactions on Intelligent Transportation Systems. 2007;8 (2):208-222. 10.1109/Tits.2006.888605.

[139] Toriumi S, Taguchi A, Matsumoto T. A Model to Simulate Delay in Train Schedule Caused by Crowded Passengers Using a Time-Space Network. Int Regional Sci Rev. 2014;37 (2):225-244. 10.1177/0160017614526883.

[140] Goverde RM, Daamen W, Hansen IA. Automatic identification of route conflict occurrences and their consequences. Computers in Railways XI. 2008:473-482.

[141] Daamen W, Goverde RM, Hansen IA. Non-discriminatory automatic registration of knock-on train delays. Networks and Spatial Economics. 2009;9 (1):47-61.

[142] Schaefer H, Pferdmenges S. An expert system for real-time train dispatching. WIT Transactions on The Built Environment. 1994;7.

[143] Chiang T, Hau H, Chiang HM, Kob SY, Hsieh CH. Knowledge-based system for railway scheduling. Data & Knowledge Engineering. 1998;27 (3):289-312.

[144] Fay A. A fuzzy knowledge-based system for railway traffic control. Engineering Applications of Artificial Intelligence. 2000;13 (6):719-729.

[145] He Zhuang LF, Chao Wen,Qiyuan Peng,Qizhi Tang. High-Speed Railway Train Timetable Conflict Prediction Based on Fuzzy Temporal Knowledge Reasoning. Engineering. 2016;2 (3):366-373. 10.1016/j.eng.2016.03.019.

[146] Ke BR, Lin CL, Chien HH, Chiu HW, Chen N. A new approach for improving the performance of freight train timetabling of a single-track railway system. Transportation Planning and Technology. 2014;38 (2):238-264. 10.1080/03081060.2014.959357.

[147] Corman F, D'Ariano A, Hansen IA, Pacciarelli D. Optimal multi-class rescheduling of railway traffic. Journal of Rail Transport Planning & Management. 2011;1 (1):14-24.

[148] Mazzarello M, Ottaviani E. A traffic management system for real-time traffic optimisation in railways. Transportation Research Part B: Methodological. 2007;41 (2):246-274.

[149] Zhu T, Mera JM, Suarez B, Maroto J. An agent-based support system for railway station dispatching. Expert Systems with Applications. 2016;61:39-52.

[150] Zhu T, de Pedro JMMS. Railway Traffic Conflict Detection via a State Transition Prediction Approach. IEEE Transactions on Intelligent Transportation Systems. 2017;18 (5):1268-1278.

[151] Yuan J, Hansen IA, Closed form expressions of optimal buffer times between scheduled

trains at railway bottlenecks; IEEE; 2008 October 12-15.

[152] Vromans M. Reliability of Railway Systems [Ph.D. thesis]: Erasmus University Rotterdam; 2005.

[153] Fischetti M, Salvagnin D, Zanette A. Fast approaches to improve the robustness of a railway timetable. Transportation Science. 2009;43 (3):321-335.

[154] Andersson EV, Peterson A, Krasemann JT. Quantifying railway timetable robustness in critical points. Journal of Rail Transport Planning & Management. 2013;3 (3):95-110.

[155] Kroon LG, Dekker R, Vromans MJ. Cyclic railway timetabling: a stochastic optimization approach. Algorithmic Methods for Railway Optimization: Springer; 2007. p. 41-66.

[156] Palmqvist C-W, Olsson NO, Hiselius L, An Empirical Study of Timetable Strategies and Their Effects on Punctuality; 2017.

[157] Goverde RMP, Hansen IA, Performance indicators for railway timetables. Beijing, China; IEEE; 2013 Aug. 30 -Sept. 1.

[158] International-Union-of-Railways. UIC Code 451-1 Timetable Recovery margins to guarantee timekeeping-Recovery margins. Paris: International Union of Railways; 5th Edition 2009.

[159] Jespersen-Groth J, Potthoff D, Clausen J, Huisman D, Kroon L, Maróti G, Nielsen MN. Disruption management in passenger railway transportation. Robust and online large-scale optimization: Springer; 2009. p. 399-421.

[160] Hansen IA. Station capacity and stability of train operations. Adv Transport. 2000;7:809-816.

[161] Rudolph R. Allowances and margins in railway scheduling. Proceedings of WCRR; 2003 October 12; Edinburgh.

[162] Vansteenwegen P, Van Oudheusden D. Developing railway timetables which guarantee a better service. European Journal of Operational Research. 2006;173 (1):337-350.

[163] Huang P, Wen C, Peng Q, Lessan J, Fu L, Jiang C. A data-driven time supplements allocation model for train operations on high-speed railways. International Journal of Rail Transportation. 2019;7 (2):140-157.

[164] HO T, CHEN, T., CHOU, C.. . Integrating of optimization and data mining techniques for high-speed train timetable design considering disturbances. Gerontechnology. 2012;11 (2):323-329.

[165] Araya S, Abe K, Fukumori K, An optimal rescheduling for online train traffic control in disturbed situations; IEEE; 1983.

[166] Araya S, ESTRAC-II An Expert System for Train Traffic Control in Disturbed Situations; 1984.

[167] Komaya K, Fukuda T, A knowledge-based approach for railway scheduling; IEEE; 1991.

[168] Tsuruta S, Matsumoto K, A knowledge-based interactive train scheduling system-aiming

at large-scale complex planning expert systems; IEEE; 1988.

[169] Vernazza G, Zunino R. A distributed intelligence methodology for railway traffic control. IEEE Transactions on Vehicular Technology. 1990;39 (3):263-270.

[170] Lange J, Werner F. Approaches to modeling train scheduling problems as job-shop problems with blocking constraints. Journal of Scheduling. 2018;21 (2):191-207.

[171] Priore P, De La Fuente D, Gomez A, Puente J. A review of machine learning in dynamic scheduling of flexible manufacturing systems. AI EDAM. 2001;15 (3):251-263.

[172] Priore P, Gómez A, Pino R, Rosillo R. Dynamic scheduling of manufacturing systems using machine learning: An updated review. AI EDAM. 2014;28 (1):83-97.

[173] Ingimundardottir H, Runarsson TP. Discovering dispatching rules from data using imitation learning: A case study for the job-shop problem. Journal of Scheduling. 2018;21 (4):413-428.

[174] LeCun Y, Bottou L, Bengio Y, Haffner P. Gradient-based learning applied to document recognition. Proceedings of the IEEE. 1998;86 (11):2278-2324.

[175] Bengio Y, Lamblin P, Popovici D, Larochelle H, Greedy layer-wise training of deep networks; 2007.

[176] Elman JL. Finding structure in time. Cognitive science. 1990;14 (2):179-211.

[177] Duan Y, Lv Y, Wang F-Y, Travel time prediction with LSTM neural network; IEEE; 2016.

[178] Raut RD, Goyal VK. Public transport bus arrival time prediction with seasonal and special emphasis on weather compensation changes using RNN. International Journal of Advanced Research in Computer and Communication Engineering. 2012;1 (6):378-382.

[179] Gopalakrishnan K, Balakrishnan H, A Comparative Analysis of Models for Predicting Delays in Air Traffic Networks; 2017.

[180] LeCun Y, Bengio Y, Hinton G. Deep learning. nature. 2015;521 (7553):436.

[181] Lin K, Zhao R, Xu Z, Zhou J. Efficient Large-Scale Fleet Management via Multi-Agent Deep Reinforcement Learning. arXiv preprint arXiv:180206444. 2018.

[182] Mo Z. Deep learning for subway pedestrian forecast based on node camera. Advances in Transportation Studies. 2017;2.

[183] Chen W, Xu Y, Wu X. Deep Reinforcement Learning for Multi-Resource Multi-Machine Job Scheduling. arXiv preprint arXiv:171107440. 2017.

[184] Voelker M. Adaptive Lenkung bei den SBB. IT13 rail. 2013.

[185] Toletti A, De Martinis V, Weidmann U. What about train length and energy efficiency of freight trains in rescheduling models? Transportation Research Procedia. 2015;10:584-594.

[186] Xu Z, Sun J. Model-driven deep-learning. National Science Review. 2017:nwx099-nwx099. 10.1093/nsr/nwx099.

[187] Central-Japan-Railway-Company. Central Japan railway company annual report 2014 2015. Available from: http://english.jr-central.co.jp/company/ir/annualreport/_pdf/ annual

report2014.pdf.

[188] China-Railway-Corporation. Punctuality reaches 98.8% 2016. Available from: http://news.gaotie.cn/yunying/2016-07-23/336706.html

[189] Yuan J, Goverde RMP, Hansen JA. Evaluating stochastic train process time distribution models on the basis of empirical detection data. Computers in Railways X: Computer System Design and Operation in the Railway and Other Transit Systems. 2006; 88:631-640. doi:10.2495/CR060621.

[190] Keiji K, Naohiko H, Shigeru M. Simulation analysis of train operation to recover knock-on delay under high-frequency intervals. Case Studies on Transport Policy. 2015;3 (1):92-98. doi:10.1016/j.cstp.2014.07.007.

[191] Yamashita T, Soeda S, Noda I. Evaluation of time delay of coping behaviors with evacuation simulator. Stud Comp Intell. 2010;325:403-414. doi:10.1007/978-3-642-16098-1_25.

[192] Zeng JW, Qian YS, Li WJ, Guang XP, Wang M. A study on the effects of redundant time on the operation of different speed-grade trains in passenger railway line traffic system by using cellular automata model. Adv Mech Eng. 2014(3):237-245. doi:Artn 302176

[193] 10.1155/2014/302176.

[194] Wen C, Li B. Train operation adjustment based on conflict resolution for high-speed rail. Journal of Transportation Security. 2013;6 (1):77-87. doi:10.1007/s12198-012-0104-9.

[195] Knapen L, Bellemans T, Usman M, Janssens D, Wets G. Within day rescheduling microsimulation combined with macrosimulated traffic. Transport Res C-Emer. 2014;45:99-118.

[196] Yalcinkaya O, Bayhan GM. A feasible timetable generator simulation modelling framework for train scheduling problem. Simul Model Pract Th. 2012;20 (1):124-141. 10.1016/j.simpat.2011.09.005.

[197] Milinkovic S, Markovic M, Veskovic S, Ivic M, Pavlovic N. A fuzzy Petri net model to estimate train delays. Simul Model Pract Th. 2013;33:144-157. doi:10.1016/j.simpat. 2012.12.005.

[198] Guo J, Meng L, Kecman P, Corman F, Modeling delay relations based on mining historical train monitoring data: a Chinese railway case. In:Proceedings of 6th International Conference on Railway Operations Modelling and Analysis – RailTokyo 2015. Tokyo; International Association of Railway Operations Research; 2015 March 23-26 2015.

[199] Ushida K, Makino S, Tomii N, Increasing robustness of dense timetables by visualization of train traffic record dataand monte carlo simulation. In:Proceedings of 9th World Congress on Railway Research. Lille; World Congress on Railway Research; May 22-26 2011.

[200] Li HF, Parikh D, He Q, Qian BY, Li ZG, Fang DP, Hampapur A. Improving rail network velocity: A machine learning approach to predictive maintenance. Transport Res C-Emer.

2014;45:17-26. doi:10.1016/j.trc.2014.04.013.

[201] Ma M, Wang P, Chu CH, Liu L. Efficient multipattern event processing over high-speed train data streams. Ieee Internet Things. 2015;2 (4):295-309. doi:10.1109/JIOT.2014. 2387883.

[202] Higgins A, Kozan E. Modeling train delays in urban networks. Transportation Science. 1998;32 (4):346-357.

[203] Krüger N, Vierth I, Fakhraei Roudsari F. Spatial, temporal and size distribution of freight train delays: evidence from Sweden. CTS-Centre for Transport Studies Stockholm (KTH and VTI), 2013.

[204] Hansen IA, Goverde RM, Van Der Meer DJ, Online train delay recognition and running time prediction. In:Proceedings of 13th International IEEE Conference on Intelligent Transportation Systems (ITSC). Beijing; IEEE; September 19-22 2010.

[205] Lacey L, Keene O, Pritchard J, Bye A. Common noncompartmental pharmacokinetic variables: are they normally or log-normally distributed? Journal of biopharmaceutical statistics. 1997;7 (1):171-178.

[206] Lai C, Xie M, Murthy D. A modified Weibull distribution. IEEE Transactions on reliability. 2003;52 (1):33-37.

[207] Garmendia M, Ribalaygua C, Ureña JM. High speed rail: implication for cities. Cities. 2012;29:S26-S31.

[208] Dong H, Ning B, Cai B, Hou Z. Automatic train control system development and simulation for high-speed railways. IEEE circuits and systems magazine. 2010;10 (2):6-18.

[209] Wu J, Nash C, Wang D. Is high speed rail an appropriate solution to China's rail capacity problems? Journal of Transport Geography. 2014;40:100-111.

[210] Jiang X, Zhang L, Chen XM. Short-term forecasting of high-speed rail demand: A hybrid approach combining ensemble empirical mode decomposition and gray support vector machine with real-world applications in China. Transportation Research Part C: Emerging Technologies. 2014;44:110-127.

[211] Lingyun M, Goverde RM. A method for constructing train delay propagation process by mining train record data. Journal of Beijing Jiaotong University. 2012;6:002.

[212] Huang Y, Verbraeck A, A dynamic data-driven approach for rail transport system simulation; Winter Simulation Conference; 2009.

[213] Takimoto T. Development of efficient operational control using object representation. Adv Transport. 2000;7:837-841.

[214] Justel A, Peña D, Zamar R. A multivariate Kolmogorov-Smirnov test of goodness of fit. Statistics & Probability Letters. 1997;35 (3): 251-259.

[215] Chen G, Silva JdAe. Regional impacts of high-speed rail: a review of methods and models. Transportation Letters. 2013;5 (3): 131-143.

[216] Preston J, Wall G, Batley R, Ibáñez J, Shires J. Impact of delays on passenger train

services: evidence from Great Britain. Transportation Research Record: Journal of the Transportation Research Board. 2009 (2117): 14-23.

[217] China-Railway-Corporation. Punctuality reaches 98.8%. http://newsgaotiecn/yunying/2016-07-23/336706html 2016-07-23.

[218] Hansen IA. Optimisation of railway capacity use by stochastic modelling. Traffic And Transportation Studies, Proceedings; 2004.

[219] Fernandez A, Cucala AP, Sanz JI. An integrated information model for traffic planning, operation and management of railway lines. Computers In Railway Six. 2004; 15: 743-752. doi: 10.2495/CR040751.

[220] Corman F, D'Ariano A, Pacciarelli D, Pranzo M. Bi-objective conflict detection and resolution in railway traffic management. Transportation Research Part C: Emerging Technologies. 2012;20 (1):79-94. doi:10.1016/j.trc.2010.09.009.

[221] Vromans MJ, Dekker R, Kroon LG. Reliability and heterogeneity of railway services. European Journal of Operational Research. 2006;172 (2): 647-665.

[222] Olsson NO, Haugland H. Influencing factors on train punctuality—results from some Norwegian studies. Transport policy. 2004;11 (4): 387-397.

[223] Dalapati P, Padhy A, Mishra B, Dutta A, Bhattacharya S. Real-time collision handling in railway transport network: an agent-based modeling and simulation approach. Transportation Letters. 2017: 1-11.

[224] Jong JC, Lin TH, Lee CK, Hu HL. The analysis of train reliability for the Taiwan High Speed Rail. Computers In Railways Xii: Computer System Design And Operation In Railways And Other Transit Systems. 2010;114:169-180. 10.2495/CR100171.

[225] Richter T. Data aggregation for detailed analysis of train delays. 2012;1:239-250. 10.2495/cr120211.

[226] Flier H, Gelashvili R, Graffagnino T, Nunkesser M. Mining railway delay dependencies in large-scale real-world delay data. Robust and online large-scale optimization: Springer; 2009. p. 354-368.

[227] Guo J, Meng L, Kecman P, Corman F. Modeling delay relations based on mining historical train monitoring data: a Chinese railway case. 6th International Conference on Railway Operations Modelling and Analysis-RailTokyo2015; 2015.

[228] Goverde RM. Punctuality of railway operations and timetable stability analysis. 2005.

[229] Huisman T, Boucherie RJ. Running times on railway sections with heterogeneous train traffic. Transportation Research Part B: Methodological. 2001;35 (3):271-292.

[230] Goverde RM, Corman F, D'Ariano A. Railway line capacity consumption of different railway signalling systems under scheduled and disturbed conditions. Journal of Rail Transport Planning & Management. 2013;3 (3):78-94.

[231] Wen C, Li Z, Lessan J, Fu L, Huang P, Jiang C. Statistical investigation on train primary delay based on real records: evidence from Wuhan–Guangzhou HSR. International Journal of Rail Transportation. 2017;5 (3):1-20.

[232] Hansen IA, Goverde RM, van der Meer DJ, Online train delay recognition and running time prediction; IEEE; 2010.

[233] Kecman P, Goverde RM. Online data-driven adaptive prediction of train event times. IEEE Transactions on Intelligent Transportation Systems. 2015;16 (1):465-474.

[234] Goverde RM. Railway timetable stability analysis using max-plus system theory. Transportation Research Part B: Methodological. 2007;41 (2):179-201.

[235] Corman F, Kecman P. Stochastic prediction of train delays in real-time using Bayesian networks. Transportation Research Part C: Emerging Technologies. 2018;95:599-615.

[236] Lessan J, Fu L, Wen C. A hybrid Bayesian network model for predicting delays in train operations. Computers & Industrial Engineering. 2018.

[237] Chapuis X, Arrival Time Prediction Using Neural Networks; 2017.

[238] Tang Y, Wen C, Huang P, Li Z, Li J, Yang Y. Support Vector Regression Models for Influenced Time Prediction in High-Speed Rail System. 2018.

[239] Chen T, Guestrin C, Xgboost: A scalable tree boosting system; ACM; 2016.

[240] Smola AJ, Schölkopf B. A tutorial on support vector regression. Statistics and computing. 2004;14 (3):199-222.

[241] Lessan J, Fu L, Wen C, Huang P, Jiang C. Stochastic Model of Train Running Time and Arrival Delay: A Case Study of Wuhan–Guangzhou High-Speed Rail. Transportation Research Record. 2018:0361198118780830.

[242] Wallander J, Mäkitalo M. Data mining in rail transport delay chain analysis. International Journal of Shipping and Transport Logistics. 2012;4 (3):269-285.

[243] Hartrumpf M, Claus T, Erb M, Albes JM. Surgeon performance index: tool for assessment of individual surgical quality in total quality management. Eur J Cardio-Thorac. 2009;35 (5):751-758. 10.1016/j.ejcts.2008.12.006.

[244] Zhang L, Liu JH, Wu RF, Gong XB. Design of Performance Testing System for Train Air Conditioning. Iceet: 2009 International Conference on Energy And Environment Technology, Vol 1, Proceedings. 2009:85-89. 10.1109/Iceet.2009.27.

[245] Hartigan JA, Wong MA. Algorithm AS 136: A k-means clustering algorithm. Journal of the Royal Statistical Society Series C (Applied Statistics). 1979;28 (1):100-108.

[246] Pedregosa F, Varoquaux G, Gramfort A, Michel V, Thirion B, Grisel O, Blondel M, Prettenhofer P, Weiss R, Dubourg V. Scikit-learn: Machine learning in Python. Journal of machine learning research. 2011;12 (Oct):2825-2830.

[247] Liu Y, Li Z, Xiong H, Gao X, Wu J, Understanding of internal clustering validation measures; IEEE; 2010.

[248] Ross SM. Introduction to probability models: Academic press; 2014.

[249] Massey Jr FJ. The Kolmogorov-Smirnov test for goodness of fit. Journal of the American statistical Association. 1951;46 (253):68-78.

[250] Harris NG, Mjøsund CS, Haugland H. Improving railway performance in Norway. Journal of Rail Transport Planning & Management. 2013;3 (4):172-180. http://dx.

doi.org/10.1016/j.jrtpm.2014.02.002.

[251] Wen C, Li J, Peng Q, Li B, Ren J. Predicting high-speed train operation conflicts using workflow nets and triangular fuzzy numbers. Proceedings of the Institution of Mechanical Engineers, Part F: Journal of Rail and Rapid Transit. 2015;229 (3):268-279.

[252] Narayanaswami S, Rangaraj N. Modelling disruptions and resolving conflicts optimally in a railway schedule. Comput Ind Eng. 2013;64 (1):469-481.

[253] Drucker H, Burges CJ, Kaufman L, Smola AJ, Vapnik V, Support vector regression machines; 1997.

[254] Brown RG, Hwang PY. Introduction to random signals and applied Kalman filtering: Wiley New York; 1992.

[255] Janecek D, Weymann F, LUKS-Analysis of lines and junctions; 2010.

[256] Wiklund M. SERIOUS BREAKDOWNS IN THE TRACK INFRASTRUCTURE: CALCULATION OF EFFECTS ON RAIL TRAFFIC. VTI MEDDELANDE. 2003(959).

[257] Awad M, Khanna R. Efficient learning machines: theories, concepts, and applications for engineers and system designers: Apress; 2015.

[258] Breiman L. Bagging predictors. Machine learning. 1996;24 (2):123-140.

[259] Altman NS. An introduction to kernel and nearest-neighbor nonparametric regression. The American Statistician. 1992;46 (3):175-185.

[260] Svozil D, Kvasnicka V, Pospichal J. Introduction to multi-layer feed-forward neural networks. Chemometrics and intelligent laboratory systems. 1997;39 (1):43-62.

[261] Rumelhart DE, Hinton GE, Williams RJ. Learning representations by back-propagating errors. Nature. 1986;323 (6088):533.

[262] Preston J, Wall G, Batley R, Ibáñez JN, Shires J. Impact of delays on passenger train services: evidence from Great Britain. Transportation Research Record. 2009;2117 (1):14-23.

[263] Burr T, Merrifield S, Duffy D, Griffiths J, Wright S, Barker G. Reducing passenger rail delays by better management of incidents. National Audit Office for the Office of Rail Regulation. 2008.

[264] Wallander J, Mäkitalo M, Data mining in rail transport delay chain analysis; 2012.

[265] Hochreiter S, Schmidhuber J. Long short-term memory. Neural computation. 1997;9 (8):1735-1780.

[266] Xingjian S, Chen Z, Wang H, Yeung D-Y, Wong W-K, Woo W-c, Convolutional LSTM network: A machine learning approach for precipitation nowcasting; 2015.

[267] Ke J, Zheng H, Yang H, Chen XM. Short-term forecasting of passenger demand under on-demand ride services: A spatio-temporal deep learning approach. Transportation Research Part C: Emerging Technologies. 2017;85:591-608.

[268] Liao S, Zhou L, Di X, Yuan B, Xiong J, Large-scale short-term urban taxi demand forecasting using deep learning; IEEE Press; 2018.

[269] Nabian MA, Alemazkoor N, Meidani H. Predicting Near-Term Train Schedule

Performance and Delay Using Bi-Level Random Forests. Transportation Research Record. 2019:0361198119840339.

[270] Goverde RM. A delay propagation algorithm for large-scale railway traffic networks. Transportation Research Part C: Emerging Technologies. 2010;18 (3):269-287.

[271] Carey M, Carville S. Testing schedule performance and reliability for train stations. J Oper Res Soc. 2000;51 (6):666-682.

[272] Wang S, Ma J, Variable-carriage vehicle scheduling Based on segment Point; 2013.

[273] Malavasi G, Ricci S. Simulation of stochastic elements in railway systems using self-learning processes. European Journal of Operational Research. 2001;131 (2):262-272.

[274] Oneto L, Fumeo E, Clerico G, Canepa R, Papa F, Dambra C, Mazzino N, Anguita D. Train Delay Prediction Systems: A Big Data Analytics Perspective. Big data research. 2018;11:54-64.

[275] Li D, Daamen W, Goverde RM. Estimation of train dwell time at short stops based on track occupation event data: A study at a Dutch railway station. Journal of Advanced Transportation. 2016;50 (5):877-896.

[276] Chollet F. Keras: Deep learning library for theano and tensorflow. URL: https://keras io/k. 2015;7 (8):T1.

[277] Tieleman T, Hinton G. Divide the gradient by a running average of its recent magnitude. coursera: Neural networks for machine learning. Technical Report. 2017.

[278] Abadi M, Barham P, Chen J, Chen Z, Davis A, Dean J, Devin M, Ghemawat S, Irving G, Isard M, Tensorflow: A system for large-scale machine learning; 2016.

[279] McKinney W. pandas: a foundational Python library for data analysis and statistics. Python for High Performance and Scientific Computing. 2011;14.

[280] Van Der Walt S, Colbert SC, Varoquaux G. The NumPy array: a structure for efficient numerical computation. Computing in Science & Engineering. 2011;13 (2):22.

[281] Rumelhart DE, Hinton GE, Williams RJ. Learning representations by back-propagating errors. Cognitive modeling. 1988;5 (3):1.

[282] Gardiner C. Stochastic methods: Springer Berlin; 2009.

[283] van der Meer DJ, Prediction of train running times and conflicts using track occupation data; 2010.

[284] Meng L, Yang Z, Li H, Jiang X, Miao J, He Z. Simulation initialization method of train running on passenger dedicated railway line. Journal of Transportation Systems Engineering and Information Technology. 2009;9 (1):62-67.

[285] Petkova B. Strategic planning for rail system design: An application for portuguese high speed rail. Industrial Engineering and Management, University of Groningen, Groningen, Netherlands. 2007.

[286] Albrecht T. The influence of anticipating train driving on the dispatching process in railway conflict situations. Networks and Spatial Economics. 2009;9 (1):85-101.

[287] Lake M, Ferreira L, Minimising the conflict between rail operations and infrastructure maintenance; Emerald Group Publishing Limited; 2002.

[288] Sauer N. Optimization of cyclic manufacturing systems with stochastic manufacturing times using event graphs. International journal of production economics. 1996 (46-47):387-399.

[289] Liebchen C, Schachtebeck M, Schöbel A, Stiller S, Prigge A. Computing delay resistant railway timetables. Comput Oper Res. 2010;37 (5):857-868. 10.1016/j.cor.2009.03.022.

[290] Caimi G, Fuchsberger M, Laumanns M, Lüthi M. A model predictive control approach for discrete-time rescheduling in complex central railway station areas. Computers & Operations Research. 2012;39 (11):2578-2593.

[291] Goverde RM. Punctuality of railway operations and timetable stability analysis: Netherlands TRAIL Research School; 2005.

[292] Huisman T. Forecasting delays on railway sections. WIT Transactions on The Built Environment. 2002;61.

[293] Pardalos PM, Resende MG. Handbook of applied optimization. 2002.

[294] Mascis A, Pacciarelli D, Pranzo M. Scheduling models for short-term railway traffic optimisation. Computer-aided systems in public transport: Springer; 2008. p. 71-90.

[295] Cheng Y. Hybrid simulation for resolving resource conflicts in train traffic rescheduling. Computers in Industry. 1998;35 (3):233-246.

[296] Yong Z, Ming Z, Xishi W. Research on a train operation simulation system under moving automatic block conditions. Journal of system simulation. 1999;11 (3):198.

[297] Xingchen Z, Hao Y, Xiaoning Z, Siji H, Anzhou H. Research on Simulation Experiment System of Jinghu High Speed Railway [J]. Journal of the China Railway Society. 1998;4.

[298] http://www.opentrack.com.cn.

[299] Rudolph R. Operational simulation of light rail. PTRC-PUBLICATIONS-P. 2000: 167-178.

[300] Tsang C, Ho T, The conflict resolution in connected railway junctions; Taylor & Francis; 2003.

[301] Yu C, A network-based train traffic simulation with changeable rescheduling strategies; IEEE; 1996.

[302] Stolk A. Automatic conflict detection and advanced decision support for optimal usage of railway infrastructure Purpose and concepts. WIT Transactions on The Built Environment. 1998;37.

[303] Hallowell SF, Harker PT. Predicting on-time performance in scheduled railroad operations: methodology and application to train scheduling. Transportation Research Part A: Policy and Practice. 1998;32 (4):279-295.

[304] Wen C. Prediction methods of train operation conflict for high-speed railway. Journal of Transportation Security. 2010;3 (4):275-286.

[305] Lindfeldt O. Evaluation of punctuality on a heavily utilised railway line with mixed traffic. Timetable Planning and Information Quality. 2010:115.

[306] Kliewer N, Suhl L. A Note on the Online Nature of the Railway Delay Management Problem. Networks. 2011;57 (1):28-37. 10.1002/net.20381.

[307] Hansen IA, Goverde RM, van der Meer DJ. Online train delay recognition and running time prediction. Intelligent Transportation Systems (ITSC), 13th International IEEE Conference on; 2010.

[308] Abid MM, Khan MB, Muhammad I. Sensitivity analysis of train schedule of a railway track network using an optimization modeling technique. European Transport Research Review. 2015;7 (1):1-7.

[309] Bosscha E. Big data in railway operations: Using artificial neural networks to predict train delay propagation: University of Twente; 2016.

[310] Yaghini M, Khoshraftar MM, SEYEDABADI S. Predicting Passenger Train Delays Using Neural Network. 2010.

[311] Wang SL, Ma JH. Variable-Carriage Vehicle Scheduling Based on Segment Point. 2013 International Conference on Computer Science And Artificial Intelligence; 2013 July 22-25.

[312] Buchmueller S, Weidmann U, Nash A. Development of a dwell time calculation model for timetable planning. Computers In Railways Xi. 2008;103:525-534. doi:10.2495/ Cr080511.

[313] Adjetey-Bahun K, Birregah B, Châtelet E, Planchet J-L. A model to quantify the resilience of mass railway transportation systems. Reliability Engineering & System Safety. 2016;153:1-14. doi: 10.1016/j.ress.2016.03.015.

[314] Corman F, D'Ariano A, Pacciarelli D, Pranzo M. A tabu search algorithm for rerouting trains during rail operations. Transportation Research Part B: Methodological. 2010;44 (1):175-192.

[315] Sato K, Fukumura N. Real-time freight locomotive rescheduling and uncovered train detection during disruption. European Journal Of Operational Research. 2012;221 (3):636-648. 10.1016/j.ejor.2012.04.025.

[316] Cacchiani V, Toth P. Nominal and robust train timetabling problems. European Journal of Operational Research. 2012;219 (3):727-737.

[317] D'Ariano A, Pacciarelli D, Pranzo M. Assessment of flexible timetables in real-time traffic management of a railway bottleneck. Transportation Research Part C: Emerging Technologies. 2008;16 (2):232-245.

[318] Abril M, Barber F, Ingolotti L, Salido M, Tormos P, Lova A. An assessment of railway capacity. Transportation Research Part E: Logistics and Transportation Review. 2008;44 (5):774-806.

[319] Cerreto F, Nielsen OA, Harrod S, Nielsen BF, Causal Analysis of Railway Running Delays; 2016.

[320] Zeng J, Xue Y, Qian Y, Li W, Xu D, Guang X, Wang M. Study on the effect of redundant time on the operation of mixed passenger and freight traffic system using cellular automata model. Measurement. 2014;47:724-733.

[321] Zeng J, Qian Y, Li W, Guang X, Wang M. A study on the effects of redundant time on the operation of different speed-grade trains in passenger railway line traffic system by using cellular automata model. Advances in Mechanical Engineering. 2014;6:302176.

[322] Javad L, Liping F, Chao W, Ping H, Chaozhe J. Stochastic Model of Train Running Time and Arrival Delay: A Case Study of Wuhan–Guangzhou High-Speed Rail. Journal of the Transportation Research Board. 2018.

[323] Hoerl AE, Kennard RW. Ridge regression: applications to nonorthogonal problems. Technometrics. 1970;12 (1):69-82.

[324] WEIK N, NIEBEL N, NIE EN N. Capacity analysis of railway lines in Germany–A rigorous discussion of the queueing based approach [J]. Journal of Rail Transport Planning & Management, 2016, 6(2): 99-115

[325] WENG J, ZHENG Y, QU X, et al. Development of a maximum likelihood regression tree-based model for predicting subway incident delay [J]. Transportation Research Part C: Emerging Technologies, 2015, 57(30-41).

[326] SCHWANH UBER W. The status of German railway operations management in research and practice [J]. Transportation Research Part A: Policy and Practice, 1994, 28(6): 495-500.

[327] GOVERDE R M, HANSEN I, HOOGHIEMSTRA G, et al. Delay distributions in railway stations; proceedings of the 9th World Conference on Transport Research, Seoul, Korea, July 22-27, 2001, F, 2001 [C]. Citeseer.

[328] LINDFELDT O. Evaluation of punctuality on a heavily utilized railway line with mixed traffic [J]. WIT Transactions on The Built Environment, 2008, 103(545-53.